# PARCC TEST PREP

## GRADE 4

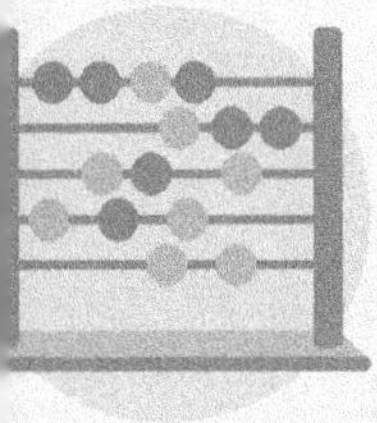

## NEW JERSEY

# MATH

Origins Publications

We help students develop their higher-order thinking skills while also improving their chances of admission into gifted and accelerated-learner programs.

Our goal is to unleash and nurture the genius in every student. We do this by offering educational and test prep materials that are fun, challenging and provide a sense of accomplishment.

Please contact us with any questions.

info@originspublications.com

---



Written and Edited by: PARCC NJ Test Prep Team



**ISBN 13: 978-1-948255-36-3**



Origins Publications
New York, NY, USA
Email:info@originspublications.com

# TABLE OF CONTENTS

# INTRODUCTION

## The PARCC Assessments

The PARCC Assessments (Partnership for Assessment of Readiness for College and Careers) are important tests designed to assess whether students are meeting the rigorous Common Core State Standards that have been implemented in schools across America. These standards, or learning goals, outline what students in each grade should learn each year. These standards emphasize just how important the new goals are: they can help show whether students are on the right track to college and beyond, even when the students are years from those life stages.

PARCC is a consortium of US states which cooperate to develop and improve the PARCC Assessments.

## PARCC Mathematics Assessment

The PARCC mathematics assessment is designed to determine whether students have mastered grade level appropriate mathematics skills. Like the Common Core State Standards, PARCC assessments focus on higher level critical thinking skills, problem solving, analysis, and real-world application.

The PARCC math assessments are given annually in grades 3-11, during a 30-day window that ends about 75% of the way through the school year. The assessments are administered in either computer-based or paper-based formats.

There are **three major task types** on PARCC Mathematics assessments.

**Type I:** Tasks assessing concepts, skills, and procedures. These questions balance conceptual understanding, fluency, and application, and can involve any or all mathematical applications. Answers are scored by machine.

**Type II:** Tasks assessing the ability to express mathematical reasoning, which call for students to respond with written arguments and justifications and to show critiques of reasoning and precision in mathematical statements. Includes a mix of machine-scored and hand-scored responses.

**Type III:** Tasks assessing models/application in real world contexts or scenarios. Questions may assess various mathematical practice standards that students have learned. Includes a mix of machine-scored and hand-scored responses.

In grade 4, students will be expected to answer 40 questions, broken down as follows:

- Type I: 33 questions
- Type II: 4 questions
- Type III: 3 questions

Each PARCC math assessment is divided into sessions, called "units." The number of units and the amount of time allotted per unit varies for each grade level.

The assessment for Grade 3-5 consist of four 60-minute sessions.

No calculator is permitted for students in grades 3-5.

### Question Format on PARCC Math Assessments

Students taking the PARCC mathematics assessment may be asked to respond to several types of questions. Most question types will likely be familiar to the student, such as multiple-choice questions, where students select the correct response from four answer choices. The mathematics assessments also contain questions called Technology Enhanced Items (TEIs), including:

**Open/Constructed Response:** A student is expected to explain or justify their answers and/or strategies in one or two complete sentences within the space, usually an answer box.

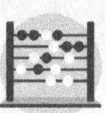

# HOW TO USE THIS BOOK

**Multi-select:** A student must select a specified number of answers that s/he thinks best responds to the question.

**Equation Editor:** A student is presented with a toolbar including a variety of variables, expressions, equations, or numbers (as appropriate to the test item) that can be used to create an answer to the question.

**Matching Item:** A student must check a box to indicate if the information from a column header matches information from a row.

**Table Item:** A student is asked to correctly enter numeric values into a provided table.

**Drag and Drop:** A student needs to drag an item from one part of the screen to another.

## Why This Book?

The objective of this book is to provide students, educators, and parents with practice materials focused on the core skills needed to help students succeed on the PARCC mathematics assessment.

A student will fare better on an assessment when s/he has practiced and mastered the skills measured by the test. A student also excels when s/he is familiar with the format and structure of the test. This book helps students do both. Students can review key material by standard through doing the skill-building exercises, as well as take practice tests to become accustomed to how the content is presented and to enhance test-taking skills. By test day, students will feel confident and be adequately prepared to do his or her best.

## This Book Includes:

- 348 skill-building exercises organised by standard in order to help students learn and review concepts in the order that they will likely be presented in the classroom. These worksheets also help identify weaknesses, and highlight and strengthen the skills needed to excel on the actual exam. A variety of question types are included in the worksheets to help students build skills in answering questions in multiple formats, so they don't get tripped up by perplexing or unfamiliar question types on test day.
- Practice test materials that are based on the official PARCC mathematics assessments released by the test administrator, and include similar question types and the same rigorous content found on the official assessments. By using these materials, students will become familiar with the types of items (including TEIs presented in a paper based format) and response formats they may see on the test. One PARCC practice test is included in the book. **Another practice test can be downloaded as a PDF online. You will find instructions on accessing this test on page 167.**
- Answer keys with detailed explanations to help students not make the same mistakes again. These explanations help clear up common misconceptions and indicate how students might arrive at an answer to a question.
- Answer keys with detailed explanations to help students not make the same mistakes again. These explanations help clear up common misconceptions and indicate how students might arrive at an answer to a question.
- Test prep tips to help students approach the test strategically and with confidence.

# TEST PREP TIPS

First of all, remind your student to pay attention in class throughout the year, asking questions as needed on homework and classwork. The curriculum should follow the exact standards and skills that will be tested on the end-of-year assessment.

Another extremely effective strategy is to practice, practice, practice. Have your student work on practice questions and complete several full length practice tests. Our practice tests are a great place to start.

However, simply answering the questions and then moving on will not yield much improvement. If your student misses a question, discuss why the correct answer is indeed correct. Come up with alternate approaches to this question type that may work better in the future. Have your student explain his or her answer to each question. This gives you the opportunity to reinforce logical thinking and correct misconceptions as needed.

Prior to the test, ensure that your student has a solid night of sleep and eats a nourishing breakfast.

For children, avoiding test anxiety is very important, so be sure to avoid over-emphasizing the test or inadvertently causing your student to feel excessive stress or pressure.

**In addition, teach your student general test-taking strategies such as the following:**

Use a "Work Folder" (if permitted) to write out problems, create charts and graphs, or draw pictures and diagrams as necessary. This portion is not graded, so do whatever you think will help you visualize and correctly solve the problem.

If you get stuck on a question, skip it and come back to it after answering easier questions.

There is no penalty for incorrect answers, so answer every question, even if you ultimately have to guess. On multiple choice questions, a 25% chance of answering correctly is still much better than no chance.

Don't panic when you get stuck on a question. Take a deep breath and remember that you are intelligent and prepared. No one is expected to answer every single question correctly.

If you follow the tips here, your student should be well on her way to a stress-free and successful performance on this important assessment.

# OPERATIONS AND ALGEBRAIC THINKING

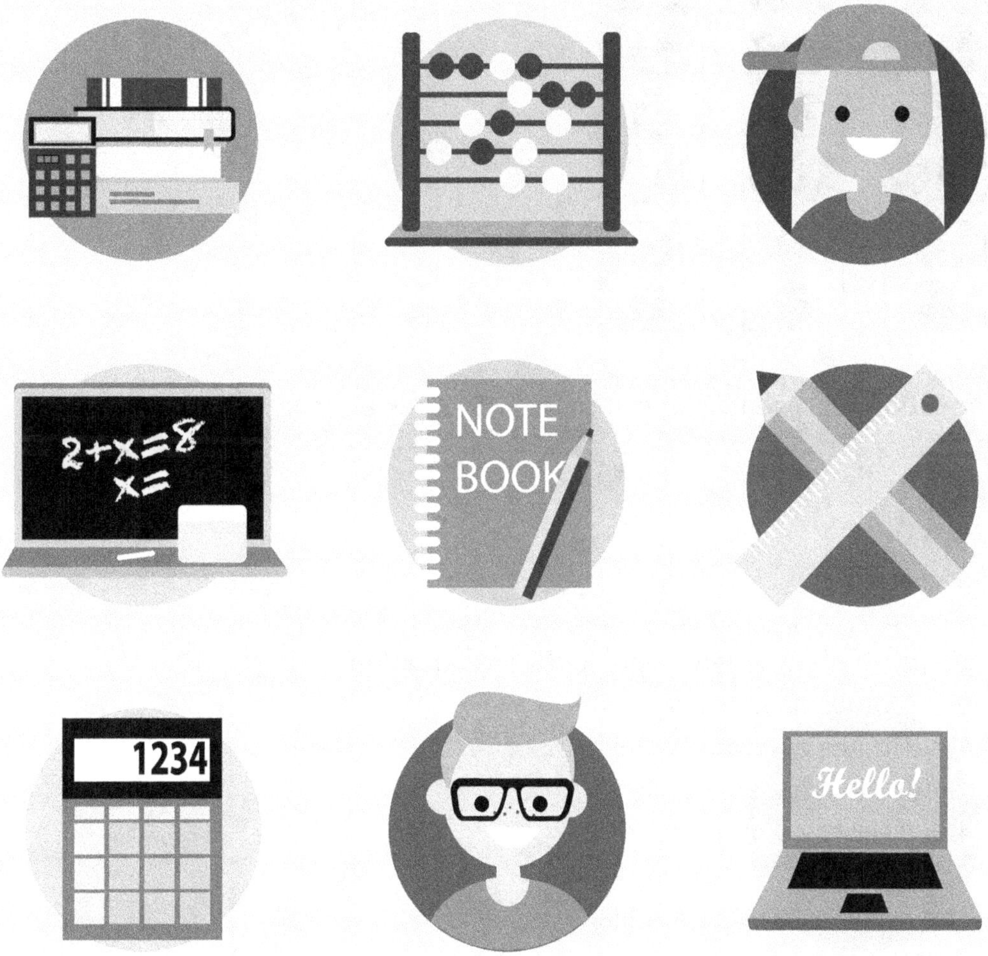

# UNDERSTAND MULTIPLICATION

**OA.A.1 Interpret a multiplication equation as a comparison, e.g., interpret 35 = 5 × 7 as a statement that 35 is 5 times as many as 7 and 7 times as many as 5. Represent verbal statements of multiplicative comparisons as multiplication equations.**

1. Which model represents the comparison 3 times as many as 4 is 12?

**A.** 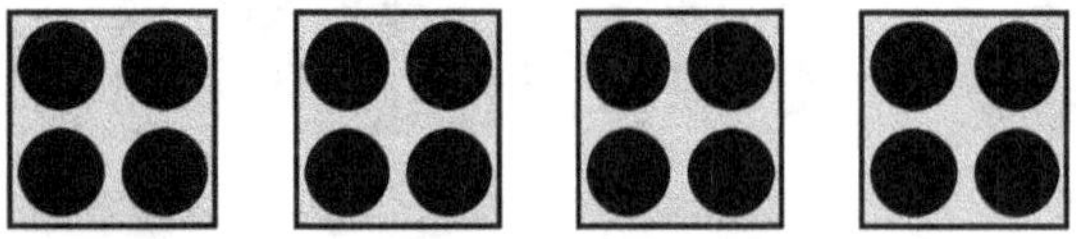

**B.** 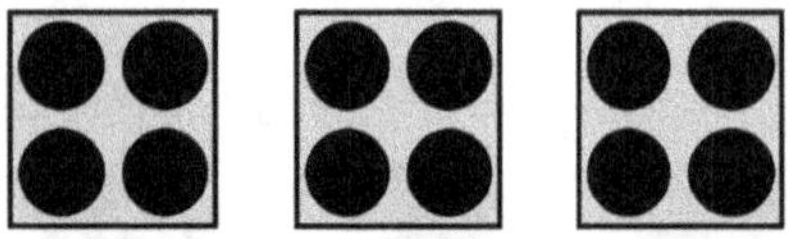

**C.** 

**D.** 

2. Which equation represents the comparison 5 times as many as 6?
   **A.** 36 = 6 x 6
   **B.** 30 = 5 x 5
   **C.** 5 x 6 = 30
   **D.** 5 x 6 = 35

3. Which comparison statement represents the equation 24 = 6 x 4?
   **A.** 24 is 6 times as many as 4
   **B.** 24 is 4 times as many as 5
   **C.** 6 times as many as 6 is 36
   **D.** 24 is 8 times as many as 3

4. Choose the number to fill in the blank:

**fifteen is _________ times as many as three**

   **A.** six
   **B.** four
   **C.** three
   **D.** five

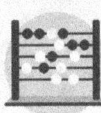

5. Choose the answer to fill in the blank:

**nine times as many as four is __________**

**A.** thirty-two
**B.** twenty-six
**C.** thirty-six
**D.** forty

6. Choose the equations that represent the comparison phrases:

**18 is 3 times as many as 6** and **18 is 6 times as many as 3**

**A.** 18 = 9 x 2, 18 = 2 x 9
**B.** 6 x 3 = 12, 3 x 6 = 12
**C.** 6 x 3 = 15, 3 x 6 = 15
**D.** 18 = 3 x 6, 18 = 6 x 3

7. Paul has twice as many pens as pencils. He has 5 pencils in his backpack. How many pens does Paul have? Choose the correct multiplication equation to solve.

**A.** 2 x 5 = 10 pens
**B.** 2 x 2 = 4 pencils
**C.** 5 + 5 = 10 pencils
**D.** 2 x 5 = 12 pens

8. Sam, Kate, Robin, and Olive went apple picking. The following chart shows the number of apples each friend picked.

| APPLE PICKING CHART | |
|---|---|
| **Name** | **Number of Apples Picked** |
| Sam | 12 |
| Kate | 6 |
| Robin | 18 |
| Olive | 2 |

A. Use the information in the chart to choose the correct answer for the following statement:

________________ picked two times as many apples as Kate.

**A.** Robin
**B.** Sam
**C.** Kate
**D.** Olive

B. Write a multiplication equation to represent the comparison statement.

Multiplication equation: ______________________________

Use the information in the apple picking chart to choose the correct answer for the following statement:

C. Robin picked ______________ times as many apples as Olive.

**A.** 9
**B.** 7
**C.** 8
**D.** 6

D. Write a multiplication equation to represent the comparison statement.

Multiplication equation: ______________________________

9. Joey is 3 times as old as his sister, Jenna. If Jenna is 7 years old, how old is Joey? Show your work.

Answer: ______________________________

10. The following chart shows the cost of pets in a pet store. Use the information in this chart to answer the questions below.

| COST OF PETS | | | |
|---|---|---|---|
| **bird** | **hamster** | **gerbil** | **fish** |
| **$20** | **$15** | **$5** | **$2** |

A. Write a multiplication equation to show the relationship between the cost of a fish and the cost of a bird.

__________ x __________ = __________

B. Sarah was in the pet store and noticed a bird cost 4 times as much as a gerbil. Is she correct? Why or why not? Explain your answer using equations or models.

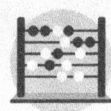

Answer: ____________________________________________________________

# USE MULTIPLICATION & DIVISION TO SOLVE WORD PROBLEMS

**OA.A.2 Multiply or divide to solve word problems involving multiplicative comparison, e.g., by using drawings and equations with a symbol for the unknown number to represent the problem, distinguishing multiplicative comparison from additive comparison.**

1. Simon sees bags of oranges at the Fresh Market. Each bag has 5 oranges. Simon needs 3 times that amount for a party. Which model shows how many bags of oranges Simon needs?

**A.** 

**B.** 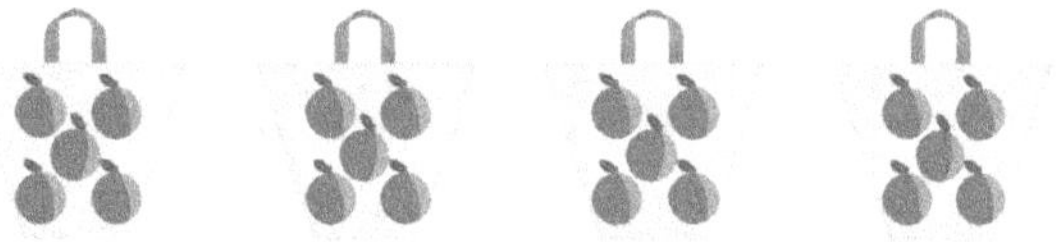

**C.** 

**D.** 

2. Tom is setting up chairs for the school play. He lines up 4 chairs. The principal says he needs 5 times that amount in each row. How many chairs should Tom set up in a row? Choose the bar model that represents this problem.

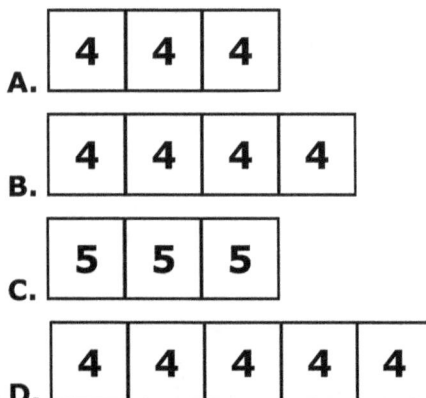

**A.**

| | | |
|---|---|---|
| 4 | 4 | 4 |

**B.**

| | | | |
|---|---|---|---|
| 4 | 4 | 4 | 4 |

**C.**

| | | |
|---|---|---|
| 5 | 5 | 5 |

**D.**

| | | | | |
|---|---|---|---|---|
| 4 | 4 | 4 | 4 | 4 |

3. James scored 4 goals last soccer season. This season, he scored 3 times as many goals as last soccer season. Which equation can you use to find how many goals James scored this soccer season?
   **A.** 4 + 3 = 7 goals
   **B.** 4 x 3 = 12 goals
   **C.** 3 + 3 = 6 goals
   **D.** 4 x 4 = 16 goals

4. Kelly has 3 times as much money as her little sister Emma. Kelly has $24. How much money does Emma have? Choose the equation that can be used to solve this problem. Use the bar model to help you solve.

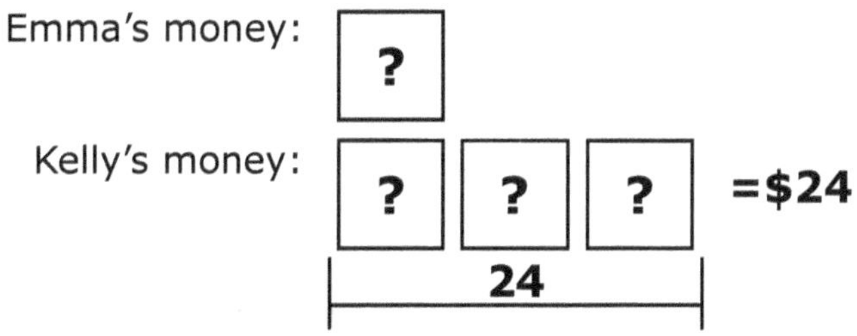


   **A.** $24 ÷ 4 = $6
   **B.** $24 ÷ 3 = $7
   **C.** $24 ÷ 3 = $8
   **D.** 4 x 3 = $12

5. Chris read 10 pages last night. His brother John read 4 times as many pages as Chris. How many pages did John read? Fill in the bar model.

   A.

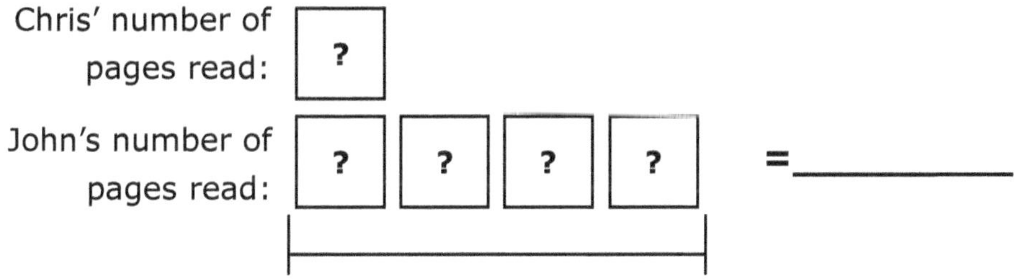


   B. Write a multiplication equation to represent this comparison statement.

   ________ x ________ = ________

6. Charlie's class has 20 students. There are 5 times as many students in the 4th grade as there are in Charlie's class. Which equation can be used to determine the number of students, *n*, in the entire 4th grade? Let *n* represent the number of students in 4th grade.

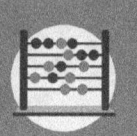

   **A.** $5 \times n = 20$

   **B.** $20 \times 5 = n$

   **C.** $20 \div n = 5$

   **D.** $5 + n = 20$

7. Mrs. Smith traveled for 24 hours last summer driving across the United States. Mr. Jones traveled for 4 hours last summer driving to the beach. How many times as many hours did Mrs. Smith travel than Mr. Jones?

   **A.** 5

   **B.** 8

   **C.** 7

   **D.** 6

8. The Blue Jays baseball team scored 6 times as many runs as the losing team. The Blue Jays scored 12 runs. Which equation can be used to find how many runs the losing team scored? Let *r* represent the losing team's runs.

   **A.** $6 \times 12 = r$

   **B.** $12 - r = 6$

   **C.** $6 \times r = 12$

   **D.** $6 + 12 = r$

9. Logan has 45 baseball cards. He has 9 times as many cards as Brendan. How many baseball cards does Brendan have? Show your work.

   A. Answer:______________________________________________

   B. Explain your thinking:

___________________________________________________________

___________________________________________________________

___________________________________________________________

___________________________________________________________

___________________________________________________________

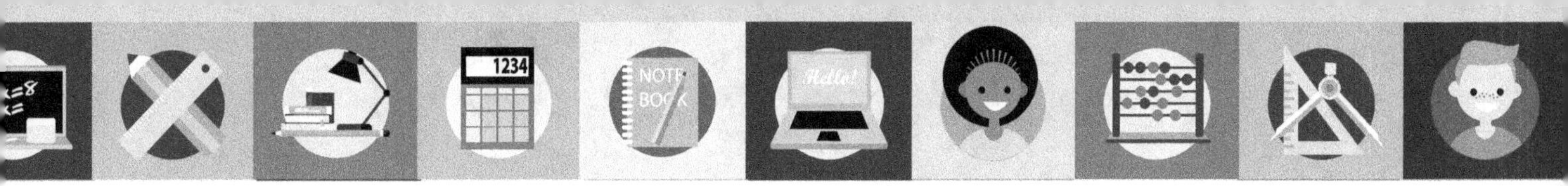


10. Lucy, Samantha, and Kristen played on the playground.
Fill in the chart to show the number of minutes each girl played on the playground.

| Girl | Minutes Played on the Playground |
|---|---|
| Lucy | |
| Samantha | |
| Kristen | |

- Lucy spent 3 times as many minutes playing as Samantha
- Samantha spent 15 more minutes playing than Kristen
- Kristen spent 20 minutes playing

11. Josh biked 12 miles last week. Mike biked 36 miles last week. Which equations can be used to find how many times the number of miles Josh biked that Mike biked? Select **ALL** the possible equations. Let *m* represent the number of unknown miles.

☐ $12 \times m = 36$
☐ $12 + 36 = m$
☐ $36 \div m = 12$
☐ $12 \div m = 36$
☐ $12 \times 36 = m$

12. Students voted on a name for their school mascot. The chart below lists the number of votes each team name received.

| Mascot Name | Number of Votes |
|---|---|
| **Tigers** | **12** |
| **Hawks** | **16** |
| **Dragons** | **48** |
| **Foxes** | **14** |

Katrina noticed 4 times as many students voted for one mascot than another. Which two mascots is she describing? Fill in the blanks.

4 times as many students voted for ____________________ than ____________________

# SOLVE & REPRESENT MULTI-STEP WORD PROBLEMS WITH EQUATIONS

**OA.A.3 Solve multistep word problems posed with whole numbers and having whole-number answers using the four operations, including problems in which remainders must be interpreted. Represent these problems using equations with a letter standing for the unknown quantity. Assess the reasonableness of answers using mental computation and estimation strategies including rounding.**

1. Alyssa is paid $5 for every hour she babysits. Mrs. Sloan paid Alyssa for 4 hours of babysitting. On her way home, Alyssa spent $6 on a coffee and a bagel. How much money does Alyssa have left?

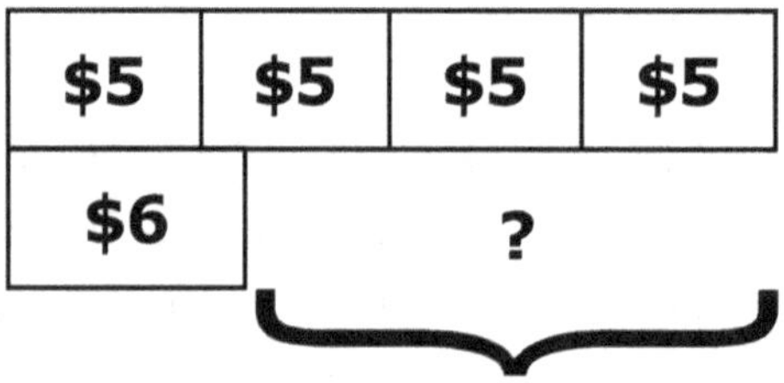


Choose the equation to solve this problem. Let *m* represent the amount of money Alyssa has left.

**A.** (4 x 5) + 6 = *m*
**B.** 4 x 5 = *m*
**C.** (4 x 5) - 6 = *m*
**D.** (5 x 6) – 4 = *m*

2. Steve mowed lawns in his neighborhood for 5 days last week. Each day he worked 2 hours in the morning and 1 hour in the afternoon. How many hours did Steve work last week? Choose the correct equation to solve this problem.

**A.** 5 + 2 + 1 = 8 hours
**B.** (2 + 1) x 5 = 15 hours
**C.** (5 x 2) + 1 = 11 hours
**D.** 2 x (5 x 1) = 10 hours

3. Carol is fixing her shed. She buys 3 pieces of wood. Each piece of wood costs $9. If she gives the cashier $40, how much money does she receive in change? Let c represent the amount of change.

**A.** (3 x 9) – 40 = *c*
**B.** 40 – 9 ÷ 3 = *c*
**C.** 40 – (3 x 9) = *c*
**D.** 40 - (9 + 3) = *c*

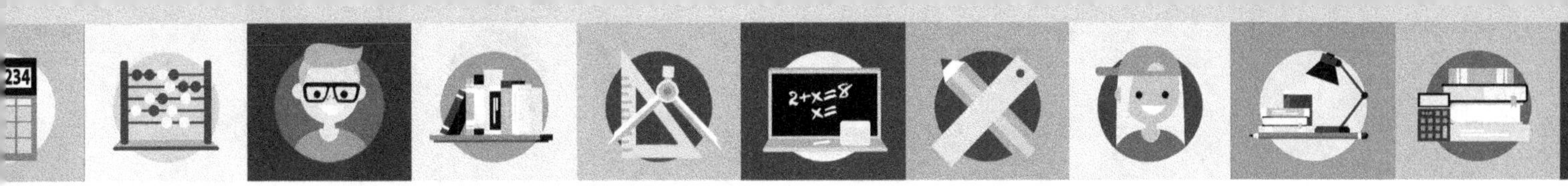


4. Fred read 300 pages in 4 days. On the first day, he read 120 pages. For the remaining 3 days, he read the same amount of pages. How many pages did Fred read for the remaining 3 days? Let $p$ represent the number of pages read.
   **A.** $(300 \div 4) \div 3 = p$
   **B.** $(300 \div 4) - 120 = p$
   **C.** $300 - (120 \div 3) = p$
   **D.** $(300 - 120) \div 3 = p$

5. Marcy's plant was 35 inches tall in June. It grew 4 inches in July. In August, it grew 2 times as much as it grew in July. How tall is Marcy's plant now?
   **A.** 47 inches
   **B.** 78 inches
   **C.** 43 inches
   **D.** 74 inches

6. Tommy and Kate are setting up 6 tables for a birthday party. They put 4 chairs at each table. How many empty chairs will there be if Tommy and Kate attend the birthday party with 19 other people? Choose the equation to solve the problem. Let $c$ represent the empty chairs.
   **A.** $(6 \times 4) - 19 = c$
   **B.** $(6 \times 4) + 19 = c$
   **C.** $21 - 6 \times 4 = c$
   **D.** $(6 \times 4) - (19 + 2) = c$

7. Jordan uses 3 eggs to make a large omelet and 2 eggs to make a small omelet. If Jordan makes 6 large omelets and 3 small omelets, how many eggs would he need? Choose the equation to solve the problem.
   **A.** $(3 \times 6) + (2 \times 3) = 24$ eggs
   **B.** $(3 \times 6) + (2 \times 6) = 30$ eggs
   **C.** $(3 \times 6) - (2 \times 3) = 1$ dozen eggs
   **D.** $(6 \times 2) + (3 + 2) = 17$ eggs

8. Mrs. Peterson is packing up the books in her classroom for the summer. Each box holds 7 books. If she has 28 math books and 31 science books to pack, how many boxes does she need?
   A. Write an equation and solve the problem.

   Equation and Answer: ______________________________

   B. Is your answer reasonable? What rounded numbers could you use to estimate the answer? Explain your thinking.

   ______________________________

   ______________________________

9. Old Town Movie Theater charges $6 for a children's ticket and $9 for an adult ticket. On Friday, the movie theater sold 25 children's tickets and twice as many adult tickets as children's tickets. How much money did the movie theater make on Friday?

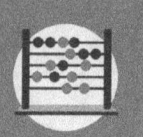

Which number completes this equation to solve the problem?

$$(25 \times 6) + (\ ?\ \times 9) =$$

**A.** 50
**B.** 25
**C.** 2
**D.** 30

10. Jessica earns $8 for each time she walks her dog. She has already earned $32. How many more times does Jessica need to walk the dog to earn enough money to buy a video game that costs $75?

**A.** 5
**B.** 7
**C.** 6
**D.** 10

11. The table shows how many toys were sold on different days at The Town Toy Store. Use the table to answer parts A and B.

| Monday | Tuesday | Wednesday | Thursday | Friday |
|---|---|---|---|---|
| 4 | 30 | 9 | 13 | 44 |

Circle **True** or **False** for each statement below.

**A.** The toys sold on Friday were 2 more toys than 7 times of what was sold on Monday.

**True or False**

**B.** The toys sold on Friday were twice what was sold on Wednesday and Thursday.

**True or False**

12. Meadow Park School is selling tickets to the school play. There will be 3 shows each week and the theater can seat 120 people for each show. The table below shows the price of the tickets.

| Type | Child | Adult | Senior |
|---|---|---|---|
| **Price** | **$5** | **$11** | **$8** |

The Friday night show sold 15 child tickets, 43 adult tickets, and 19 senior tickets. The amount of money made on the Saturday night show was 4 times the amount of money made for the Friday show. How much money did the Saturday night show make?

Show your work.

Answer: ______________________________

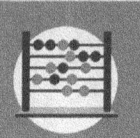

# UNDERSTAND AND USE FACTORS AND MULTIPLES

**OA.2.4 Find all factor pairs for a whole number in the range 1-100. Recognize that a whole number is a multiple of each of its factors. Determine whether a given whole number in the range 1-100 is a multiple of a given one-digit number. Determine whether a given whole number in the range 1-100 is prime or composite.**

1. What are **all** the factors of 8?
    - **A.** 1, 2, 4, 6
    - **B.** 1 ,2, 8
    - **C.** 1, 2, 4, 8
    - **D.** 1, 8, 4

2. Which number is a multiple of 7?
    - **A.** 20
    - **B.** 14
    - **C.** 32
    - **D.** 54

3. What are **all** the common factors of 6, 24, and 30?
    - **A.** 1, 2, 3, 6
    - **B.** 1, 2, 4
    - **C.** 1, 2, 4, 6
    - **D.** 1, 2, 3, 12

4. Which number is a factor of 32 and a multiple of 4?
    - **A.** 10
    - **B.** 18
    - **C.** 16
    - **D.** 6

5. Main Street Ice Cream Shop sold $96 worth of ice cream cakes on Saturday. Each cake cost an equal amount. Which number could be the cost of each cake?
    - **A.** 18
    - **B.** 22
    - **C.** 9
    - **D.** 12

6. Jonah ate 17 gummy bears. How many factor pairs does 17 have and is it a prime or a composite number?
   **A.** 17 is prime because it has 0 factor pairs.
   **B.** 17 is composite because it has 1 factor pair.
   **C.** 17 is prime because it has 1 factor pair.
   **D.** 17 is composite because it has 2 factor pairs.

7. Gavin runs 6 miles every day. Which could NOT be the number of miles Gavin runs after some number of days?
   **A.** 48
   **B.** 30
   **C.** 18
   **D.** 16

8. Which number sentence proves that 27 is a composite number?
   **A.** 27 x 1 = 27
   **B.** 3 x 27 = 81
   **C.** 27 ÷ 9 = 3
   **D.** 2 x 13 = 27

9. Lisa is baking cupcakes for a party. She uses a cupcake tray that makes 12 cupcakes.

A. Which of these numbers could be the total number of cupcakes she baked? Circle **ALL** the possible answers.

| | | | |
|---|---|---|---|
| **14** | **24** | **50** | **44** |
| **36** | **12** | **38** | **40** |

B. Fill in the blank using *factors* or *multiples.*

The numbers I circled are ______________________________ of 12.

10. A group of 16 friends are playing board game. They need to divide evenly into teams. Draw a model to show two ways they can split into teams. Then decide if 16 is a prime or composite number.

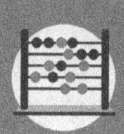

A. Draw 2 different ways the friends can split into even teams.

One Way: Another Way:

B. Fill in the blank using *prime* or *composite.*

16 is a ______________________________ number because

____________________________________________________

____________________________________________________

11. The number line below shows a factor pair of a number. Choose the correct statement that describes the factor pair the number line shows.

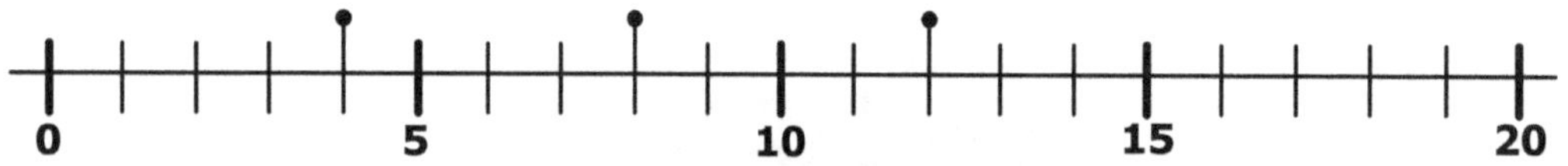


**A.** A factor pair of 12 is 6 and 2
**B.** A factor pair of 12 is 4 and 3
**C.** A factor pair of 12 is 1 and 12
**D.** A factor pair of 12 is 12 and 24

12. Hayden arranged her cookies in 6 rows with 6 cookies on a tray. What other ways can Hayden arrange her cookies?

Fill in the chart to show the different ways Hayden can organize her cookies.

| Hayden's Cookies | Rows | Columns |
|---|---|---|
| Option 1 | 6 | 6 |
| Option 2 | | |
| Option 3 | | |
| Option 4 | | |

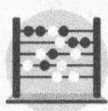

# GENERATE & IDENTIFY ARITHMETIC & SHAPE PATTERNS

**OA.C.5 Generate a number or shape pattern that follows a given rule. Identify apparent features of the pattern that were not explicit in the rule itself. *For example, given the rule "Add 3" and the starting number 1, generate terms in the resulting sequence and observe that the terms appear to alternate between odd and even numbers. Explain informally why the numbers will continue to alternate in this way.***

1. Which number comes next in this pattern?

**95, 86, 77, 68, 59, ________**

**A.** 52
**B.** 48
**C.** 50
**D.** 49

2. Which operation can be used to find the next number in the pattern?

**20, 40, 80, 160, ________**

**A.** Add 20 to the previous number.
**B.** Multiply the previous number by 2.
**C.** Divide the previous number by 2.
**D.** Add 40 to the previous number.

3. A pattern starts at 5 and follows the rule "Add 3, multiply by 2, add 3...". What is the fourth number in the pattern?

**5, ______, _______, ______**

**A.** 18
**B.** 32
**C.** 20
**D.** 19

4. The first 5 numbers in a pattern are shown below. Which statement is true about every number in the pattern? Select **ALL** the possible answers.

**12, 24, 36, 48, 60**

☐ It is a multiple of 12.
☐ It is divisible by 8.
☐ It is a factor of 60.
☐ It is multiple of 4.

5. The table shows the number of flowers Katia puts in each vase.

| Number of Vases | Number of Flowers |
|---|---|
| 2 | 16 |
| 5 | 40 |
| 7 | 56 |
| 9 | 72 |

Which of the following describes the relationship between the number of vases and the number of flowers in each vase?

**A.** Number of vases + 14 = Number of flowers
**B.** Number of vases x 8 = Number of flowers
**C.** Number of vases x 6 = Number of flowers
**D.** Number of vases +24 = Number of flowers

6. Jacob sorted buttons into groups in a specific pattern. The first 3 sets of the pattern is shown below. Draw Set 4 and Set 5 of the pattern.

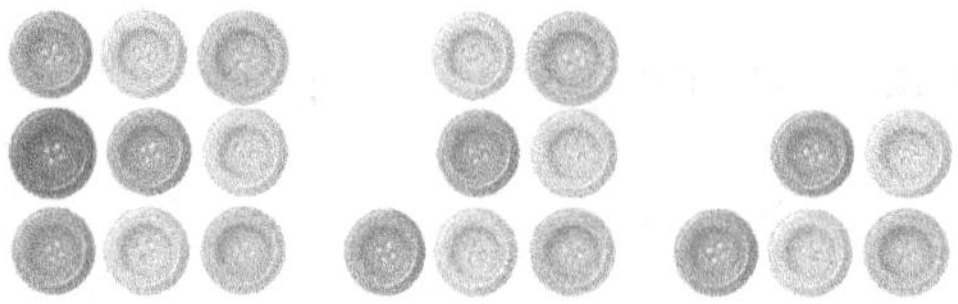

**Set 1** **Set 2** **Set3** **Set 4** **Set 5**

7. A pattern is shown below.

**6, 15, 24, 33, 42, 51, 60....**

A. Circle all the numbers that could be in the pattern.

| | | | |
|---|---|---|---|
| **68** | **78** | **75** | **69** |
| **85** | **87** | **96** | **99** |

B. Explain the pattern in this problem.

8. Jackson scored 100 points in a video game. Then he doubled his score each of the next 3 times he played. What were Jackson's scores for next 3 times he played the game?

**A.** 300, 600, 900
**B.** 200, 400, 800
**C.** 200, 300, 400
**D.** 200, 400, 600

9. What would be the 90th number in the pattern shown below?

**10, 20, 30, 40, 50**

**A.** 900
**B.** 90
**C.** 990
**D.** 99

10. Latoya writes the pattern below.

**6, 12, 18, 24, 30, 36, 42, 48,**

If she continues the pattern to 120, will the number 72 be a number in the pattern? Choose the answer that explains why or why not.

**A.** Yes, 72 is a factor of 120.
**B.** Yes, 72 is a multiple of 6.
**C.** No, 120 is not a multiple of 72.
**D.** No, 72 is not a factor of 120.

11. In a soccer tournament, after each round of games, 6 teams are cut out of the tournament. This pattern continues until there is a final round of 2 teams left to play the championship game. If there are 44 teams to start, how many rounds of soccer games will be played in order to get down to the final 2 teams for the championship game?

**A.** 5 rounds of games
**B.** 9 rounds of games
**C.** 8 rounds of games
**D.** 7 rounds of games.

12. On a 3rd grade school trip, there is 1 adult chaperone for a set number of students. The table below shows the relationship between the number of adults and the number of students on the field trip.

| | | | | | |
|---|---|---|---|---|---|
| **Number of Adults** | **4** | **6** | **9** | **13** | |
| **Number of Students** | **48** | **72** | **108** | | **180** |

A. Write an equation that can be solved to find the number of students when there are 13 adults. Then solve the problem and write the missing number in the table.

Equation: ______________________________

B. Write an equation that can be solved to find the number of adults when there are 180 students. Then solve the problem and write the missing number in the table.

Equation: ______________________________

# NUMBERS AND OPERATIONS IN BASE 10

# UNDERSTAND PLACE VALUE

**NBT.A.1 Recognize that in a multi-digit whole number, a digit in one place represents ten times what it represents in the place to its right. *For example, recognize that 700 ÷ 70 = 10 by applying concepts of place value and division.***

Use the place value chart below to answer questions 1-3.

| Hundred Thousands | Ten Thousands | Thousands | Hundreds | Tens | Ones |
|---|---|---|---|---|---|
| | | 4 | 4 | 4 | 4 |

1. What is the value of the 4 in the thousands place?
   **A.** 400
   **B.** 4
   **C.** 4,000
   **D.** 40

2. What number is 10 times the value of the 4 in the tens place? Choose the equation to solve.
   **A.** 10 x 40 = 400
   **B.** 4 x 10 = 40
   **C.** 40 x 4 = 160
   **D.** 10 x 400 = 4000

3. The value of the 4 in the thousands place is ten times the value of the 4 in the ________ place. Choose the word to fill in the blank.
   **A.** thousands
   **B.** tens
   **C.** ones
   **D.** hundreds

4. How many times greater is 15,000 than 15?
   **A.** 10 times greater
   **B.** 1,000 times greater
   **C.** 100times greater
   **D.** 10,000 times greater

5. Which number with the digit 8 represents a value ten times greater than the value represented by the 8 in 48,921?
   **A.** 93,834
   **B.** 13,718
   **C.** 86,502
   **D.** 10,780

6. Which pair of numbers correctly completes the equation?

$$\_\_\_\_\_\_\_\_\_\_ \times 1{,}000 = \_\_\_\_\_\_\_\_\_\_$$

**A.** 450 and 450,000
**B.** 450 and 45,000
**C.** 45 and 4,500
**D.** 45 and 450,000

7. What is the value of the expression below?

$$3{,}200{,}000 \div 32{,}000 =$$

**A.** 1
**B.** 10
**C.** 100
**D.** 1,000

8. In which pairs of numbers does the 4 in the first number represent a value 100 times greater than the 4 in the second number. Circle **ALL** the correct answers.

| | | |
|---|---|---|
| **2400 and 14** | **3,475 and 9,408** | **14,922 and 87,341** |
| **40,135 and 9,477** | **5,640 and 324** | **4,823 and 7,314** |

9. How many groups of 100 do you need to make the number 32,000?
**A.** 32
**B.** 320
**C.** 100
**D.** 10

Write an equation to prove your answer: ____________________________

10. Select the answer to make this equation true:

$$10{,}007 \times \_\_\_\_\_\_\_\_\_\_ = 1{,}000{,}700$$

**A.** 107
**B.** 170
**C.** 10
**D.** 100

11. A craft store sold 1,300 boxes of glue sticks last month. If the store sold 130,000 glue sticks, how many glue sticks were in each box?

Write an equation to solve the problem:________________________________________

Answer:____________________________________________________________

12. A toy store orders 50,000 bouncy balls. They can order the bouncy balls in boxes of 100 or boxes of 1,000 bouncy balls. If the toy store wants to order the least amount of boxes, should they order boxes with 100 containing bouncy balls or boxes containing 1,000 bouncy balls?

Write 2 equations to solve the problem:

A. ______________________________

B. ______________________________

Explain your answer:

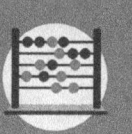

# UNDERSTAND & COMPARE MULTI-DIGIT NUMBERS

**NBT.A.2 Read and write multi-digit whole numbers using base-ten numerals, number names, and expanded form. Compare two multi-digit numbers based on meanings of the digits in each place, using >, =, and < symbols to record the results of comparisons.**

1. Which phrase represents the number 10,043?
   **A.** ten thousand, four hundred three
   **B.** ten thousand, four hundred thirty
   **C.** ten thousand, forty-three
   **D.** ten thousand, thirty-four

2. What is 358,201 written in expanded form?
   **A.** 300,000 + 5,000 + 200 + 1
   **B.** 300,000 + 58,000 + 200 + 1
   **C.** 300,000 + 50,000 + 8,000 + 201
   **D.** 300,000 + 50,000 + 8,000 + 200 + 1

3. What is this number written in standard form?

   **(2 x 10,000) + (3 x 1,000) + (9 x 100) + (4 x 10)**

   **A.** 23,940
   **B.** 23,904
   **C.** 23,914
   **D.** 32,904

4. How is this number written in standard form?

   **14 thousands + 5 thousands + 8 tens + 6 ones**

   **A.** 14,086
   **B.** 14,806
   **C.** 19,086
   **D.** 19,860

5. Which digit in the number 487,912 proves that the number is greater than 478,953?
   **A.** 9
   **B.** 8
   **C.** 7
   **D.** 5

6. Which number is seven tens less than 789,498?
   **A.** 789,479
   **B.** 789,478
   **C.** 789,528
   **D.** 789,428

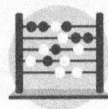

7. How many tens are in 4,000?
   **A.** 40
   **B.** 400
   **C.** 4
   **D.** 4,000

8. Which number below is the greatest?
   **A.** 8 ten thousands and 97 tens
   **B.** 872,498
   **C.** (800 x 1,000) + (70 x 100) + (2 x 1000) + (40 x 10)
   **D.** 80 ten thousands + 70 hundreds + 20 tens + 9 ones

9. Which number is less than 40 hundreds, 56 tens and 3 ones?

   A. First write the number in standard form:

   **40 hundreds = ______ + 56 tens =______ + 3 ones =______= ______**

   B. Select the number that is less than the one above.
   **A.** 4,536
   **B.** 4,566
   **C.** 40,563
   **D.** 4,635

10. What other ways could you write 7,629? Choose **ALL** the correct answers.
   **A.** 7,000 + 600 +9
   **B.** (70 x 10) + (6 x 100) + (2 x 10)
   **C.** 7 thousands + 62 tens + 9 ones
   **D.** (70 x 100) + (60 x 10) + (2 x 10) + (9 x 1)
   **E.** 76 hundreds + 2 tens + 9 one

11. Write the correct number on the line. Then fill in the equation to prove your answer.

   A. How many hundreds are in 700,000? __________

   __________ x __________ = 700,000

B. How many thousands are in 700,000? __________

__________ x __________ = 700,000

C. How many tens are in 700,000? __________

__________ x __________ = 700,000

12. Fill in the blanks to show three different ways to represent the number:

**317,568**

A. ______ hundred thousands, ______ ten thousands, ______ thousands

______ hundreds, ______ tens, ______ ones

B. ______ hundred thousands, ______ ten thousands, ______ hundreds,

______ tens, ______ ones

C. ______ ten thousands, ______ hundreds, ______ ones

# UNDERSTAND PLACE VALUE

**NBT.A.3 Use place value understanding to round multi-digit whole numbers to any place.**

1. What is 875,235 rounded to the nearest ten thousand?
   **A.** 875,000
   **B.** 880,000
   **C.** 890,000
   **D.** 870,000

2. What is 78,432 rounded to the nearest hundred?
   **A.** 78,430
   **B.** 79,400
   **C.** 78,400
   **D.** 78,500

3. Which number will round to 840 when rounded to the nearest tens' place?
   **A.** 845
   **B.** 848
   **C.** 847
   **D.** 843

4. What is 499,830 rounded to the nearest thousand?
   **A.** 500,000
   **B.** 490,000
   **C.** 499,000
   **D.** 498,000

5. Which number will round to 1,000 when rounded to the nearest hundreds' place?
   **A.** 943
   **B.** 983
   **C.** 912
   **D.** 939

6. When rounded to the nearest hundred, which number will round up to the next hundred?
   **A.** 17,549
   **B.** 308,248
   **C.** 35,671
   **D.** 1,935

7. What number below could be the number that when rounded to the thousands' place, it is 68,000?
   **A.** 67,345
   **B.** 67,498
   **C.** 68,723
   **D.** 68,457

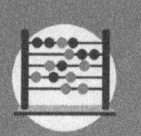

8. Angelo rounds the amount of money he made each week to the nearest hundred. Which number does NOT round to 1,300?
   **A.** 1,321
   **B.** 1,357
   **C.** 1,298
   **D.** 1,255

9. Old Town Bakery rounded their actual sales of 134,948 to 130,000. Which place value did the bakery round to?
   **A.** hundred thousand
   **B.** thousand
   **C.** ten thousand
   **D.** hundred

10. Circle all the numbers that will equal 414,000 when rounded to the thousands' place.

**413,802**  **414,502**  **413,276**

**414,498**  **413,734**  **414,258**

11. Complete the table by filling in the missing number. All numbers are rounded to the tens place.

    A. What is the lowest possible number that would round to the number listed in the table?

    B. What is the highest possible number that would round to the number listed in the table?

| Number Rounded to the Nearest Ten | Lowest Possible Number | Highest Possible Number |
|---|---|---|
| example: 650 | 645 | 654 |
| 4,320 | | |
| 17,660 | | |
| 812,710 | | |

12. The table shows the total amount of money Papa's Pizzeria made in 4 days.

| Days | Thursday | Friday | Saturday | Sunday |
|---|---|---|---|---|
| Sales | $10,048 | $9,730 | $10,569 | $10,365 |

A. On which day or days will the sales rounded to the nearest thousand be greater than the actual sales?

______________________________

B. On which day will the sales rounded to the nearest thousand be closest to the actual sales?

______________________________

C. On which day will the sales rounded to the nearest thousand be farthest from the actual sales?

______________________________

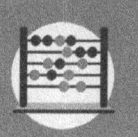

# ADD & SUBTRACT MULTI-DIGIT NUMBERS

**NBT.B.4 Fluently add and subtract multi-digit whole numbers using the standard algorithm.**

1. What is the sum of 9,237 + 5,871?
   **A.** 15,108
   **B.** 14,108
   **C.** 15,198
   **D.** 15,098

2. What is difference of 7,652 – 4,239?
   **A.** 4,333
   **B.** 3,327
   **C.** 3,337
   **D.** 3,413

3. What is the sum of 45,873 + 139,592?
   **A.** 175,465
   **B.** 184,465
   **C.** 185,465
   **D.** 185,455

4. The normal price of motorcycle is $13,500. On Friday, the shop has a sale and the price of the motorcycle is on sale for $1,299 less than the normal price. What is the price of the motorcycle when it is on sale?
   **A.** $12,399
   **B.** $12,201
   **C.** $12,311
   **D.** $12,211

5. The Great Amusement Park tracks how many people visit on the weekends. On Friday, 5,398 visit the park. On Saturday, 7,450 people visit the park and on Sunday 8,957 people visit. How many total people visited the park over the weekend?
   **A.** 21,805
   **B.** 22,995
   **C.** 21,705
   **D.** 22,805

6. Which expression has a sum of 2,000?
   **A.** 1,115 + 385 +495 =
   **B.** 1,756 + 344=
   **C.** 1,463 + 537=
   **D.** 1,372 + 250 + 478=

7. Which number is 20 hundreds less than 5,975,321?
   **A.** 5,975,121
   **B.** 5,955,321
   **C.** 5,973,121
   **D.** 5,973,321

8. Which number makes this equation true?

   **5,763 + ________________ = 28,754**

   **A.** 22,911
   **B.** 22,991
   **C.** 23,991
   **D.** 22,981

9. Which number makes this equation true?

   **112,572 - ________________ = 39,678**

   **A.** 72,894
   **B.** 72,804
   **C.** 72,104
   **D.** 72,994

10. The Peters Family pays rent each year for their vacation home in the mountains. The table shows their rent for 3 years.

| Year | Rent |
| --- | --- |
| 2013 | $19,350 |
| 2014 | $20,720 |
| 2015 | $22,090 |

   How much does the rent increase each year?
   **A.** $1,380
   **B.** $1,360
   **C.** $1,370
   **D.** $1,330

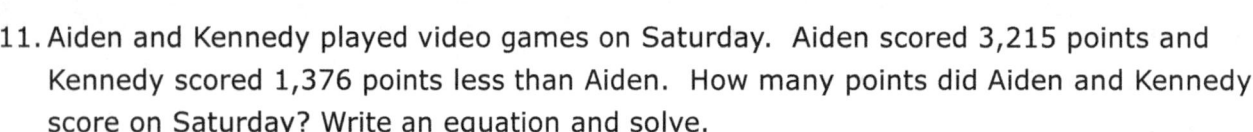

11. Aiden and Kennedy played video games on Saturday. Aiden scored 3,215 points and Kennedy scored 1,376 points less than Aiden. How many points did Aiden and Kennedy score on Saturday? Write an equation and solve.

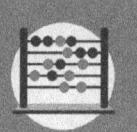

Show your work.

A. Equation and Answer: ______________________________

B. Explain how your solved the problem.

______________________________

______________________________

______________________________

______________________________

12. Our Town Movie theater tracks their sales for each season. The table below shows the movie theater's number of sales.

| **Season** | **Winter** | **Spring** | **Summer** | **Fall** |
|---|---|---|---|---|
| **Sales (amount of money made)** | **$24,671** | **$19,255** | **$20,498** | **$22,319** |

A. How much more money did the movie theater make in the winter and fall than in the spring and summer?

Show your work:

Answer: ______________________________

B. How much more money did the movie theater make in its highest selling season versus its lowest selling season?

Show your work:

Answer: ______________________________

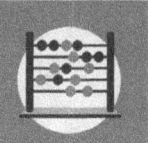

# MULTIPLY MULTI-DIGIT NUMBERS & REPRESENT MULTIPLICATION

**NBT.B.5 Multiply a whole number of up to four digits by a one-digit whole number, and multiply two two-digit numbers, using strategies based on place value and the properties of operations. Illustrate and explain the calculation by using equations, rectangular arrays, and/or area models.**

1. What is the value of 549 times 8?
   **A.** 4,372
   **B.** 4,382
   **C.** 4,392
   **D.** 4,032

2. What is the product of 2,974 x 5?
   **A.** 14,870
   **B.** 14,770
   **C.** 14,850
   **D.** 14,570

3. Mrs. Rogers handed out stickers to her students. If each of the 24 students receives 15 stickers, how many stickers does Mrs. Rogers need to purchase?
   **A.** 260
   **B.** 360
   **C.** 560
   **D.** 350

4. Which expression can be used to find the product of 45 x 5?
   **A.** (40 x 50) =
   **B.** (40 x 50) + 5=
   **C.** (40 x 5) x 5
   **D.** (40 x 5) + (5 x 5)=

5. Which expression has a value of 630?
   **A.** 60 x 30 =
   **B.** (9 x 7) x 10=
   **C.** (60 x 10) + (3 x 30)=
   **D.** (21 x 3) x 100=

6. Complete the area model to find the product.

**83 x 79**

A.

| | 80 | 3 |
|---|---|---|
| **70** | | |
| **9** | | |

B. Fill in the equation: _______ + _______ + _______ + _______ = _______

7. Which pairs of numbers could be added to this table?

| Number A | Number B |
|---|---|
| 640 | 64,000 |
| 39,006 | 3,900,600 |
| 8,703 | 870,300 |

**A.** 10,007 and 1,000,700
**B.** 5,060 and 50,060
**C.** 9,834 and 983,040
**D.** 12,031 and 120,310

8. Which would **NOT** be a correct way to find the product of 37 x 52?
**A.** (37 x 50) + (37 x 2)=
**B.** (50 x 30) + (50 x 7) + (30 x 2) + (7 x 2) =
**C.** (30 x 50) + (30 x 7) + (30 x 2) + (7 x 2) =
**D.** (52 x 30) + (52 x 7)=

9. Bob's Bakery is counting the amount of pastries sold in 4 days. For the first 3 days, the bakery sold 147 pastries each day. On the 4th day, the bakery sold 138 pastries. How many pastries did the bakery sell in 4 days?
**A.** 588 pastries
**B.** 579 pastries
**C.** 559 pastries
**D.** 479 pastries

10. Robin ordered 25 trays of cookies for her restaurant with 38 cookies on each tray. If she will host 935 people at her restaurant over the weekend and each person eats one cookie, how many cookies will she have left over?

   **A.** 25 cookies
   **B.** 35 cookies
   **C.** 20 cookies
   **D.** 15 cookies

11. Sean is planting vegetables in his garden. The garden has 2 rows with 3 sections in each row. Each garden section has an area of 64 square feet.

   What is the total area of the garden?

   Show your work:

   Write an equation using parenthesis to solve: ______________________________

   Total area of garden: __________________________________________________

12. Bennett brings 3 gallons of water to his football game. His teammate, Jordan, brings 3 times as many gallons of water as Bennett. If one gallon of water contains 128 fluid ounces, how many ounces of water did Bennett and Jordan bring to their football game?

   Show your work:

   Answer:_____________________________________

Explain the steps you used to solve the problem.

______________________________________________________________________________

______________________________________________________________________________

______________________________________________________________________________

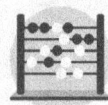

# DIVIDE MULTI-DIGIT NUMBERS & REPRESENT DIVISION

**NBT.B.6 Find whole-number quotients and remainders with up to four-digit dividends and one-digit divisors, using strategies based on place value, the properties of operations, and/or the relationship between multiplication and division. Illustrate and explain the calculation by using equations, rectangular arrays, and/or area models.**

1. What is 966 divided by 3?
   **A.** 323
   **B.** 322
   **C.** 332
   **D.** 302

2. What is the value of 7200 ÷ 9?
   **A.** 80
   **B.** 8,000
   **C.** 800
   **D.** 8

3. Mario earns $8 for every hour he works at the movie theater. Mario made $264 last week. How many hours did Mario work last week?
   **A.** 33
   **B.** 32
   **C.** 43
   **D.** 31

4. Which number makes this equation true?

   **462 ÷ ________ = 77**

   **A.** 8
   **B.** 9
   **C.** 7
   **D.** 6

5. Which of the expressions below can be used to find n in 7 x $n$ = 196
   **A.** 196 ÷ 7 = $n$
   **B.** 196 x 7 = $n$
   **C.** $n$ ÷ 196 = 7
   **D.** 7 ÷ $n$ = 196

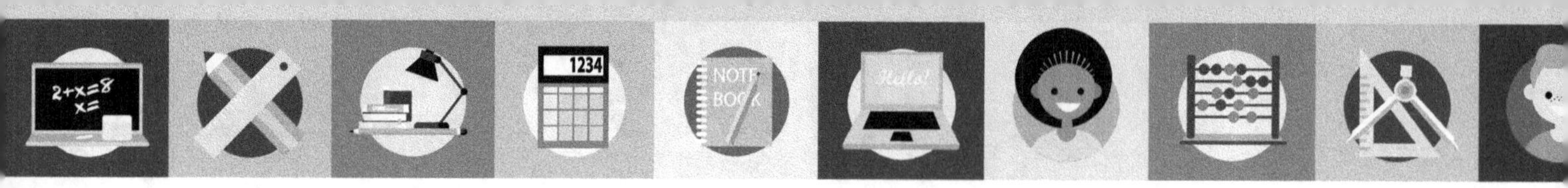


6. The array below shows a set of 24 circles.

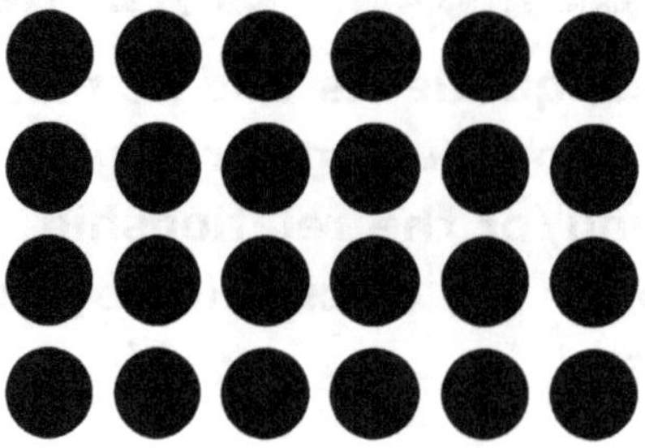

Which of these equations can be matched to this array? Circle **ALL** the correct answers.

| | | | |
|---|---|---|---|
| **4 x 6 = 24** | **24 x 4 = 96** | **6 x 4 = 24** | **6 x 24 = 144** |
| **96 ÷ 4 = 24** | **24 ÷ 6 = 4** | **144 ÷ 6 = 24** | **24 ÷ 4 = 6** |

7. Which of these statements describes a situation where there will be 4 muffins left over?
   **A.** 48 muffins divided into 12 bags
   **B.** 58 muffins divided into 4 bags
   **C.** 60 muffins divided into 8 bags
   **D.** 78 muffins divided into 6 bags

8. The diagram below shows 23 buttons sorted into groups.

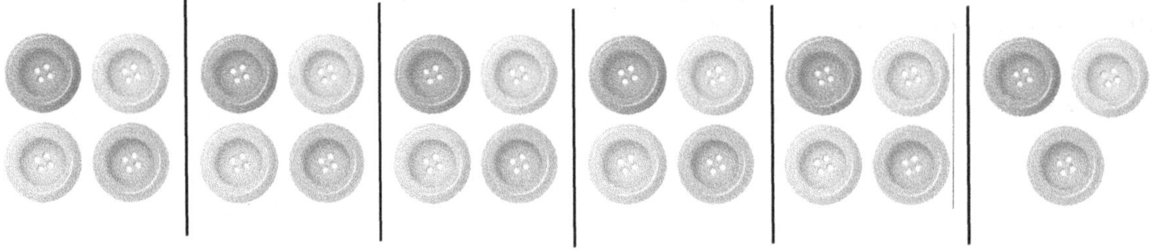

Which division equation shows how the buttons were sorted?
   **A.** 23 ÷ 5 = 4
   **B.** 23 ÷ 5 = 4, remainder 3
   **C.** 23 ÷ 4 = 4, remainder 3
   **D.** 20 ÷ 5 =4

9. Addison shaded 148 squares on a grid to make a rectangle. If she shaded 4 rows, how many squares did she shade in each row?
   **A.** 37
   **B.** 38
   **C.** 27
   **D.** 36

10. Payton has $256 saved up from working. If he spends $9 day on lunch, how many days will it take Peyton to spend all his money? How much money will he have left over?

**A.** 256 ÷ 9 = 28 days, $0 remaining
**B.** 256 x 9 = 2,304 days, $0 remaining
**C.** 256 ÷ 9 = 28 days, $3 remaining
**D.** 256 ÷ 9 = 28 days, $4 remaining

11. Lola estimated that 353 divided by 5 will be about 70 and 614 divided by 3 will be about 200.

Fill in the blanks to show the estimated equations Lola used to find her rounded quotients.

A. __________ ÷ __________ **= 70**

B. __________ ÷ __________ **= 200**

12. The table below shows the number of tickets sold for a Saturday night football game.

| Type of Ticket | Adult Ticket | Children's Tickets |
|---|---|---|
| **Regular** | **5,785** | **3,624** |
| **VIP** | | |

A. There were 5 times more regular adult tickets sold than VIP adult tickets. How many adult VIP were sold?

Answer: ____________________

B. There were 4 times more regular children's tickets sold than VIP children's tickets. How many VIP children's tickets were sold?

Answer: ____________________

C. Of all the adults at the game, half of the adults were supporting the home team. How many adults were cheering for the home team?

Answer: ____________________

# NUMBERS AND OPERATIONS – FRACTIONS

# UNDERSTAND, IDENTIFY & GENERATE EQUIVALENT FRACTIONS

**NF.A.1 Explain why a fraction *a/b* is equivalent to a fraction *(n × a)/(n × b)* by using visual fraction models, with attention to how the number and size of the parts differ even though the two fractions themselves are the same size. Use this principle to recognize and generate equivalent fractions.**

1. The shaded part of the model below represents a fraction. The entire bar model represents 1.

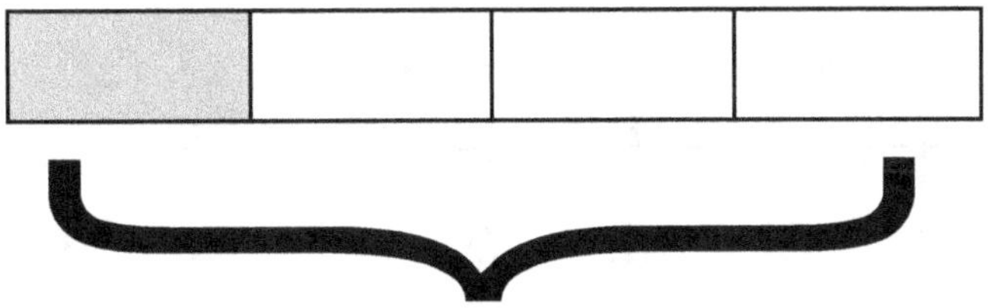

**1**

Which model below represents an equivalent fraction to the bar model above?

**A.** 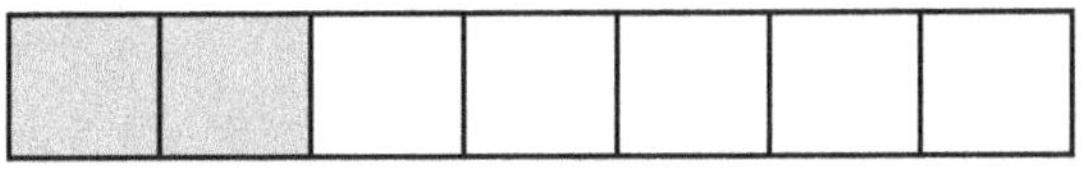

**B.** 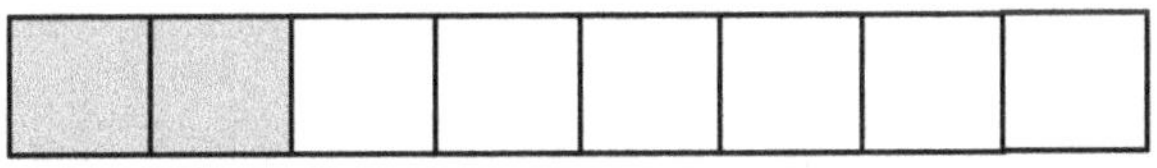

**C.** 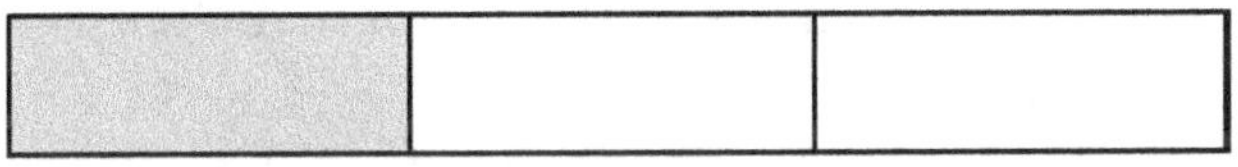

**D.** 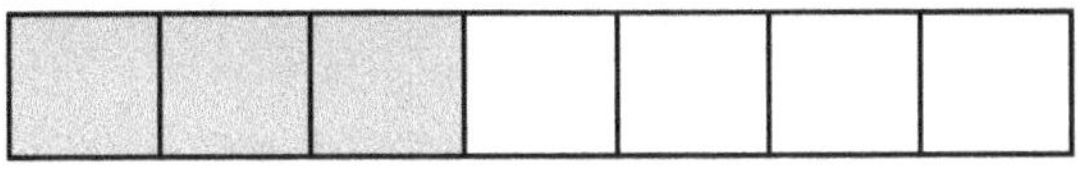

2. Which fraction is equivalent to the shaded region of this bar model?

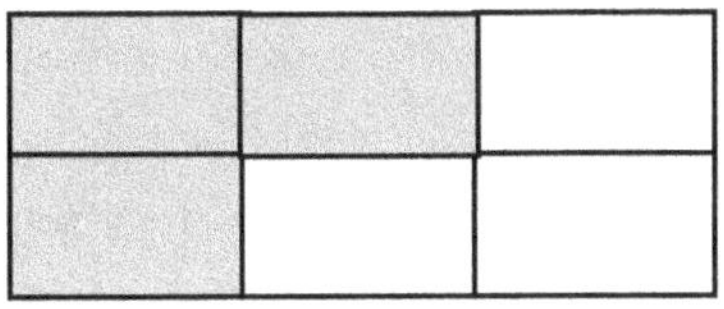

**A.** $^{1}/_{3}$
**B.** $^{2}/_{3}$
**C.** $^{2}/_{6}$
**D.** $^{1}/_{2}$

3. What fraction is shaded in on the bar model?

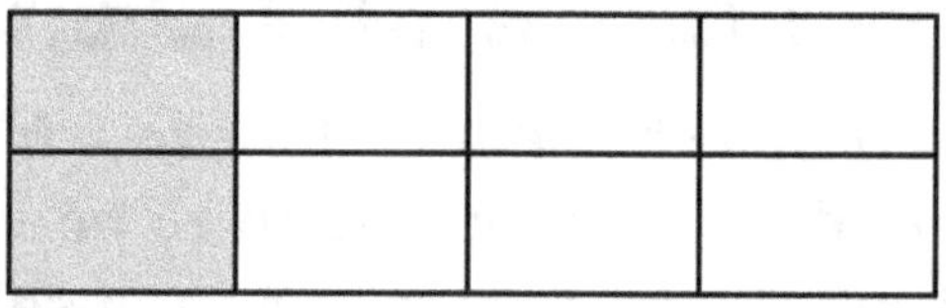

**A.** $^{2}/_{3}$
**B.** $^{1}/_{2}$
**C.** $^{1}/_{4}$
**D.** $^{2}/_{6}$

4. The point on the number lines represents a fraction.

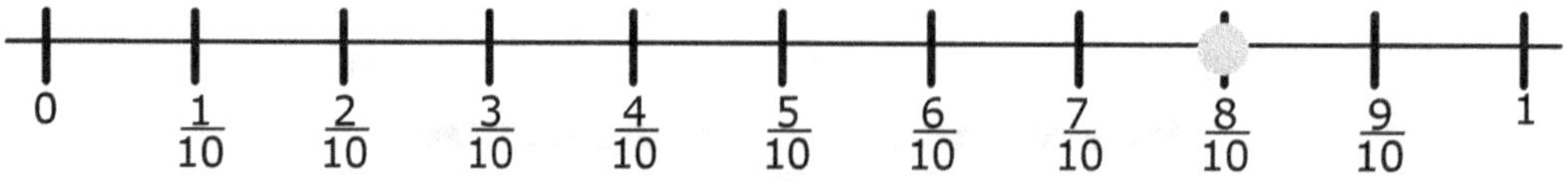


Which fraction is equivalent to the fraction represented on the number line?

**A.** $^{4}/_{5}$
**B.** $^{3}/_{8}$
**C.** $^{3}/_{5}$
**D.** $^{4}/_{6}$

5. Clara has set of 12 stickers. She has 8 plain stickers and 4 striped stickers.

Which fraction below is equivalent to the fraction that represents the striped stickers?

**A.** $^{1}/_{4}$
**B.** $^{2}/_{8}$
**C.** $^{1}/_{3}$
**D.** $^{3}/_{6}$

6. Which fraction is equivalent to $^{2}/_{5}$ ?

**A.** $^{4}/_{12}$
**B.** $^{4}/_{15}$
**C.** $^{5}/_{10}$
**D.** $^{6}/_{15}$

7. Which pair of fractions below are equivalent?

**A.** $\frac{4}{12}$ and $\frac{3}{8}$
**B.** $\frac{1}{10}$ and $\frac{10}{100}$
**C.** $\frac{3}{18}$ and $\frac{1}{9}$
**D.** $\frac{2}{8}$ and $\frac{4}{24}$

8. Which fraction below can be simplified to form an equivalent fraction?

**A.** $\frac{4}{32}$
**B.** $\frac{8}{31}$
**C.** $\frac{7}{20}$
**D.** $\frac{9}{25}$

9. The shaded part of the model below represents a fraction.

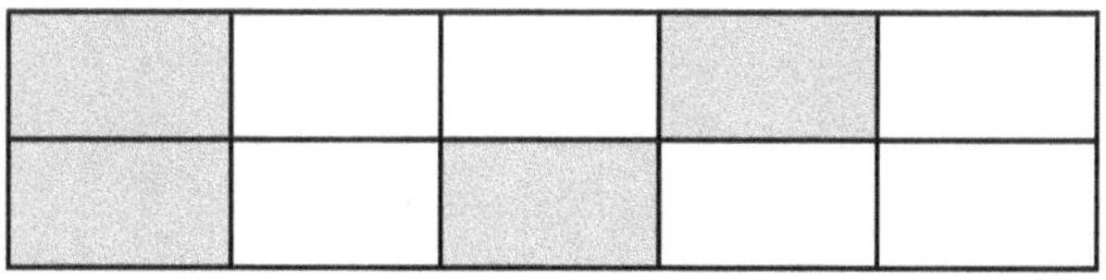

Circle **ALL** the fractions that represent the shaded part of this model.

$\frac{12}{30}$ $\frac{3}{6}$ $\frac{8}{20}$ $\frac{2}{5}$ $\frac{6}{20}$

10. Landon is organizing muffins for a party. He has 18 muffins and divides them into 3 groups.

Choose the fraction that represents the muffins in each group and a matching equivalent fraction.

**A.** $\frac{3}{12}$ and $\frac{9}{18}$
**B.** $\frac{6}{18}$ and $\frac{1}{3}$
**C.** $\frac{3}{18}$ and $\frac{1}{9}$
**D.** $\frac{6}{18}$ and $\frac{4}{24}$

11. Draw 3 separate number lines below to show how $^{1}/_{4}$, $^{2}/_{8}$, $^{3}/_{12}$ are equivalent.

Place an X on the number line to label each fraction: $^{1}/_{4}$, $^{2}/_{8}$, $^{3}/_{12}$

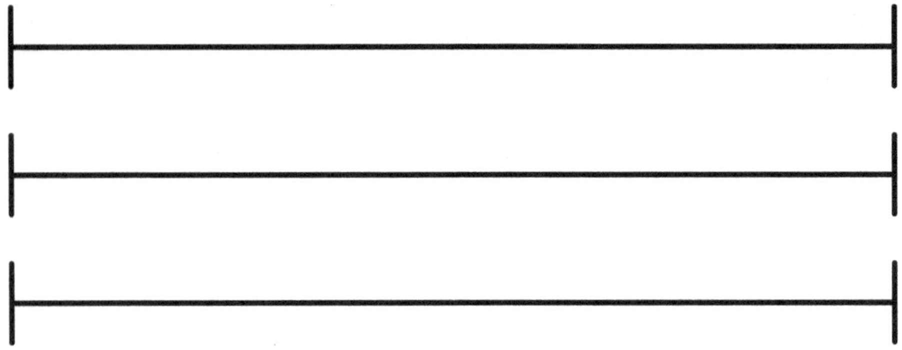

Explain using mathematical reasoning how you know these fractions are equivalent.

________________________________________

________________________________________

________________________________________

12. Tasha is counting her collection of buttons. Out of 30 buttons, 5 are white. She adds 6 more buttons to her collection with the same fraction of white buttons. How many white buttons did she add to her collection?

Answer: ____________________________________ buttons

Explain how you found your answer:

________________________________________

________________________________________

________________________________________

# UNDERSTAND, IDENTIFY & GENERATE EQUIVALENT FRACTIONS

**NF.A.2 Compare two fractions with different numerators and different denominators, e.g., by creating common denominators or numerators, or by comparing to a benchmark fraction such as 1/2. Recognize that comparisons are valid only when the two fractions refer to the same whole. Record the results of comparisons with symbols >, =, or <, and justify the conclusions, e.g., by using a visual fraction model.**

1. Which fraction below is the smallest?

    **A.** $^{3}/_{12}$
    **B.** $^{1}/_{2}$
    **C.** $^{1}/_{6}$
    **D.** $^{3}/_{4}$

2. Which fraction below is the largest?

    **A.** $^{4}/_{8}$
    **B.** $^{1}/_{9}$
    **C.** $^{2}/_{6}$
    **D.** $^{9}/_{10}$

3. The shaded model below compares two fractions.

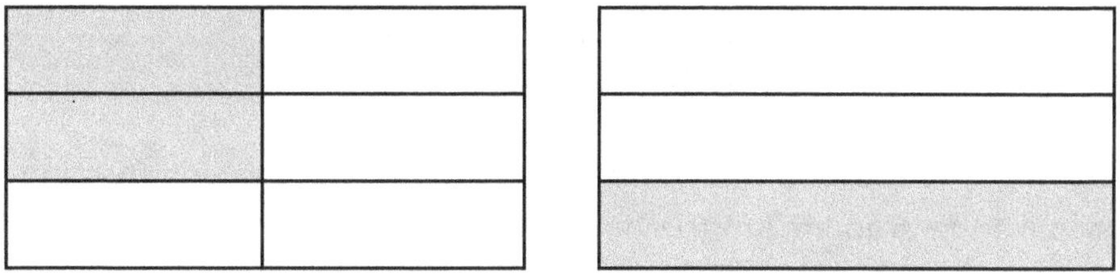

    Which expression correctly compares the shaded fraction models?

    **A.** $^{1}/_{3} < {}^{2}/_{6}$
    **B.** $^{2}/_{6} = {}^{1}/_{3}$
    **C.** $^{5}/_{6} > {}^{1}/_{3}$
    **D.** $^{2}/_{6} < {}^{1}/_{3}$

4. Which expression correctly compares the fractions?

    **A.** $^{1}/_{3} < {}^{3}/_{6}$
    **B.** $^{1}/_{5} > {}^{3}/_{4}$
    **C.** $^{2}/_{6} > {}^{7}/_{8}$
    **D.** $^{8}/_{10} < {}^{4}/_{12}$

5. Choose the fraction that makes the comparison true.

$$^{1}/_{5} < \frac{\square}{\square}$$

**A.** $^{1}/_{7}$

**B.** $^{2}/_{11}$

**C.** $^{1}/_{10}$

**D.** $^{2}/_{8}$

6. Which fraction listed below is smaller than $^{1}/_{2}$ ?

**A.** $^{4}/_{7}$

**B.** $^{5}/_{8}$

**C.** $^{1}/_{6}$

**D.** $^{2}/_{3}$

7. Amari and Joanna each shaded in a hundreds square like the one below.

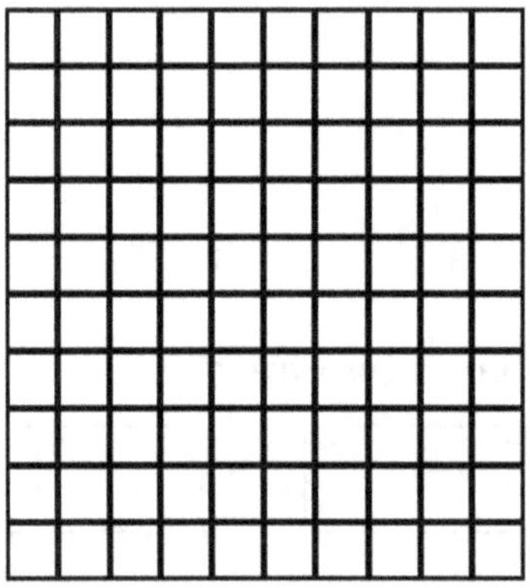

Amarai shaded $^{8}/_{10}$ of the grid and Joanna shaded in $^{75}/_{100}$. Which fraction below can be used to compare the amount Amari shaded to Joanna's amount?

**A.** $^{8}/_{100}$

**B.** $^{80}/_{100}$

**C.** $^{7}/_{10}$

**D.** $^{5}/_{10}$

8. Hailey and Jonah are eating lunch. Hailey ate $^{2}/_{3}$ of her sandwich. Jonah ate $^{3}/_{5}$ of his sandwich. Which pair of fractions correctly compares who ate more of their sandwich?

**A.** $^{2}/_{3} = {}^{10}/_{15} > {}^{3}/_{5} = {}^{9}/_{15}$

**B.** $^{2}/_{3} = {}^{8}/_{15} > {}^{3}/_{5} = {}^{6}/_{15}$

**C.** $^{2}/_{3} = {}^{6}/_{9} > {}^{3}/_{5} = {}^{6}/_{10}$

**D.** $^{2}/_{3} = {}^{8}/_{15} > {}^{3}/_{5} = {}^{6}/_{15}$

9. Bella, Colby and Sierra each read the same book for their 4th grade reading assignment. Bella read $^{5}/_{6}$ of the book, Colby read $^{2}/_{4}$ of the book, and Sierra read $^{9}/_{12}$ of the book. Who read the least amount?

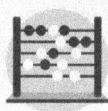

   **A.** Bella
   **B.** Sierra
   **C.** Colby
   **D.** Both Bella and Colby

10. Order the fractions from least to greatest.

**40/100** **3/5** **1/4** **4/20**

Least Greatest

________ ________ ________ ________

11. Alexa's teacher told her to practice her math facts for $^{4}/_{5}$ of an hour. She practiced for $^{3}/_{4}$ of an hour. Did Alexa practice her math facts for the required time?

Answer:____________________________________________

Explain how you know:

__________________________________________________

__________________________________________________

12. Raquel and Sean compare how much money they each have. Raquel has $12 and spent $4 on ice cream and Sean has $18 and spent $9 on a sandwich. Who spent a greater fraction of their money?

Answer:____________________________________________

Write a comparison statement using <, >, = to compare the fractions:

__________________________________________________

# UNDERSTAND & USE FRACTIONS: DECOMPOSE FRACTIONS, ADD AND SUBTRACT FRACTIONS, ADD & SUBTRACT MIXED NUMBERS, SOLVE WORD PROBLEMS WITH FRACTIONS

**NF.B.3 Understand a fraction $^a/_b$ with a > 1 as a sum of fractions $^1/_b$ .**

**NF.B.3A Understand addition and subtraction of fractions as joining and separating parts referring to the same whole.**

**NF.B.3B Decompose a fraction into a sum of fractions with the same denominator in more than one way, recording each decomposition by an equation. Justify decompositions, e.g., by using a visual fraction model.**
***Examples:*** $^3/_8 = {^1/_8} + {^1/_8} + {^1/_8}$ ; $^3/_8 = {^1/_8} + {^2/_8}$ ; $2\,^1/_8 = 1 + 1 + {^1/_8} = {^8/_8} + {^8/_8} + {^1/_8}$ .

**NF.B.3C Add and subtract mixed numbers with like denominators, e.g., by replacing each mixed number with an equivalent fraction, and/or by using properties of operations and the relationship between addition and subtraction.**

**NF.B.3D Solve word problems involving addition and subtraction of fractions referring to the same whole and having like denominators, e.g., by using visual fraction models and equations to represent the problem.**

1. Which addition expression represents the total amount show in the shaded fraction models?

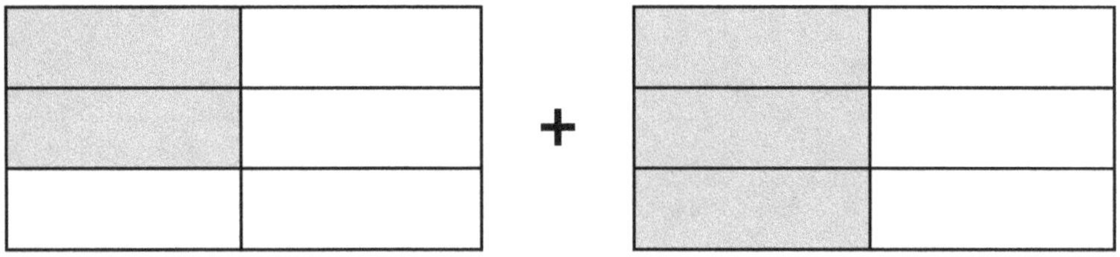

**A.** $^2/_3 + {^1/_2}$
**B.** $^2/_6 + {^3/_6}$
**C.** $^2/_6 + {^4/_6}$
**D.** $^4/_6 + {^3/_6}$

2. Find the sum: $^3/_8 + {^4/_8}$

**A.** $^6/_8$
**B.** $^7/_{16}$
**C.** $^7/_8$
**D.** $^{12}/_{64}$

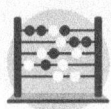

3. Find the difference: $^{8}/_{10}$ - $^{5}/_{10}$

   **A.** $^{2}/_{10}$
   **B.** $^{3}/_{5}$
   **C.** $^{4}/_{10}$
   **D.** $^{3}/_{10}$

4. Which expression represents the shaded fraction below?

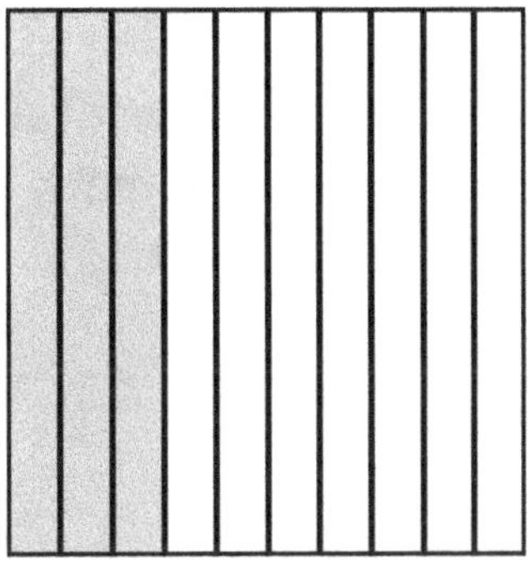

   **A.** $^{1}/_{10} + ^{1}/_{10} + ^{1}/_{10}$
   **B.** $^{3}/_{10} + ^{3}/_{10} + ^{3}/_{10}$
   **C.** $^{1}/_{10} + ^{1}/_{10}$
   **D.** $^{1}/_{3} + ^{1}/_{3} + ^{1}/_{3}$

5. Which sum is greater than 1?

   **A.** $^{4}/_{7} + ^{3}/_{7}$
   **B.** $^{4}/_{5} + ^{2}/_{5}$
   **C.** $^{9}/_{18} + ^{8}/_{18}$
   **D.** $^{4}/_{12} + ^{6}/_{12}$

6. Dane ate $^{4}/_{7}$ of one whole pizza. How much of the pizza pie is left?

   **A.** $^{5}/_{7}$
   **B.** $^{4}/_{7}$
   **C.** $^{3}/_{7}$
   **D.** $^{2}/_{7}$

7. What is $3\ ^{3}/_{4} + 2\ ^{2}/_{4}$ ?

   **A.** $6\ ^{5}/_{4}$
   **B.** $5\ ^{1}/_{4}$
   **C.** $5\ ^{5}/_{8}$
   **D.** $6\ ^{1}/_{4}$

8. This week, Avery spent $4\ ^{2}/_{6}$ hours reading on Wednesday and $2\ ^{4}/_{6}$ hours reading on Friday. How many hours did Avery spend reading this week?
   - **A.** $6\ ^{5}/_{6}$ hours
   - **B.** 7 hours
   - **C.** $7\ ^{6}/_{6}$ hours
   - **D.** $6\ ^{6}/_{12}$ hours

9. Cindy is training for a half-marathon. Her farthest run yet was $8\ ^{1}/_{4}$ miles. How many more miles does Cindy have to run in order to reach the 13 mile half-marathon race?
   - **A.** $4\ ^{3}/_{4}$ miles
   - **B.** $5\ ^{1}/_{4}$ miles
   - **C.** $5\ ^{3}/_{4}$ miles
   - **D.** $4\ ^{1}/_{4}$ miles

10. The chart below shows the amount of some ingredients needed to make a cake.

| Ingredient | Amount |
|---|---|
| **flour** | **3 cups** |
| **sugar** | **$1\ ^{1}/_{3}$ cups** |
| **milk** | **$1\ ^{2}/_{3}$ cups** |

A. How many more cups of flour than sugar is used to make a cake?

_______________ cups

B. How many total cups of ingredients are listed in the chart?

_______________ cups

11. Madison shared an apple pie with her friends. Carly ate $^{1}/_{6}$ of the pie, Don ate $^{1}/_{2}$ of the pie, and Madison ate $^{1}/_{6}$ of the pie. What fraction of the apple pie is left over?

Show your work:

Answer:_______________________________________________

12. Mrs. Hamilton ordered 3 chocolate cakes, 2 vanilla cakes, and 3 ice cream cakes for her holiday party.

- $2\ ^{1}/_{2}$ of the chocolate cake was eaten
- $1\ ^{3}/_{8}$ of the vanilla cake was eaten
- $2\ ^{3}/_{4}$ of the ice cream cake was eaten

A. What fraction of all the cakes was eaten?

Answer:____________________________________________

B. What fraction of all the cakes was left over?

Answer:____________________________________________

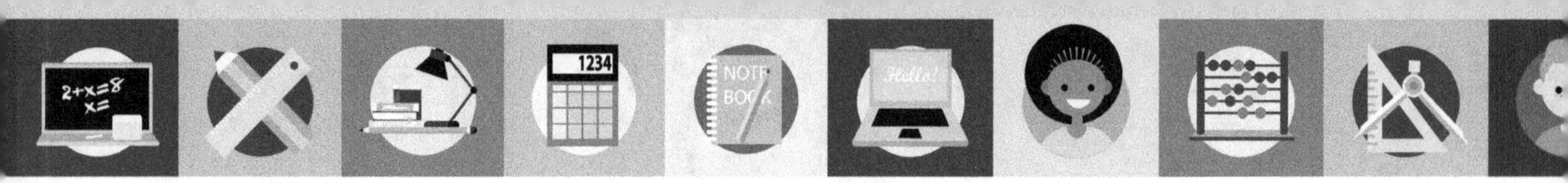


# MULTIPLY FRACTIONS: MULTIPLY FRACTIONS BY WHOLE NUMBERS, SOLVE WORD PROBLEMS BY MULTIPLYING FRACTIONS

**NF.B.4 Apply and extend previous understandings of multiplication to multiply a fraction by a whole number.**

**NF.B.4.A Understand a fraction $^{a}/_{b}$ as a multiple of $^{1}/_{b}$.** ***For example, use a visual fraction model to represent $^{5}/_{4}$ as the product $5 \times (^{1}/_{4})$, recording the conclusion by the equation $^{5}/_{4} = 5 \times (^{1}/_{4})$.***

**NF.B.4.B Understand a multiple of $^{a}/_{b}$ as a multiple of $^{1}/_{b}$, and use this understanding to multiply a fraction by a whole number.** ***For example, use a visual fraction model to express $3 \times (^{2}/_{5})$ as $6 \times (^{1}/_{5})$, recognizing this product as $^{6}/_{5}$. (In general, $n \times (^{a}/_{b}) = {}^{(n \times a)}/_{b}$.)***

**NF.B.4.C Solve word problems involving multiplication of a fraction by a whole number, e.g., by using visual fraction models and equations to represent the problem.** ***For example, if each person at a party will eat $^{3}/_{8}$ of a pound of roast beef, and there will be 5 people at the party, how many pounds of roast beef will be needed? Between what two whole numbers does your answer lie?***

1. The fraction model below shows 3 cakes. The shaded parts of the model represent the fractional pieces of a cake that has icing.

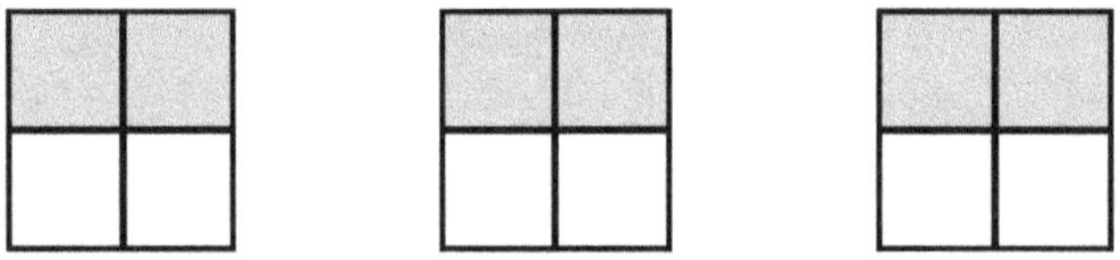

Which expression shows the total amount of cakes that have icing?

**A.** $2 \times {}^{1}/_{2}$

**B.** $6 \times {}^{1}/_{2}$

**C.** $3 \times {}^{2}/_{4}$

**D.** $3 \times {}^{1}/_{3}$

2. The shaded part of each model represents a fraction. Which shaded parts of the model below show $\mathbf{2 \times {}^{1}/_{3}}$ ?

**A.** 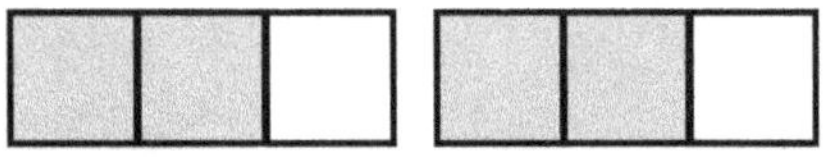

**B.** 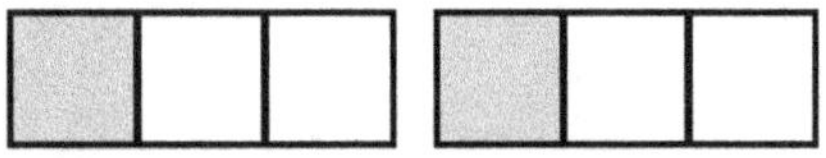

**C.** 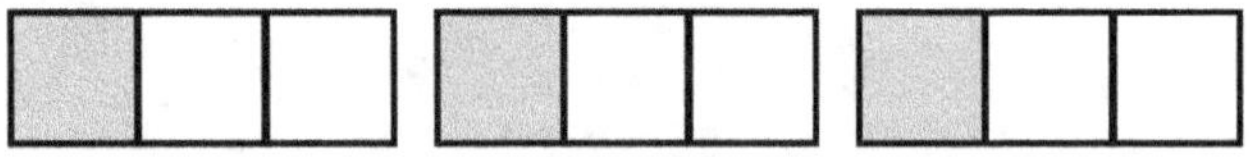

**D.** 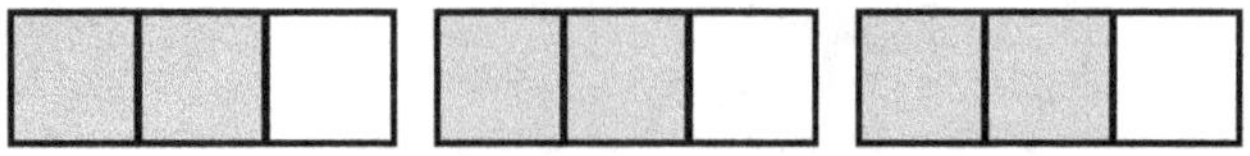

3. Use the expression **3 x $^2/_3$** and the fraction model of this expression to solve the problem below.

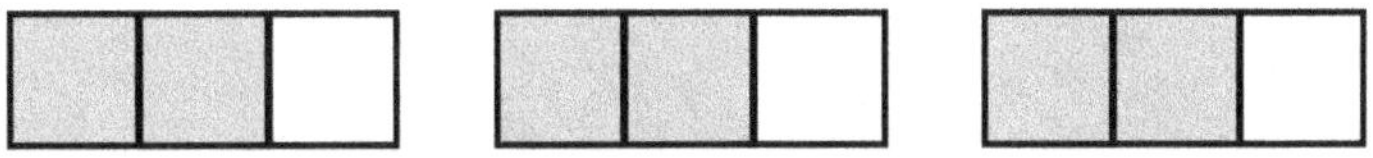

Which expression is the same as **3 x $^2/_3$** ?

**A.** $^1/_3 + ^1/_3$

**B.** $^2/_3 + ^2/_3$

**C.** $^2/_3 \times ^2/_3$

**D.** $^2/_3 + ^2/_3 + ^2/_3$

4. Use the expression 3 x $^2/_3$ and the fraction model of this expression to solve the problem below.

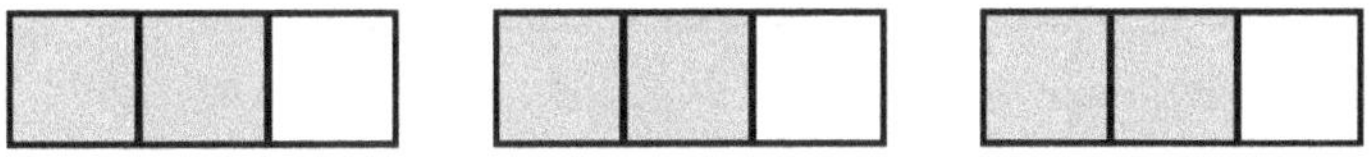

What is the value of **3 x $^2/_3$** ?

**A.** $^6/_3$

**B.** $^2/_3$

**C.** $^3/_3$

**D.** $^6/_9$

5. Each shaded part of the model below represents a fraction. Use the model to help you solve this problem.

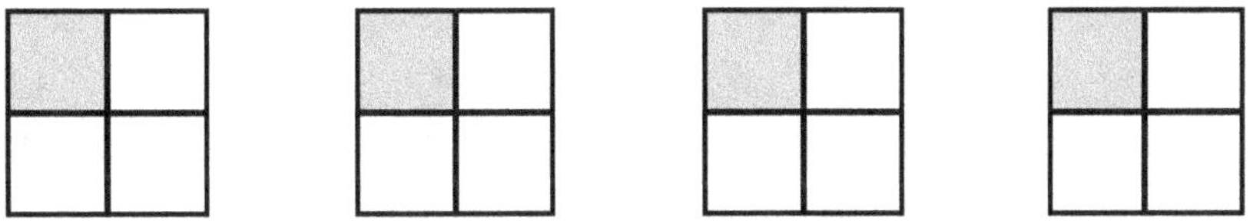

Which number completes this equation? **$^1/_4$ x ____ = 1**

**A.** 1

**B.** 4

**C.** 3

**D.** 2

6. What is the value of **5 x $^2/_5$** ?

**A.** $^{10}/_2$

**B.** 3

**C.** $^{10}/_5$

**D.** $^{10}/_{25}$

7. What is the value of **n** in the equation below?

$$n \times {}^{1}/_{2} = 3$$

**A.** 5
**B.** 4
**C.** 3
**D.** 6

8. Shade the model below to show the expression: $^{2}/_{6} \times 4$

A. 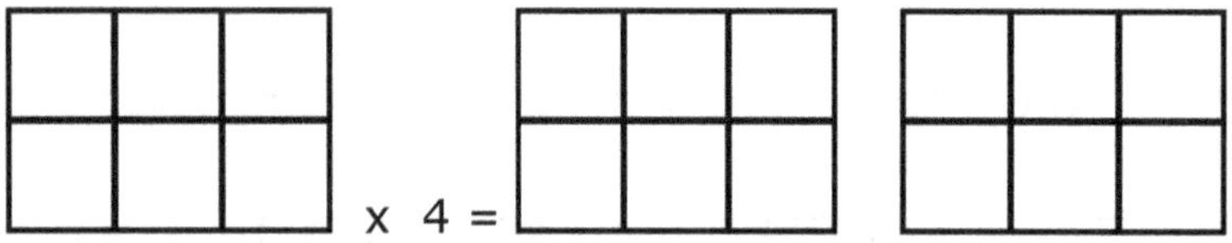


B. What is the product of $^{2}/_{6} \times 4$ ? ______________________

**C.** Write your answer as a mixed number: ______________________

9. Tomas is making 5 smoothies for his friends. He uses $^{1}/_{3}$ cup of milk for each smoothie. How much milk does Tomas need to make all the smoothies?

**A.** $1\ ^{2}/_{3}$ cups
**B.** 2 cups
**C.** $^{10}/_{5}$ cups
**D.** $1\ ^{1}/_{3}$ cups

10. Mia is planting a row of plants in her garden. Each plant is $^{3}/_{4}$ foot long. Mia's garden is 6 feet long. How many plants can Mia plant in her garden?

A. Write a multiplication equation to solve: ______________________

B. Solve and explain your answer:

11. Josh is using tiles to redo his bathroom floor. Each tile is $1\,^{1}/_{2}$ feet long. He does not want to cut any tiles and the length of this bathroom floor is a whole number. How many tiles could he use in order to equal a whole number of feet without cutting any tiles?

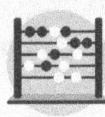

    A. 3 tiles
    B. 5 tiles
    C. 4 tiles
    D. 7 tiles

12. Carly, Lucy, and Aiden are in a running club. Carly runs $^{3}/_{4}$ mile each day for 5 days. Lucy runs $^{2}/_{6}$ mile each day for 8 days. Aiden runs $^{4}/_{5}$ mile each day for 4 days.

    Who ran the most amount of miles? ___________________________

    Who ran the least amount of miles? ___________________________

# UNDERSTAND & USE EQUIVALENT FRACTIONS INVOLVING DENOMINATORS OF 10 TO 100

**NF.C.5 Express a fraction with denominator 10 as an equivalent fraction with denominator 100, and use this technique to add two fractions with respective denominators 10 and 100.** ***For example, express $^{3}/_{10}$ as $^{30}/_{100}$, and add $^{3}/_{10}$ + $^{4}/_{100}$ = $^{34}/_{100}$.***

1. Which fraction does the shaded model below represent?

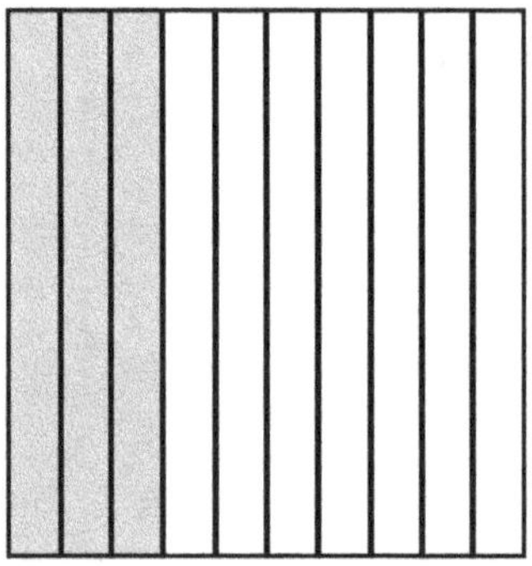

**A.** $^{3}/_{100}$
**B.** $^{3}/_{10}$
**C.** $^{33}/_{100}$
**D.** $^{30}/_{10}$

2. Which fraction does the shaded model below represent?

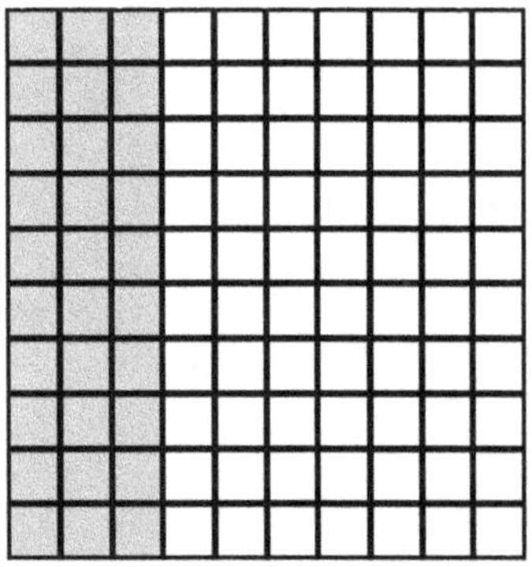

**A.** $^{3}/_{100}$
**B.** $^{33}/_{10}$
**C.** $^{30}/_{100}$
**D.** $^{30}/_{10}$

3. Which pair of fractions are equivalent?

**A.** $^{30}/_{100} = {}^{3}/_{10}$

**B.** $^{33}/_{10} = {}^{3}/_{10}$

**C.** $^{30}/_{100} = {}^{30}/_{10}$

**D.** $^{30}/_{10} = {}^{3}/_{100}$

4. Which fraction is equivalent to $^{40}/_{100}$?

**A.** $^{40}/_{10}$

**B.** $^{4}/_{100}$

**C.** $^{400}/_{100}$

**D.** $^{4}/_{10}$

5. Which fraction could be equivalent to a fraction with a denominator of 10?

**A.** $^{80}/_{100}$

**B.** $^{8}/_{100}$

**C.** $^{88}/_{100}$

**D.** $^{80}/_{10}$

6. What is the sum of $^{7}/_{10}$ and $^{20}/_{100}$ ?

**A.** $^{27}/_{100}$

**B.** $^{90}/_{100}$

**C.** $^{27}/_{10}$

**D.** $^{72}/_{100}$

7. What is the sum of $^{3}/_{10}$ and $^{5}/_{100}$ ?

**A.** $^{53}/_{100}$

**B.** $^{305}/_{100}$

**C.** $^{35}/_{100}$

**D.** $^{35}/_{10}$

8. Which fraction is needed to solve the equation below?

$$^{3}/_{10} + \_\_\_\_\_\_\_\_ = {}^{85}/_{100}$$

**A.** $^{65}/_{100}$

**B.** $^{8}/_{10}$

**C.** $^{82}/_{100}$

**D.** $^{55}/_{100}$

9. Sally owns a greenhouse. She plants sunflowers in $^{6}/_{10}$ of the greenhouse and daisies in $^{25}/_{100}$ of the greenhouse. In what fraction of the greenhouse does Sally plant daisies and sunflowers?

    **A.** $^{85}/_{100}$

    **B.** $^{31}/_{100}$

    **C.** $^{31}/_{10}$

    **D.** $^{85}/_{10}$

10. Arlo has 100 sports trading cards. Of those cards, $^{4}/_{10}$ are football cards and $^{33}/_{100}$ are soccer cards.

    A. Shade the model below to show the number of soccer and football cards.

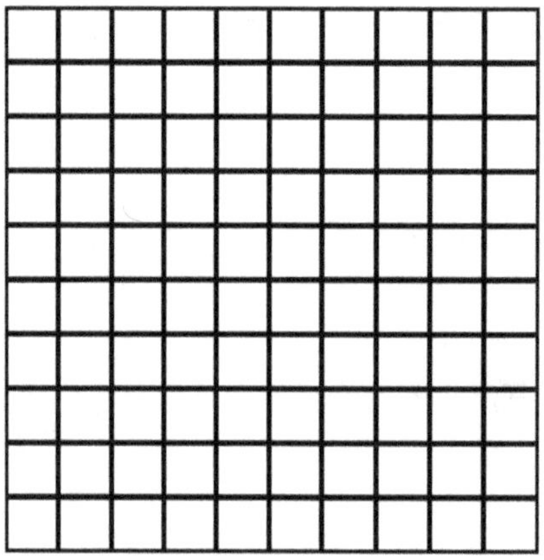

    B. How many sports cards does Arlo have altogether? Write the sum as a fraction:

    ______________________________________________

    C. The rest of Arlo's sports cards are baseball cards. What fraction of Arlo's cards are baseball cards?

    ______________________________________________

11. Lisa says the sum of $^{3}/_{10}$ and $^{4}/_{100}$ is $^{7}/_{100}$ .

    A. What mistake did Lisa make?

______________________________________________

______________________________________________

B. Write an equation that shows how to correctly add the fractions.

________________________________________________________

12. Noelle has $100 to spend for her birthday. She uses $^{58}/_{100}$ of her birthday money to purchase a new jacket and $^{2}/_{10}$ to purchase a hat. How much of her birthday money does Noelle have left?

Show your work:

Write your answer in a dollar amount: ______________________________

# CONVERT FRACTIONS TO DECIMALS

**4 NF.C.6 Use decimal notation for fractions with denominators 10 or 100. *For example, rewrite 0.62 as 62/100; describe a length as 0.62 meters; locate 0.62 on a number line diagram.***

1. The shaded model below represents $^{4}/_{10}$ .

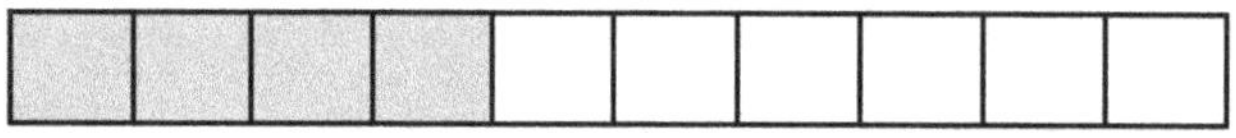

What decimal represents the shaded model?

**A.** 0.04
**B.** 0.4
**C.** 0.6
**D.** 4.0

2. The shaded model below represents $^{37}/_{100}$.

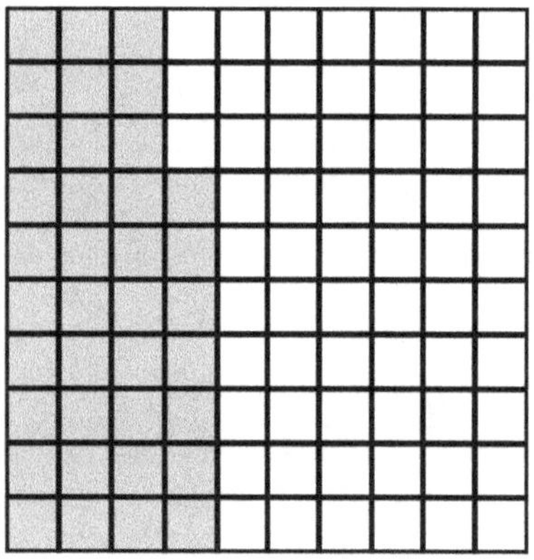

What decimal represents the shaded model?

**A.** 3.70
**B.** 0.037
**C.** 0.37
**D.** 37.0

3. The shaded model below represents 1 $^{34}/_{100}$.

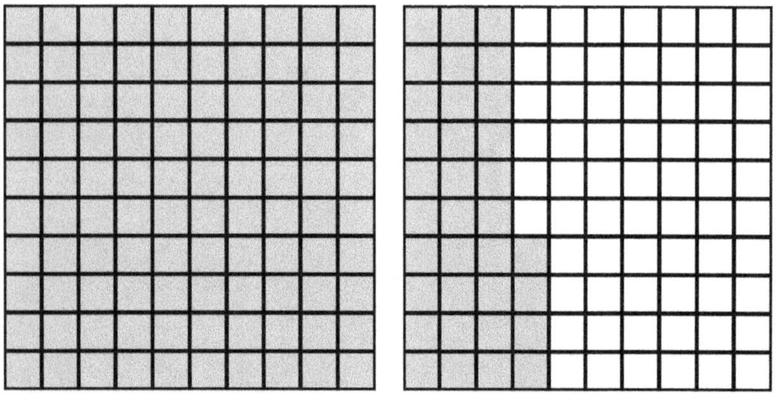

What decimal represents the shaded model?

**A.** 1.34
**B.** 0.134
**C.** 13.4
**D.** 0.34

4. Which model represents 0.62?

A. 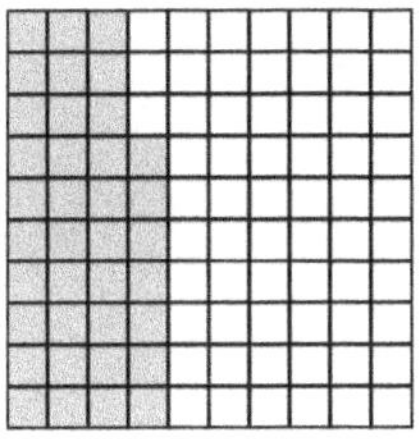 B.  C. 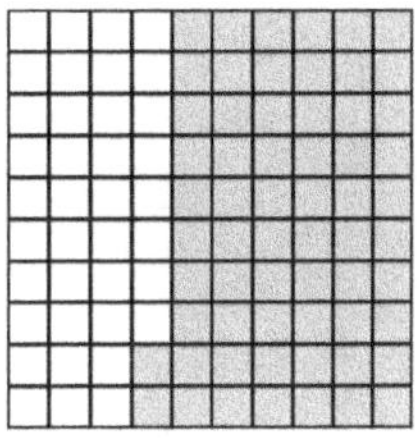 D. 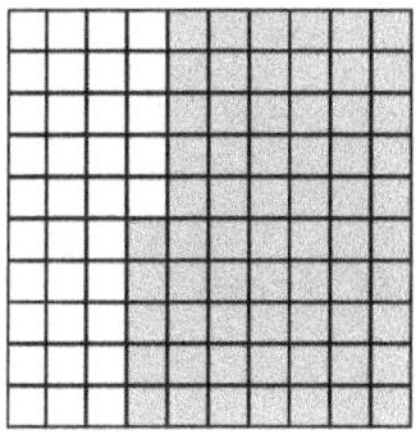

5. What is the decimal equivalent for $2\ ^{6}/_{100}$ ?
   **A.** 0.26
   **B.** 2.60
   **C.** 2.66
   **D.** 2.06

6. Which decimal equivalent represents the fraction $^{8}/_{10}$ ?
   **A.** 0.08
   **B.** 0.80
   **C.** 8.0
   **D.** 0.008

7. Which fraction is equivalent to 0.2?
   **A.** 20/100
   **B.** 2/100
   **C.** 200/100
   **D.** 20/10

8. What decimal represents point A on the number line?

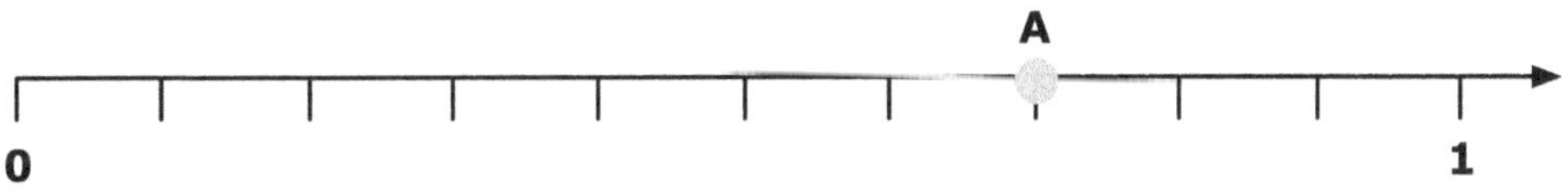


   **A.** 0.07
   **B.** 7.0
   **C.** 0.7
   **D.** 0.77

9. What decimal represents point B on the number line?

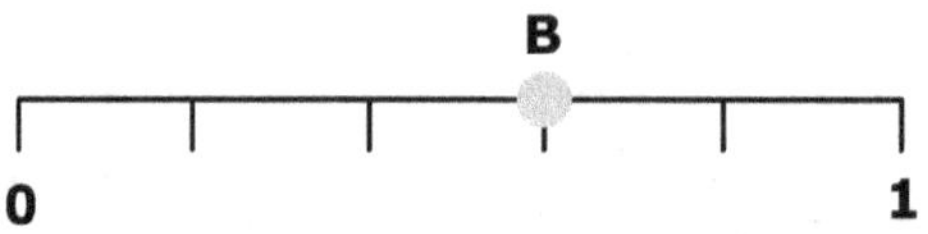


**A.** 0.06
**B.** 0.7
**C.** 0.8
**D.** 0.6

10. Circle **ALL** the fractions that are equivalent to 0.5.

| | | | |
|---|---|---|---|
| **4/20** | **50/100** | **1/2** | **6/12** |
| **5/100** | **2/4** | **20/50** | **5/10** |

11. Use the chart below to complete this problem.

A. Convert the fractions to an equivalent fraction with a denominator of 10 or 100.

B. Then write the equivalent decimal for each fraction.

| Fraction | Fraction with a Denominator of 10 | Equivalent Decimal |
|---|---|---|
| $\frac{2}{5}$ | | |
| $2\frac{1}{2}$ | | |
| **Fraction** | **Fraction with a Denominator of 100** | **Equivalent Decimal** |
| $\frac{3}{4}$ | | |
| $\frac{12}{20}$ | | |

12. Kara is measuring her lawn to put up a fence. She writes out the measurements as she measures the lawn. What is the length of Kara's lawn in meters? Write your answer as a decimal and a fraction.

$$(10 \times 1) + (6 \times 1) + (4 \times {}^{1}/_{10}) + (7 \times {}^{1}/_{100}) =$$

Decimal: ____________________ meters

Fraction:____________________meters

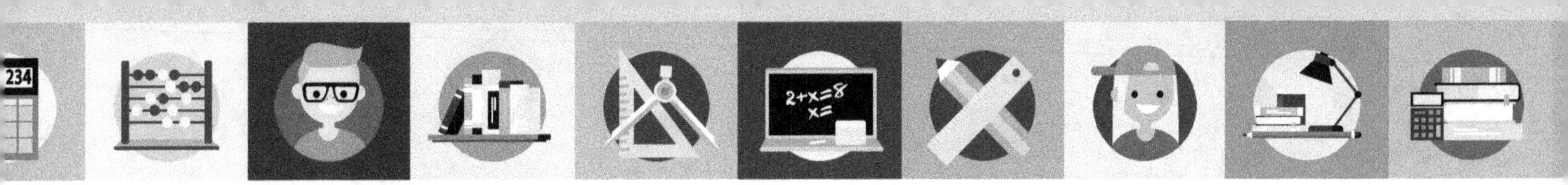


# COMPARE DECIMALS

**NF.C.7 Compare two decimals to hundredths by reasoning about their size. Recognize that comparisons are valid only when the two decimals refer to the same whole. Record the results of comparisons with the symbols >, =, or <, and justify the conclusions, e.g., by using a visual model.**

1. The models below represent two decimals. Which expression correctly compares the decimals?

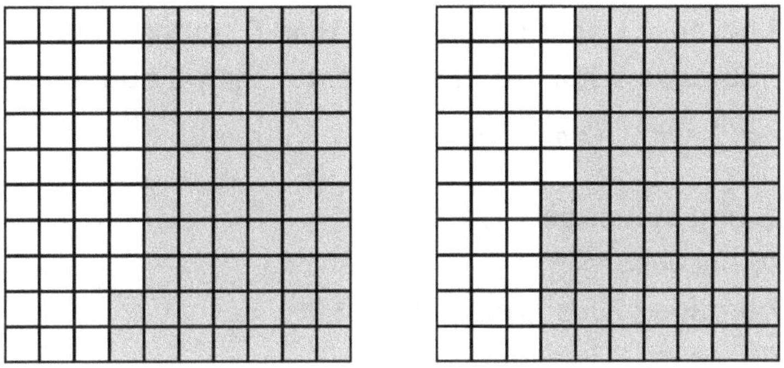

   **A.** 0.65 < 0.62
   **B.** 0.62 < 0.65
   **C.** 6.5 > 6.2
   **D.** 6.2 > 6.5

2. Which decimal is less than 0.52?
   **A.** 0.76
   **B.** 0.57
   **C.** 1.0
   **D.** 0.51

3. The model below represents a decimal. Which decimal is larger than the one represented in this model?

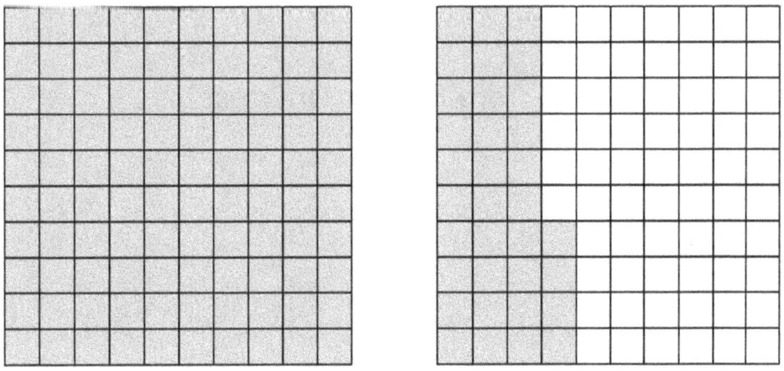

   **A.** 1.14
   **B.** 1.33
   **C.** 1.38
   **D.** 1.29

4. Which expression correctly compares 0.8 and 0.76?
   **A.** 0.8 > 0.76
   **B.** 0.76 > 0.8
   **C.** 0.8 = 0.76
   **D.** 0.80 = 0.76

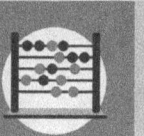

5. Which statement and reasoning is true about the decimals 0.6 and 0.59?
   **A.** 0.59 > 0.6 because 59 > 6.
   **B.** 0.59 < 0.6 because 6 tenths is greater than 5 tenths
   **C.** 0.59 > 0.6 because 9 hundredths is greater than 0 hundredths
   **D.** 0.59 > 0.6 because $^{59}/_{100} > {}^{6}/_{10}$

6. Which of the following statements is true?
   **A.** 0.04 > 0.40 because $^{4}/_{100}$ is greater than $^{4}/_{10}$
   **B.** 0.79 > 1.7 because 79 is greater than 17
   **C.** 0.08 = 0.8 because 8 is equal to 8
   **D.** 0.7 < 0.89 because $^{70}/_{100}$ is less than $^{89}/_{100}$

7. Which expression correctly compares the decimals?
   **A.** 3.25 > 3.52
   **B.** 4.06 > 4.60
   **C.** 0.7 = 0.70
   **D.** 9.95 < 9.94

8. Which of the following decimals is greater than 0.03 but less than 0.3?
   **A.** 0.28
   **B.** 0.34
   **C.** 0.02
   **D.** 0.40

9. Which list of decimals is ordered from least to greatest?
   **A.** 0.22, 0.04, 1.2
   **B.** 0.08, 0.84, 0.9
   **C.** 0.01, 0.10, 0.03
   **D.** 0.19, 0.08, 0.2

10. Use the number line to answer parts A and B.

A. Plot the decimals on the number line by placing a dot on the number line and writing the decimal above the line.

**0.31, 0.04, 0.22, 0.16**

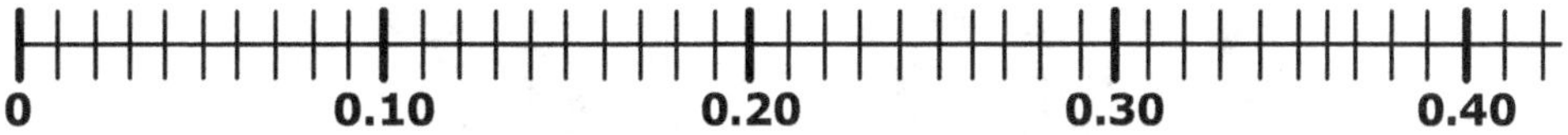


B. Order the decimals from least to greatest:

________, ________, ________, ________

11. Plot the decimals on the number line below using a dot to indicate where the decimal is and write the decimal above the line:

**1.5, 2.3, 0.5**

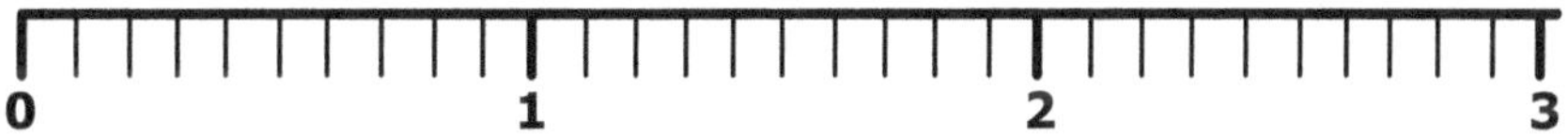


A. Use the number line to name a decimal that is less than 1.5 but greater than 0.5

________________________________________

B. Use the number line to name a decimal that is greater than 2.3

________________________________________

12. Josie wrote the expression 10.07 > 10.4. Is she correct or incorrect? Explain your reasoning using pictures, words or expressions.

# MEASUREMENT AND DATA

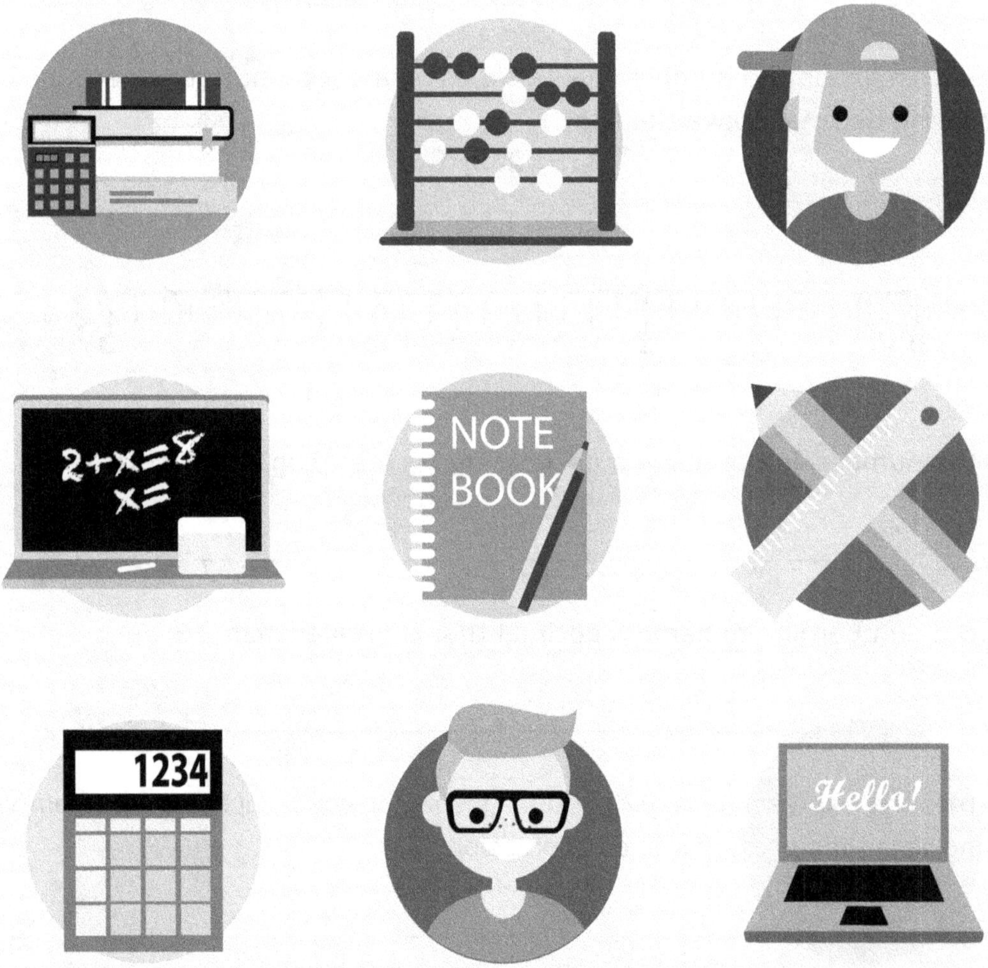

# COMPARE, CONTRAST & RECORD UNITS OF MEASUREMENT

**MD.A.1 Know relative sizes of measurement units within one system of units including km, m, cm; kg, g; lb, oz.; l, ml; hr, min, sec. Within a single system of measurement, express measurements in a larger unit in terms of a smaller unit. Record measurement equivalents in a two-column table.**

1. Which is the largest unit of measurement listed below?
   **A.** 1 kilometer
   **B.** 1 millimeter
   **C.** 1 centimeter
   **D.** 1 meter

2. Which is the smallest unit of measurement listed below?
   **A.** 1 yard
   **B.** 1 mile
   **C.** 1 inch
   **D.** 1 foot

3. What is most reasonable estimate of the length of this hot dog?

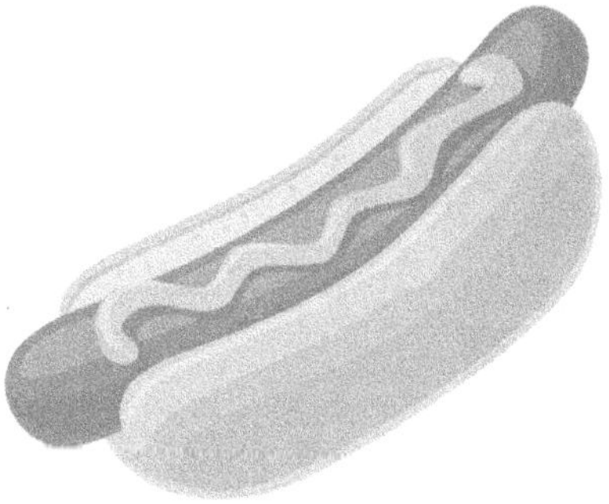

   **A.** 6 yards
   **B.** 6 inches
   **C.** 6 miles
   **D.** 6 feet

4. What is the most reasonable estimate for the mass of a car?

   **A.** 20 pounds
   **B.** 2 kilograms
   **C.** 20 ounces
   **D.** 2 tons

5. Ayesha bought a half-gallon of orange juice. How many pints are in a half-gallon?
   **A.** 6 pints
   **B.** 4 pints
   **C.** 8 pints
   **D.** 2 pints

6. Jeremy drove 5 kilometers to a friend's house. How many meters did Jeremy drive?
   **A.** 5,000 meters
   **B.** 500 meters
   **C.** 50,000 meters
   **D.** 50 meters

7. Samuel worked 8 hours on Friday. Which of the following times is equal to 8 hours?
   **A.** 600 minutes
   **B.** 4,800 minutes
   **C.** 480 minutes
   **D.** 3,600 seconds

8. Caylee drinks 1 liter of soda. How many milliliters did Caylee drink?

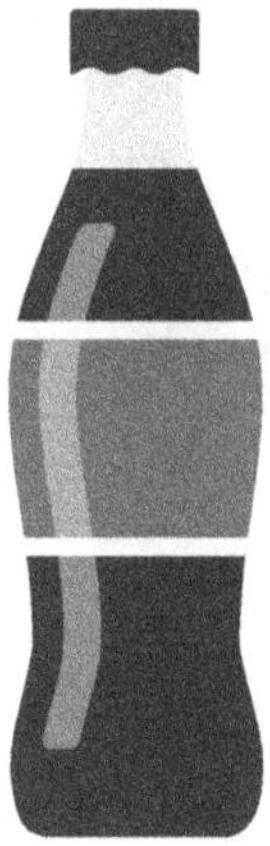

   **A.** 10,000 milliliters
   **B.** 100 milliliters
   **C.** 1,100 milliliter
   **D.** 1,000 milliliters

9. The length of John's driveway is 120 feet. What is the length of his driveway in yards?
   **A.** 400 yards
   **B.** 40 yards
   **C.** 3,600 yards
   D. 360 yards

10. Carson bought 4 liters of soda. He plants to drink the same amount each day for 5 days until the soda is gone. How many milliliters of soda will he drink each day?

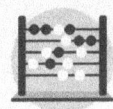

Show your work:

Answer:________________________________________________

11. Fill in the chart to show the relationship between inches, feet and yards.

| Inches | Feet | Yards |
|---|---|---|
| 36 | 3 | 1 |
| | | 2 |
| | | 3 |
| | | 4 |

Use the chart to help you fill in the blanks.

A. 1 foot is ______ times as long as 1 inch.

B. 1 yard is ______ times as long as 1 foot.

C. 1 yard is ______ times as long as 1 inch.

12. The Harrigon Family is having a party. They ordered a large sub-style sandwich that is 5 feet long. List two ways they can cut the sub into equal-size pieces in inches.

A. One way:
Divide the sub into _________ pieces that are each _________ inches long.

B. Another way:
Divide the sub into _________ pieces that are each _________ inches long.

# SOLVE WORD PROBLEMS USING MEASUREMENTS

**MD.A.2 Use the four operations to solve word problems involving distances, intervals of time, liquid volumes, masses of objects, and money, including problems involving simple fractions or decimals, and problems that require expressing measurements given in a larger unit in terms of a smaller unit. Represent measurement quantities using diagrams such as number line diagrams that feature a measurement scale.**

1. Mary's Chihuahua weighs 9 pounds. At her next visit to the vet, the Chihuahua gained 2 pounds. How many ounces does the Chihuahua weigh now?
   **A.** 172 ounces
   **B.** 176 ounces
   **C.** 170 ounces
   **D.** 128 ounces

2. To ride a rollercoaster at the amusement park, a person must be 55 inches tall. Carlos is 5 feet tall. Is he tall enough to ride the roller coaster? Choose the answer that describes his situation.
   **A.** No, he is 5 inches shorter than 55 inches.
   **B.** No, he is 4 inches shorter than 55 inches.
   **C.** Yes, he is 5 inches taller than 55 inches.
   **D.** Yes, he is 10 inches taller than 55 inches.

3. A stick of gum is 6 centimeters long. How long is the stick of gum in millimeters?
   **A.** 60 millimeters
   **B.** 6.0 millimeters
   **C.** 600 millimeters
   **D.** 0.6 millimeters

4. Carla made 6 liters of lemonade. She fills eight 550-milliliter pitchers. How much lemonade does she have left?
   **A.** 1,000 milliliters
   **B.** 1,400 milliliters
   **C.** 600 milliliters
   **D.** 1,600 millimeters

5. 10 bags of candy weigh 5 kilograms. All candy bags are the same weight. How much does each bag weigh in grams?
   **A.** 1,000 grams
   **B.** 500 grams
   **C.** 50 grams
   **D.** 5,000 grams

6. Jordan drove 60 miles per hour for 5 hours. If he continues at the same rate for the next 2 hours, how many miles will Jordan drive in all?
   **A.** 300 miles
   **B.** 350 miles
   **C.** 420 miles
   **D.** 480 miles

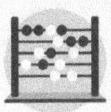

7. One pound of apples costs $2.60. Maggie bought 2.5 pounds of apples. She paid with a $10 bill. How much change did Maggie receive?
   **A.** $3.50
   **B.** $3.00
   **C.** $3.35
   **D.** $4.00

8. Karina is having a party. She buys 1/2 gallon of soda, 3 quarts of orange juice, and 1 gallon of lemonade. She is serving the drinks in pint-sized glasses. How many pint-sized glasses will Karina be able to fill using all the drinks?
   **A.** 16 pints
   **B.** 20 pints
   **C.** 12 pints
   **D.** 18 pints

9. The main stage in the concert auditorium can hold 10,000 pounds. The band's lighting equipment weighs 3.5 tons and the stage props weigh 1,500 pounds. How much more weight can be added to the stage until it reaches maximum weight limit?
   **A.** 1,600 pounds
   **B.** 2,000 pounds
   **C.** 1,500 pounds
   **D.** 1,700 pounds

10. David is making pizza for a party. He needs a total of 5 pounds of shredded cheese and he has a 20-ounce bag of shredded cheese. The store sells 12-ounce bags of shredded cheese.

    A. How many more ounces of shredded cheese does David need to make the pizzas?

    ______________________________________________

    B. How many bags of cheese does he need to buy at the store?

    ______________________________________________

11. Levi spent 4 hours running errands on Saturday. First, he spent 25 minutes at the post office. Then he spent 1 $^{3}/_{4}$ hour at the supermarket. Next, he went to car wash, which took him 35 minutes. How much time does Levi have left to go to the mall?

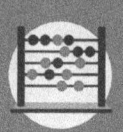

Show your work:

Answer: ______________________________________________

12. A train comes and goes from the station every 45 minutes. The first train leaves at 5:30 am.

A. Plot the times the train leaves between 5:30 am and 9:00 am but by placing a dot on the number line.

B. If Jane arrives at the train station at 7:30 am, how long will she have to wait for the train?

______________________________________________

C. If Kip arrives at the train station at 8:45 am, how long will he have to wait for the next train?

______________________________________________

# FIND AREA AND PERIMETER; SOLVE PROBLEMS INVOLVING AREA AND PERIMETER

**MD.A.3 Apply the area and perimeter formulas for rectangles in real world and mathematical problems.** ***For example, find the width of a rectangular room given the area of the flooring and the length, by viewing the area formula as a multiplication equation with an unknown factor.***

1. The rectangle below has a length of 12 inches and a width of 7 inches. What is the area of the rectangle? (Picture not to scale)

    **A.** 80 square inches
    **B.** 72 square inches
    **C.** 84 square inches
    **D.** 74 square inches

2. Which expression can be used to find the perimeter of the rectangle below? (Picture not to scale)

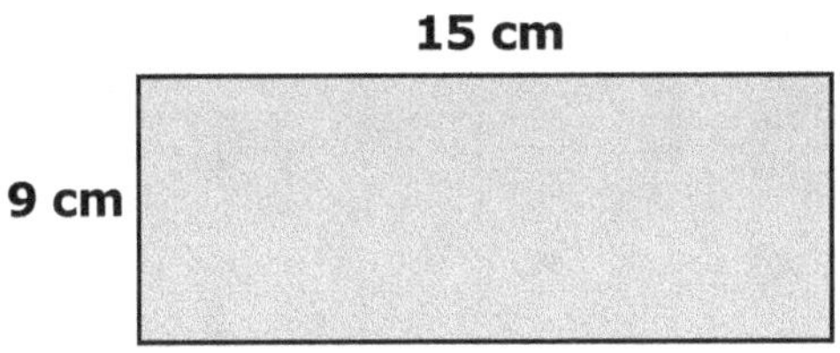


    **A.** 9 x 15
    **B.** 15 + 9
    **C.** 15 + 9 x 2
    **D.** 15 + 9 + 15 + 9

3. Tom's room has an area of 48 square feet. If the length of the room is 12 feet, what is the width of the room?
    **A.** 5 feet
    **B.** 4 feet
    **C.** 6 feet
    **D.** 7 feet

4. Which expression can be used to find the perimeter of a garage that is 16 feet long and 13 feet wide?
   **A.** 2 x (13 + 16)
   **B.** 13 x 16
   **C.** 16 + 13 + 2
   **D.** 16 + 13 + 16 + 13 + 16

5. The garden has an area of 126 square yards. Which could be the length and width of the garden?
   **A.** 12 yards by 11 yards
   **B.** 8 yards by 15 yards
   **C.** 14 yards by 9 yards
   **D.** 13 yards by 11 yards

6. Jason's back yard has a perimeter of 62 meters. The length is 16 meters. What is the width of Jason's back yard?
   **A.** 16 meters
   **B.** 14 meters
   **C.** 46 meters
   **D.** 15 meters

7. Larry drew a rectangle that has a length of 8 inches and a width of 13 inches. What other rectangle has the same perimeter as Larry's rectangle?
   **A.** 11 inches by 9 inches
   **B.** 9 inches by 12 inches
   **C.** 8 inches by 14 inches
   **D.** 10 inches by 8 inches

8. Melissa draws one rectangle that has a length of 18 cm and a width of 9 cm. The other rectangle she draws has a length of 15 cm and a width of 10 cm. What is the total area of the two rectangles?
   **A.** 312 square cm
   **B.** 310 square cm
   **C.** 300 square cm
   **D.** 242 square cm

9. Mrs. James is planning out her flowerbed. She knows the perimeter is 64 yards and the length of one side is 14 yards. What is the area of her flowerbed?
   **A.** 504 square yards
   **B.** 332 square yards
   **C.** 252 square yards
   **D.** 224 square yards

10. Annie is deciding to put up a fenced-in play area for her dogs outside. She needs the area to be 560 square feet. Fill in the blanks to find the possible dimensions of the play area.

**20 x ______________ = 560** **10 x ______________ = 560**

**14 x ______________ = 560** **70 x ______________ = 560**

11. Jake is making drawings of the possible dimensions for a rectangular poster. His teacher says the poster has to have a perimeter of 24 inches. On the grid below, draw the 3 possible dimensions of his poster.

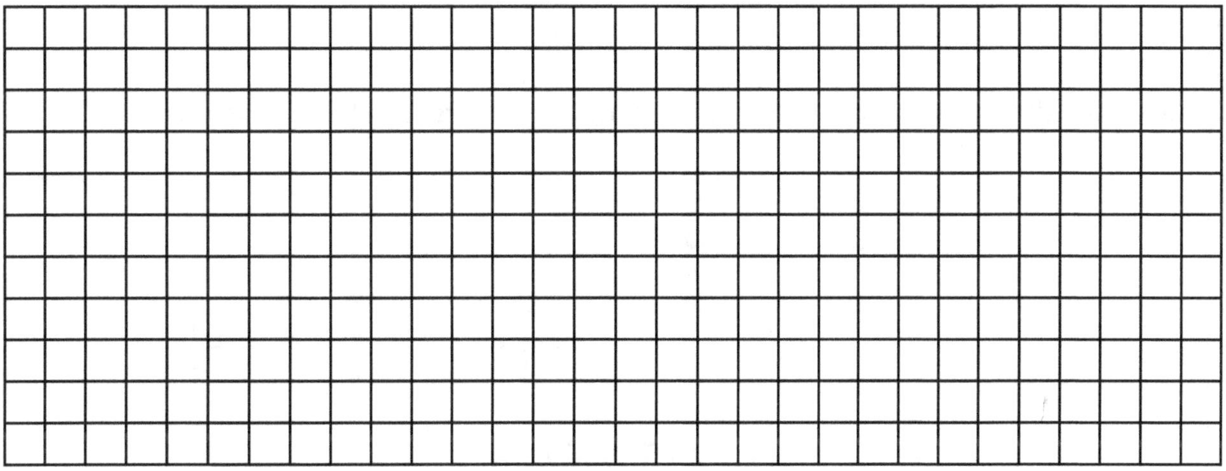

Jake wants to make a poster with the largest area. What should be the length and width of the poster?

________________________________________________

12. The model below represents the playground at the park.

A. Find the missing measurements. (Picture not to scale)

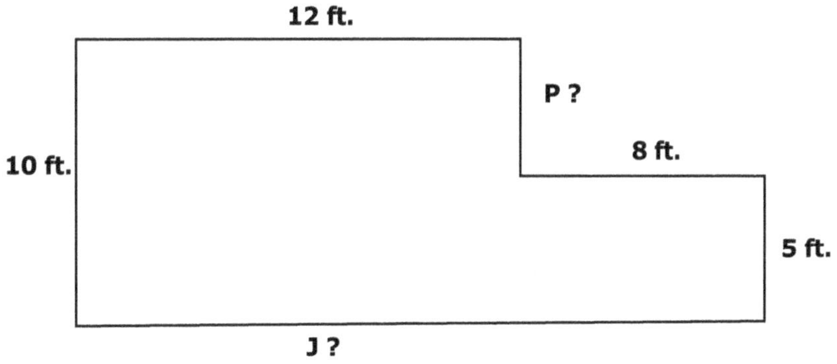


B. What is the perimeter of the playground? ____________________

C. What is the area of the playground? ____________________

# DISPLAY AND INTERPRET DATA IN LINE PLOTS AND SOLVE PROBLEMS USING LINE PLOTS

**MD.B.4 Make a line plot to display a data set of measurements in fractions of a unit (1/2, 1/4, 1/8). Solve problems involving addition and subtraction of fractions by using information presented in line plots.** ***For example, from a line plot find and interpret the difference in length between the longest and shortest specimens in an insect collection.***

Use the following line plot to answer questions 1-3.

The line plot shows the number of pets the students in Mrs. Master's class own.

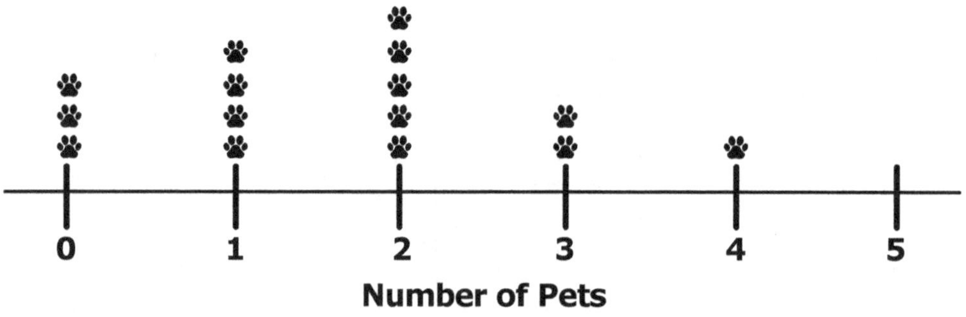


1. How many students are in Mrs. Master's class?
   **A.** 16
   **B.** 14
   **C.** 15
   **D.** 17

2. How many more students have 2 pets than 4 pets?
   **A.** 4
   **B.** 5
   **C.** 6
   **D.** 3

3. Which number of pets was most common?
   **A.** 4
   **B.** 2
   **C.** 5
   **D.** 3

Use the line plot to answer questions 4-6.

The line plot below shows the amount of snowfall in December in Colorado.

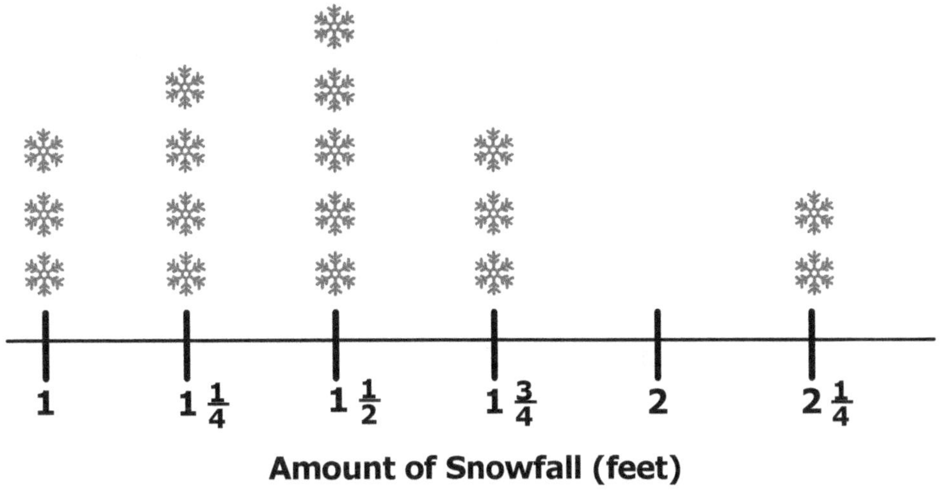


4. Which amount of snowfall was not recorded?
   **A.** 2 ft.
   **B.** $2\frac{1}{4}$ ft.
   **C.** $1\frac{3}{4}$ ft.
   **D.** 1 ft.

5. How many times was $1\frac{1}{4}$ ft. of snow recorded?
   **A.** 5
   **B.** 2
   **C.** 4
   **D.** 3

6. How many times was the snowfall recorded in December?
   **A.** 15
   **B.** 16
   **C.** 18
   **D.** 17

The list of fractions shows the distance students ran in gym class (in miles).

$^{1}/_{2}$ $^{3}/_{4}$ $^{1}/_{4}$ $^{3}/_{4}$ $^{7}/_{8}$ $^{1}/_{4}$ $^{1}/_{2}$ $^{3}/_{8}$ $^{1}/_{4}$ $^{3}/_{4}$ $^{1}/_{2}$ $^{3}/_{8}$

7. Use the data to complete the line plot below. Answer questions 8-10 using the line plot.

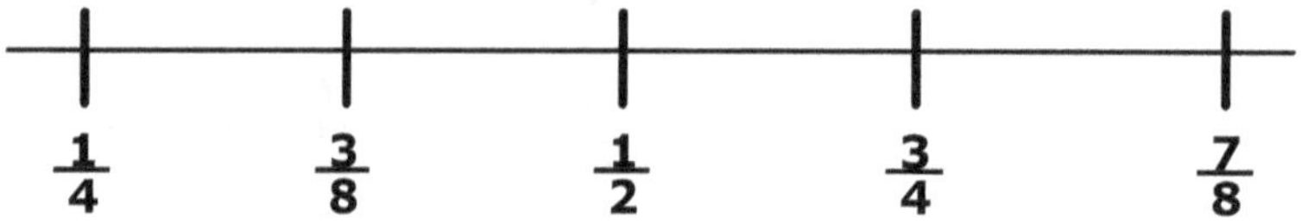


8. How many students ran $^{1}/_{2}$ mile or more?
   **A.** 5
   **B.** 6
   **C.** 8
   **D.** 7

9. What is the difference between the longest distance and the shortest distance run?
   **A.** $^{4}/_{8}$
   **B.** $^{3}/_{8}$
   **C.** $^{5}/_{8}$
   **D.** $^{1}/_{4}$

10. What was the least common distance run?
   **A.** $^{3}/_{8}$
   **B.** $^{7}/_{8}$
   **C.** $^{1}/_{2}$
   **D.** $^{1}/_{4}$

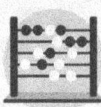

11. Use the information in the chart to make a line plot.

The chart shows the ages of 4th grade students.

| Name | Colin | Avery | Sue | Lacey | Devin | Arthur | Maggie | Ava | Quinn |
|---|---|---|---|---|---|---|---|---|---|
| Age (years) | $9\frac{1}{4}$ | $9\frac{3}{4}$ | $9\frac{1}{2}$ | $10\frac{1}{4}$ | $9\frac{3}{4}$ | 10 | $10\frac{1}{4}$ | $9\frac{3}{4}$ | $9\frac{1}{2}$ |

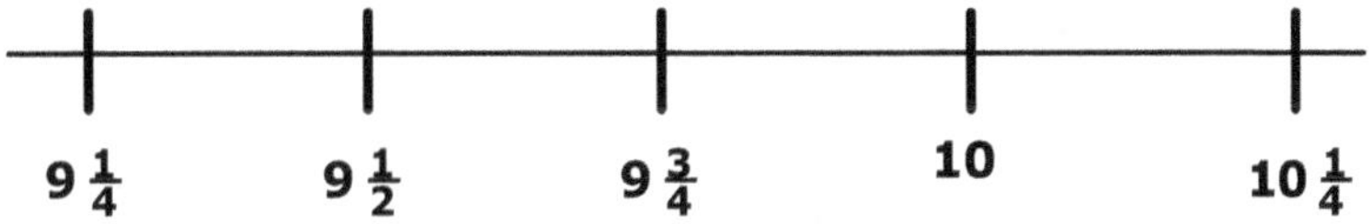


12. Colin says their combined age is 90 years old. Is he correct? Why or why not? Show your work and explain how you know.

# RECOGNIZE ANGLES & UNDERSTAND ANGLES MEASUREMENT

**MD.C.5 Recognize angles as geometric shapes that are formed wherever two rays share a common endpoint, and understand concepts of angle measurement:**

**MD.C.5A An angle is measured with reference to a circle with its center at the common endpoint of the rays, by considering the fraction of the circular arc between the points where the two rays intersect the circle. An angle that turns through 1/360 of a circle is called a "one-degree angle," and can be used to measure angles.**

**MD.C.5B An angle that turns through n one-degree angles is said to have an angle measure of *n* degrees**

1. What type of angle is the angle below?

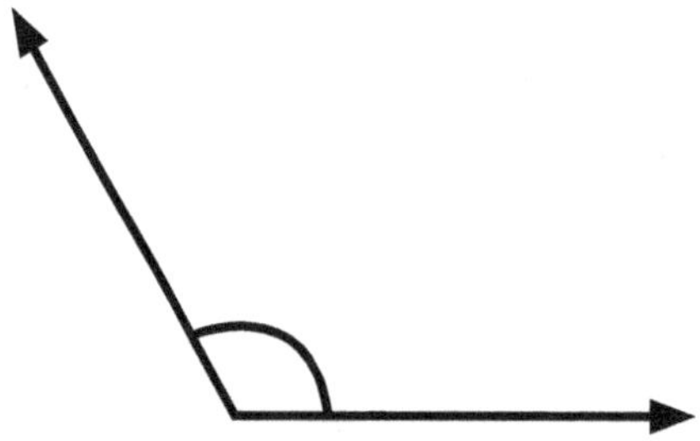

**A.** right angle
**B.** obtuse angle
**C.** acute angle
**D.** straight angle

2. What type of angle is the angle below?

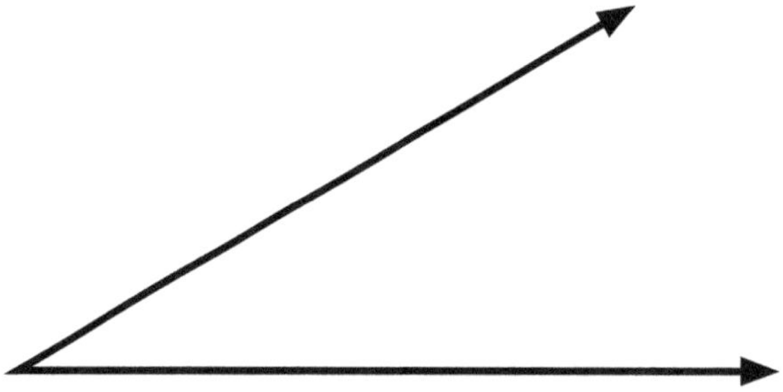

**A.** straight angle
**B.** obtuse angle
**C.** right angle
**D.** acute angle

3. What type of angle is the angle below?

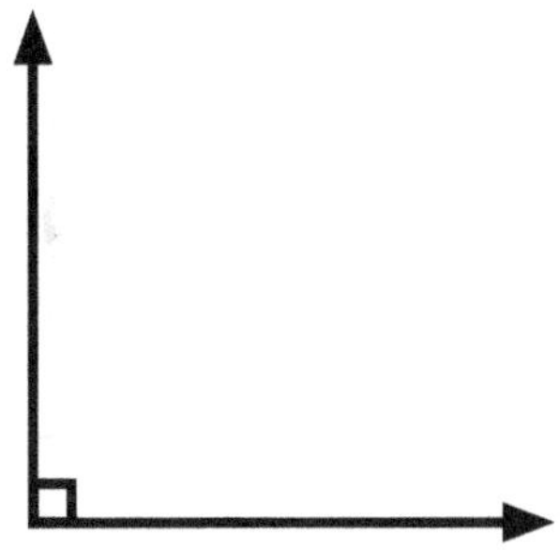

**A.** right angle
**B.** acute angle
**C.** straight angle
**D.** obtuse angle

4. What is the measure of the angle shown below?

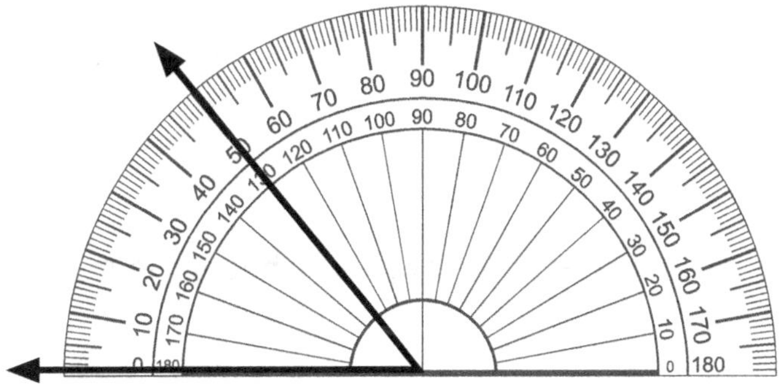

**A.** 130 °
**B.** 55 °
**C.** 50 °
**D.** 65 °

5. What is the measure of the angle shown below?

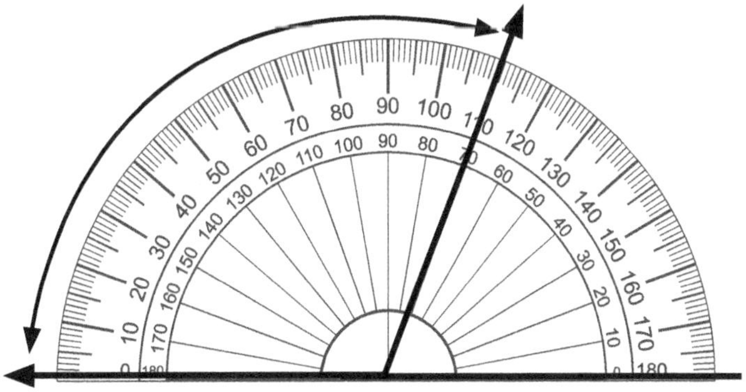

**A.** 120 °
**B.** 110 °
**C.** 100 °
**D.** 70 °

6. Which angle is less than 90° ?

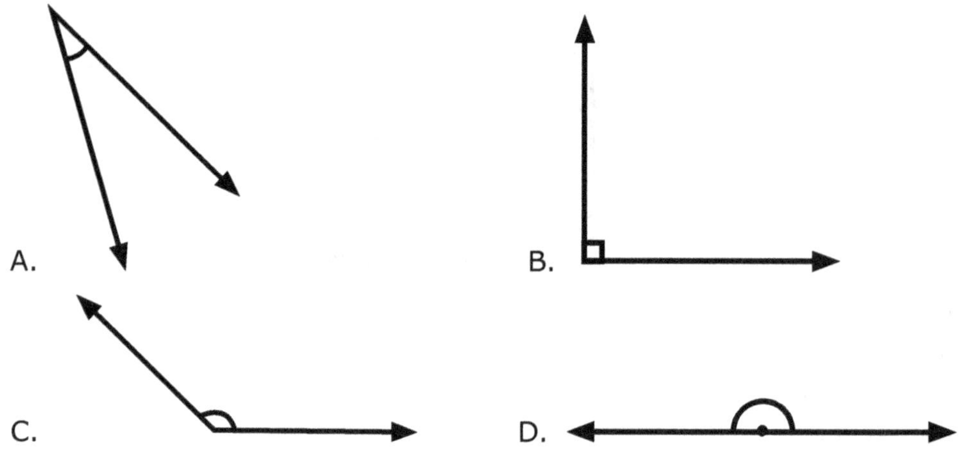


7. An angle that makes a full turn through a circle measures how many degrees?
   **A.** 180°
   **B.** 300°
   **C.** 0°
   **D.** 360°

8. An angle turns through 77 one-degree angles. What is the measure of the angle?
   **A.** 7°
   **B.** 17°
   **C.** 77°
   **D.** 71°

9. An angle turns through $^{1}/_{4}$ of a circle. In degrees, what is the measure of a $^{1}/_{4}$ angle turn in circle?
   **A.** 180°
   **B.** 90°
   **C.** 270°
   **D.** 360°

10. How many third-size turns does it take to make one full turn on the circle below?

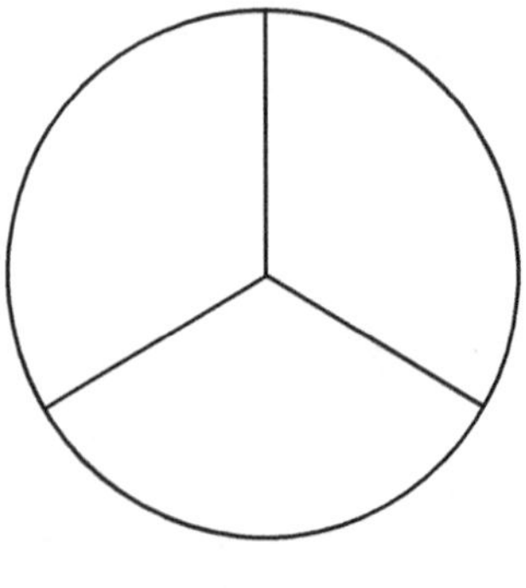

A. Answer: ______________________________

B. What is the measure of each angle shown on the circle above?

__________________________________________________

11. Clive says an angle that turns through $^{1}/_{5}$ of a circle is greater than an angle that turns through $^{1}/_{6}$ of a circle. Is he correct?

A. Explain your answer using the models below. Label the parts of the circle in degrees.

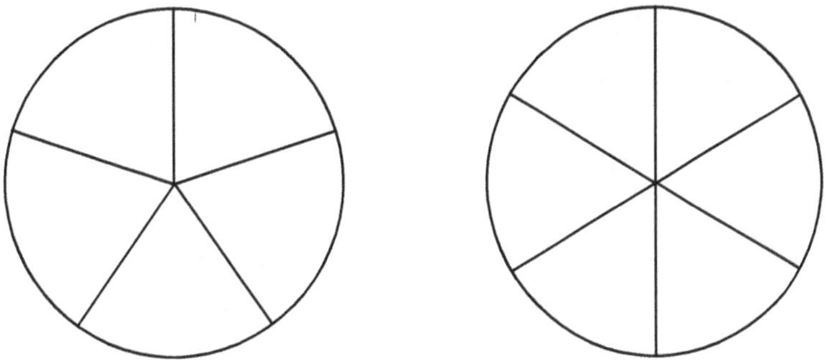

B. Answer:

______________________________________________

______________________________________________

______________________________________________

12. Antoine is making a chart of how many angle turns it takes to make a full circle using a specific number of degrees. Fill in the chart below.

| **Angle measure in degrees** | **Number of turns to make a FULL turn** |
|---|---|
| 180° | 2 turns |
| 90° | |
| 30° | |
| 40° | |
| 60° | |

# MEASURE AND SKETCH ANGLES

**MD.C.6 Measure angles in whole-number degrees using a protractor. Sketch angles of specified measure.**

1. What is the measure of the angle shown below?

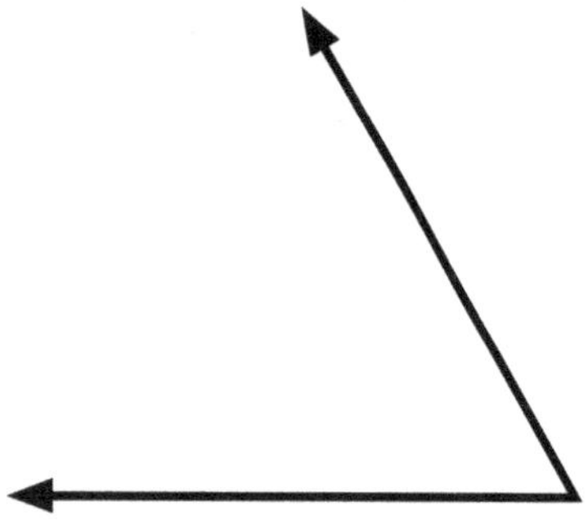

**A.** 60°
**B.** 75°
**C.** 120°
**D.** 50°

2. What is the measure of the angle shown below?

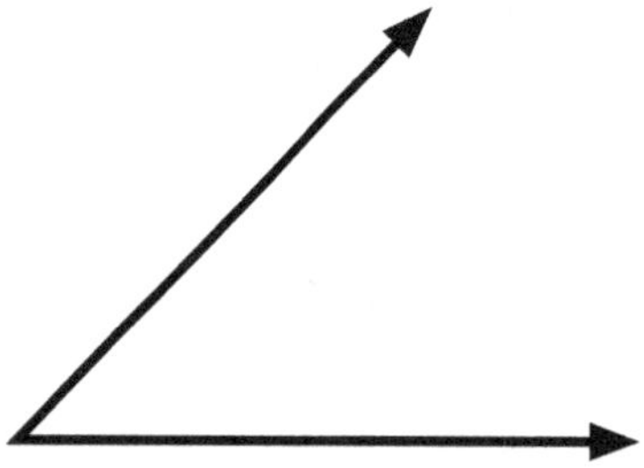

**A.** 50°
**B.** 45°
**C.** 40°
**D.** 140°

3. What is the measure of the angle shown below?

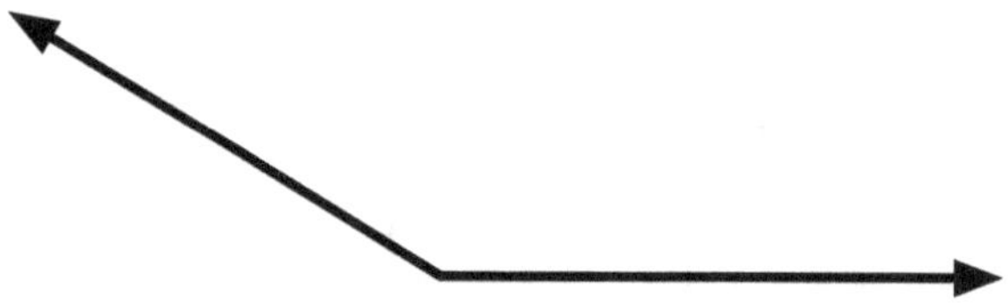

**A.** 140°
**B.** 30°
**C.** 155°
**D.** 150°

4. Without using a protractor, what is the measure of the angle shown below?

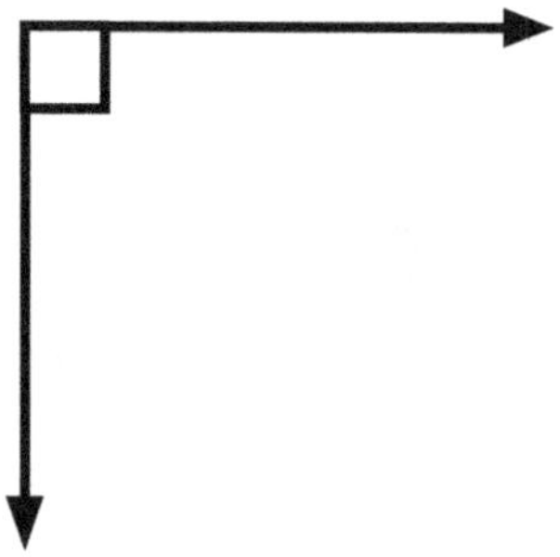

**A.** 180°
**B.** 80°
**C.** 90°
**D.** 100°

5. What is the measure of the angle shown below?

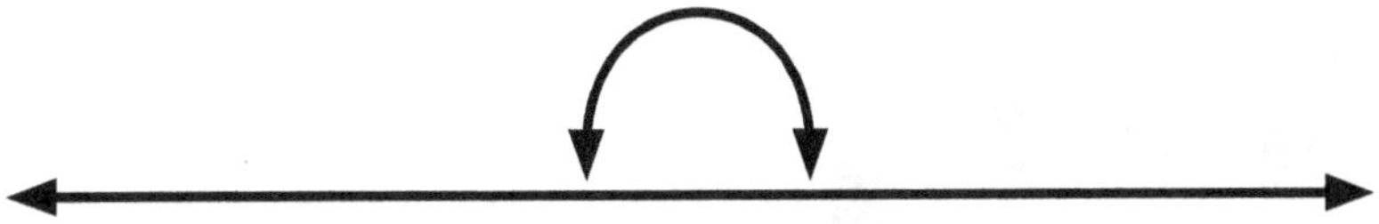

**A.** 180°
**B.** 360°
**C.** 90°
**D.** 170°

6. Which picture shows the correct way to measure an angle with a protractor?

**A.** 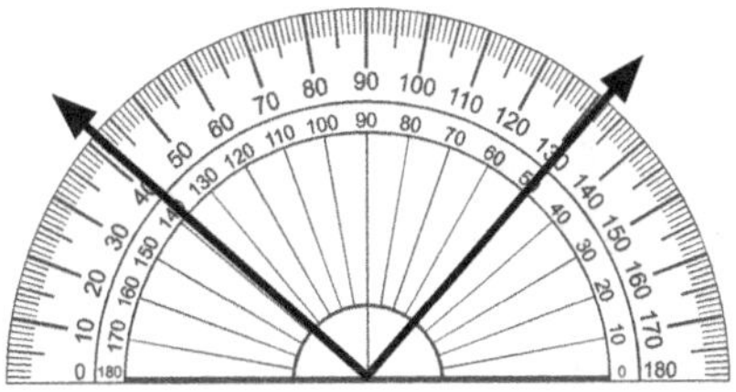

**B.** 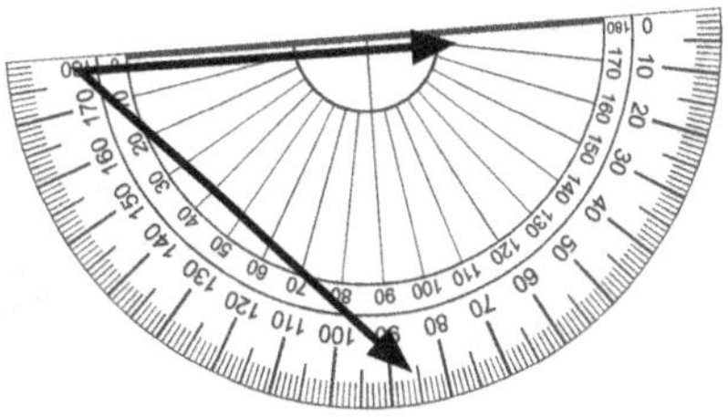

**C.** 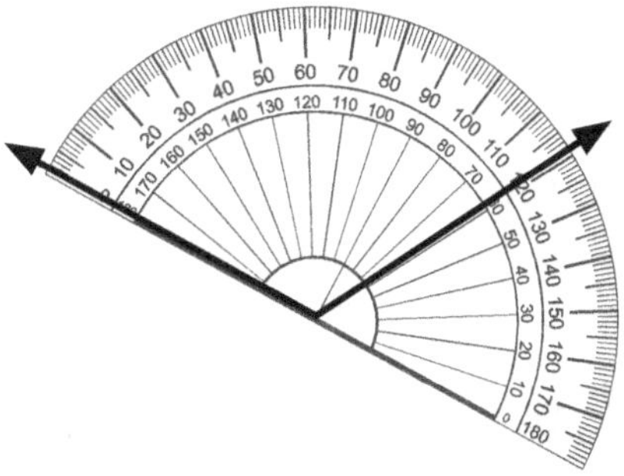

**D.** 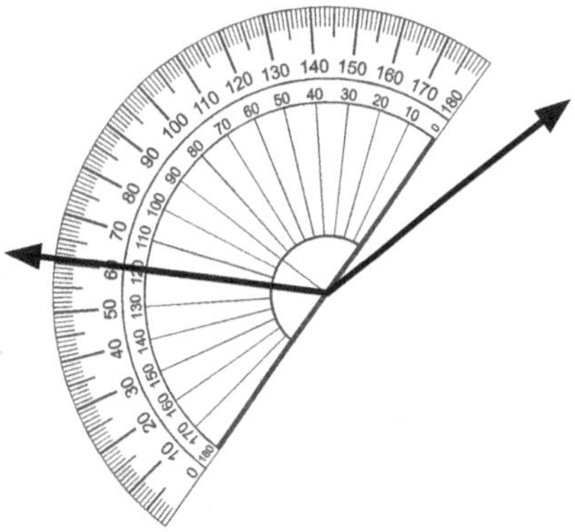

7. Which point could be the vertex of a 60° angle?

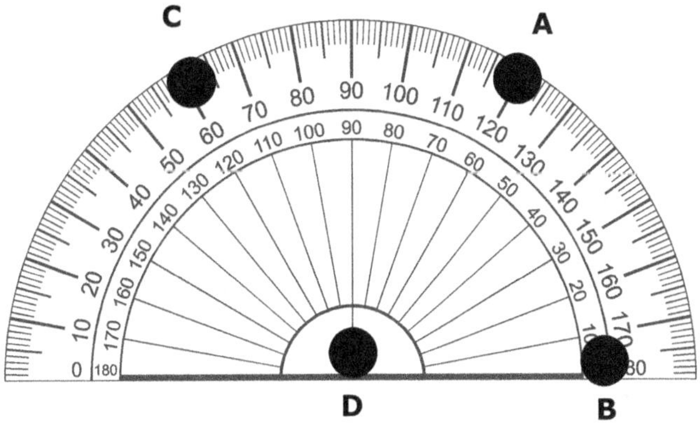


**A.** point A
**B.** point B
**C.** point C
**D.** point D

8. Which point could be used to create an 80° angle?

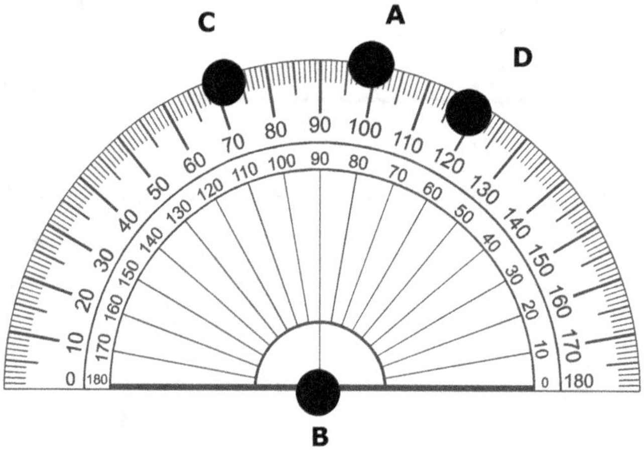


**A.** point A
**B.** point B
**C.** point C
**D.** point D

9. Which set of points can be used to draw an angle that measures 140°?

**A.**

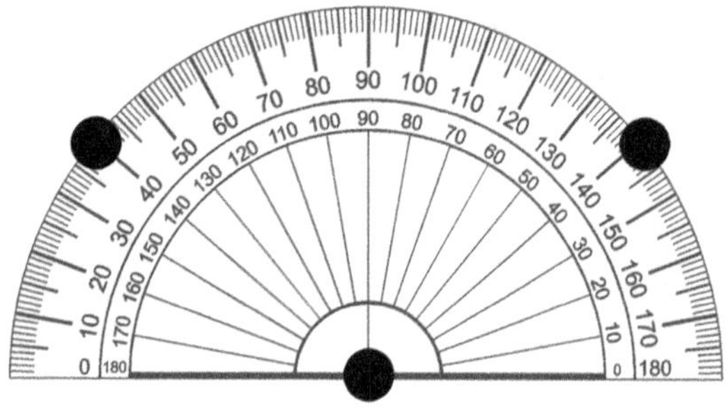

**B.**

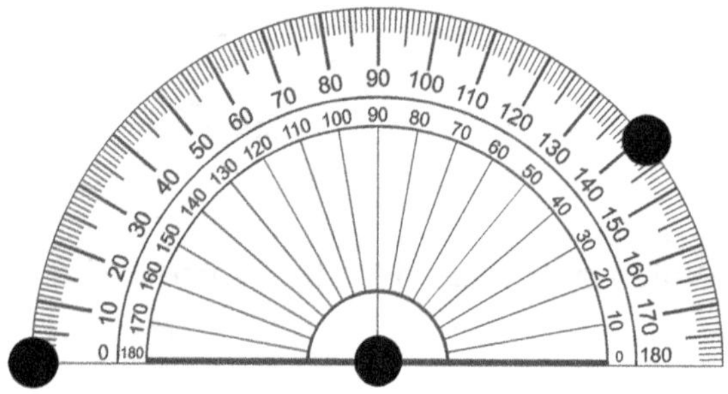

**C.**

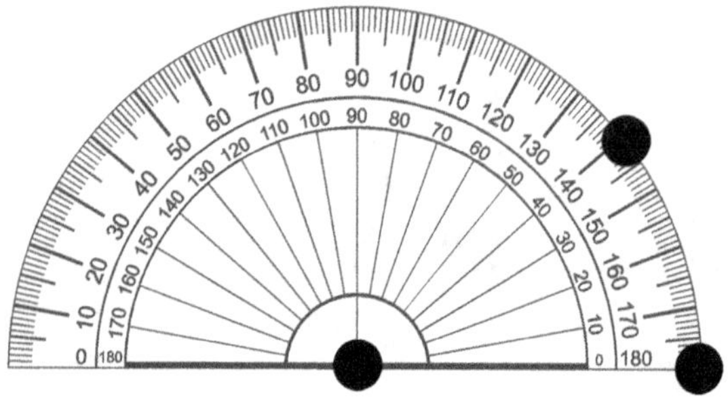

**D.**

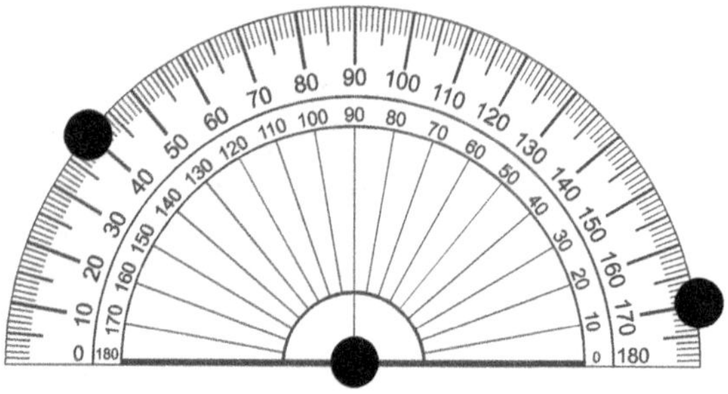

10. Draw a triangle using the line shown below for one side.

A. The triangle has angles that measure 90°, 30°, and 60°. Use your protractor to draw the proper angles.

B. What is the sum of the interior angles of a triangle? ______________________

11. Use your protractor to draw these angles in the space below.

A. Draw an angle with a measure of 50°.

B. Draw an angle with a measure of 150°.

C. Draw an angle with a measure of 136°

12. Draw a trapezoid that has two 130° angles and two 50° angles.

What do you notice about the sum of the interior angles of a trapezoid?

# MEASURE AND SKETCH ANGLES

**MD.C.7 Recognize angle measure as additive. When an angle is decomposed into non-overlapping parts, the angle measure of the whole is the sum of the angle measures of the parts. Solve addition and subtraction problems to find unknown angles on a diagram in real world and mathematical problems, e.g., by using an equation with a symbol for the unknown angle measure.**

1. What is the measure of the unknown angle x?

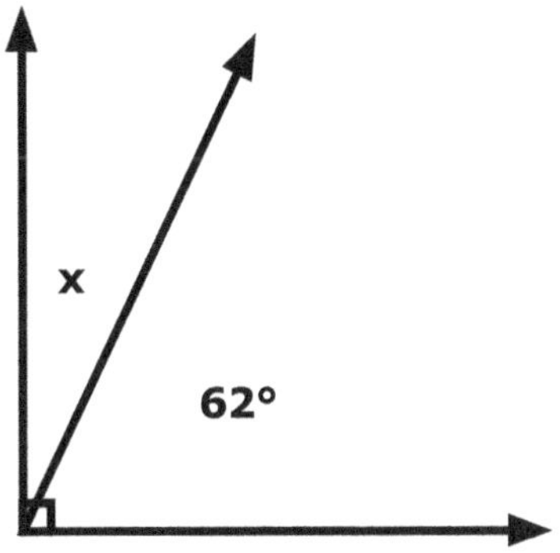


**A.** 25°
**B.** 28°
**C.** 38°
**D.** 18°

2. What is the measure of the unknown angle x? (Angles are not drawn to scale.)

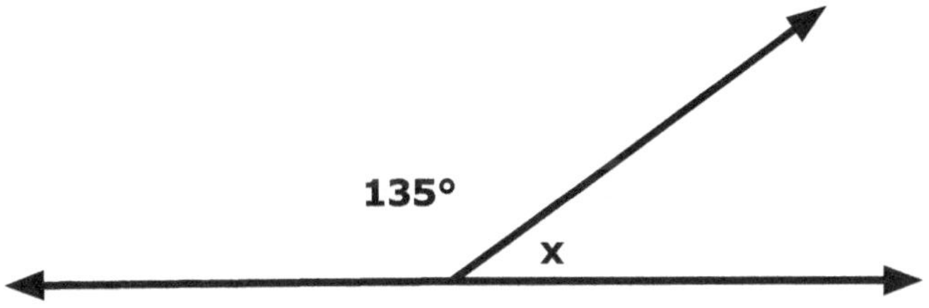

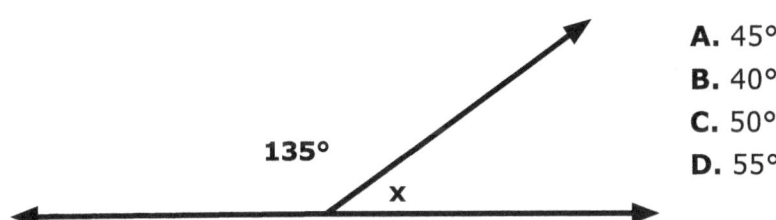

**A.** 45°
**B.** 40°
**C.** 50°
**D.** 55°

3. What is the measure of the unknown angle x? (Angles are not drawn to scale.)

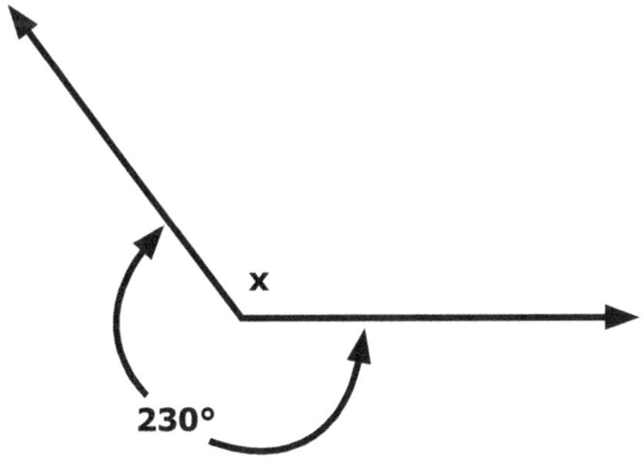

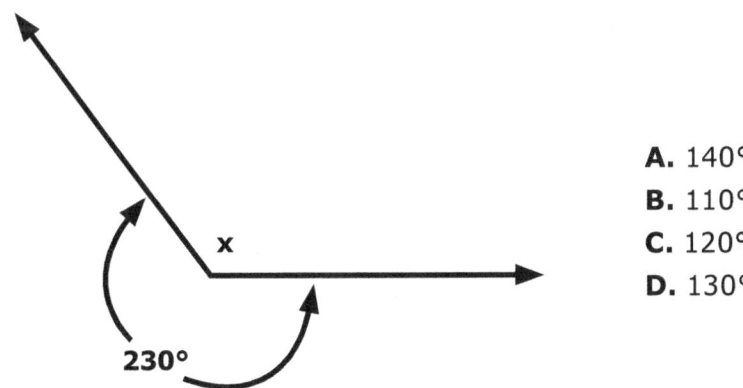

**A.** 140°
**B.** 110°
**C.** 120°
**D.** 130°

4. The measure of angle B is 48°. What fraction of a complete circle is angle B?
   **A.** $^{48}/_{90}$
   **B.** $^{48}/_{360}$
   **C.** $^{48}/_{180}$
   **D.** $^{48}/_{340}$

5. What is the measure of the unknown angle x? (Angles are not drawn to scale.)

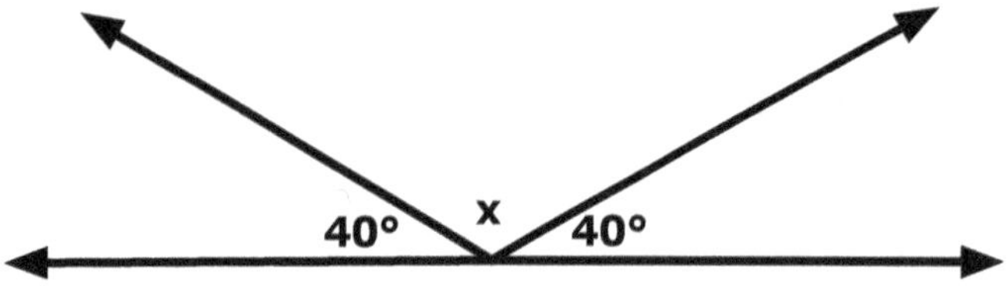


   **A.** 105°
   **B.** 190°
   **C.** 100°
   **D.** 95°

6. What is the measure of the unknown angle x?

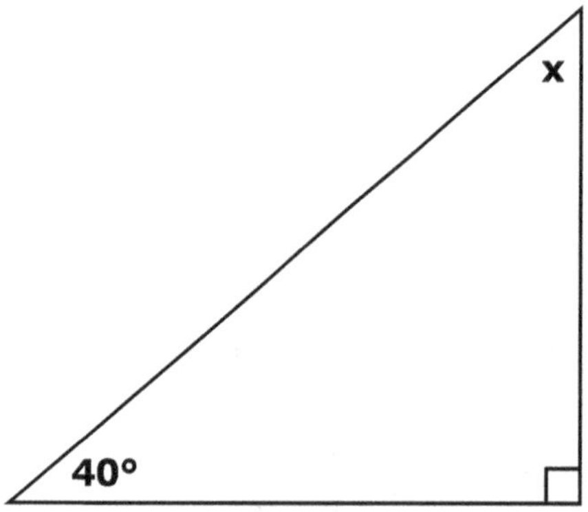


   **A.** 50°
   **B.** 60°
   **C.** 55°
   **D.** 45°

7. The circle below represent a cake cut into equal pieces. What is the angle measure of each angle?

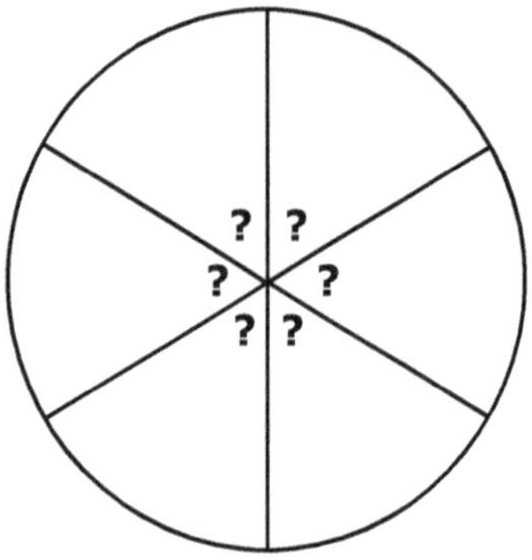


   **A.** 50°
   **B.** 80°
   **C.** 60°
   **D.** 40°

8. Kevin opens the car door 75° and then it gets stuck. The car door should open 110° to get the passengers get in. How many more degrees are needed to fully open the door?
   **A.** 30°
   **B.** 40°
   **C.** 55°
   **D.** 35°

9. Jeremy is using a rolling compass to draw a perfect circle. He turned the pencil 156° and then another 44°. How many more degrees does Jeremy need to turn the pencil in order to make a complete circle?
   **A.** 151°
   **B.** 160°
   **C.** 170°
   **D.** 161°

10. The diagram below shows a swing in a playground. Kayla swings 40° forward and then 100° back. How many degrees forward does the swing have to move to return to is starting position? (Picture is not to scale)

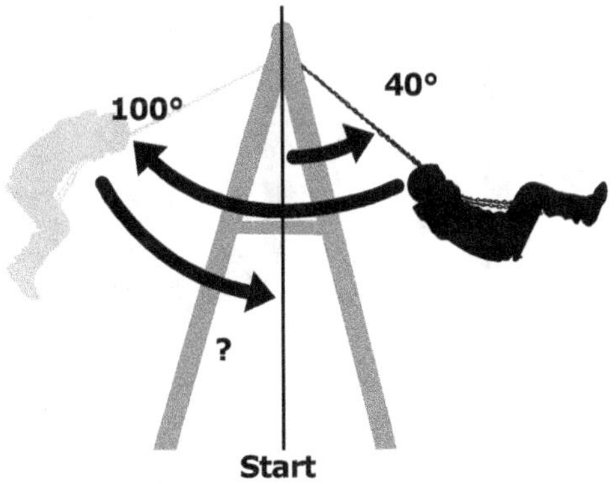


Answer:

______________________

______________________

______________________

11. The rhombus below has opposite angles that are congruent. The obtuse angle measures 110° and the acute angle measures 70°.

Label the angles correctly in the rhombus.

Draw a line on the rhombus to divide it into 2 congruent triangles that have the exact same angle measures.

What are the angle measures of the triangle?

________, ________, ________

12. Meghan is making a poster for her project. She uses a rectangular shaped piece of paper and draws a line directly in the middle of one corner to the other side of the rectangle to make a triangle.

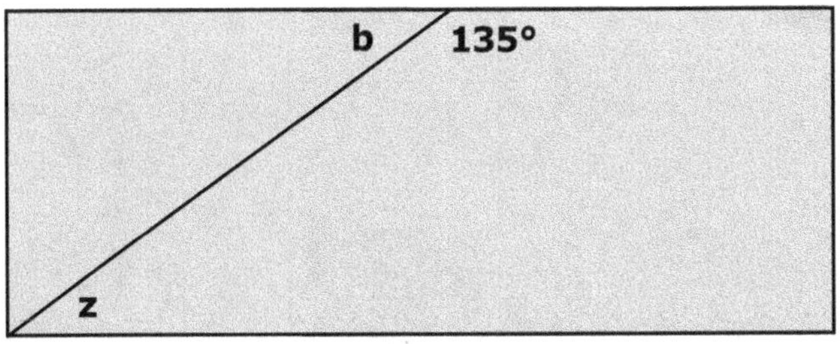


A. What is the measure of angle b?

______________________

B. What is the measure of angle z?

______________________

# GEOMETRY

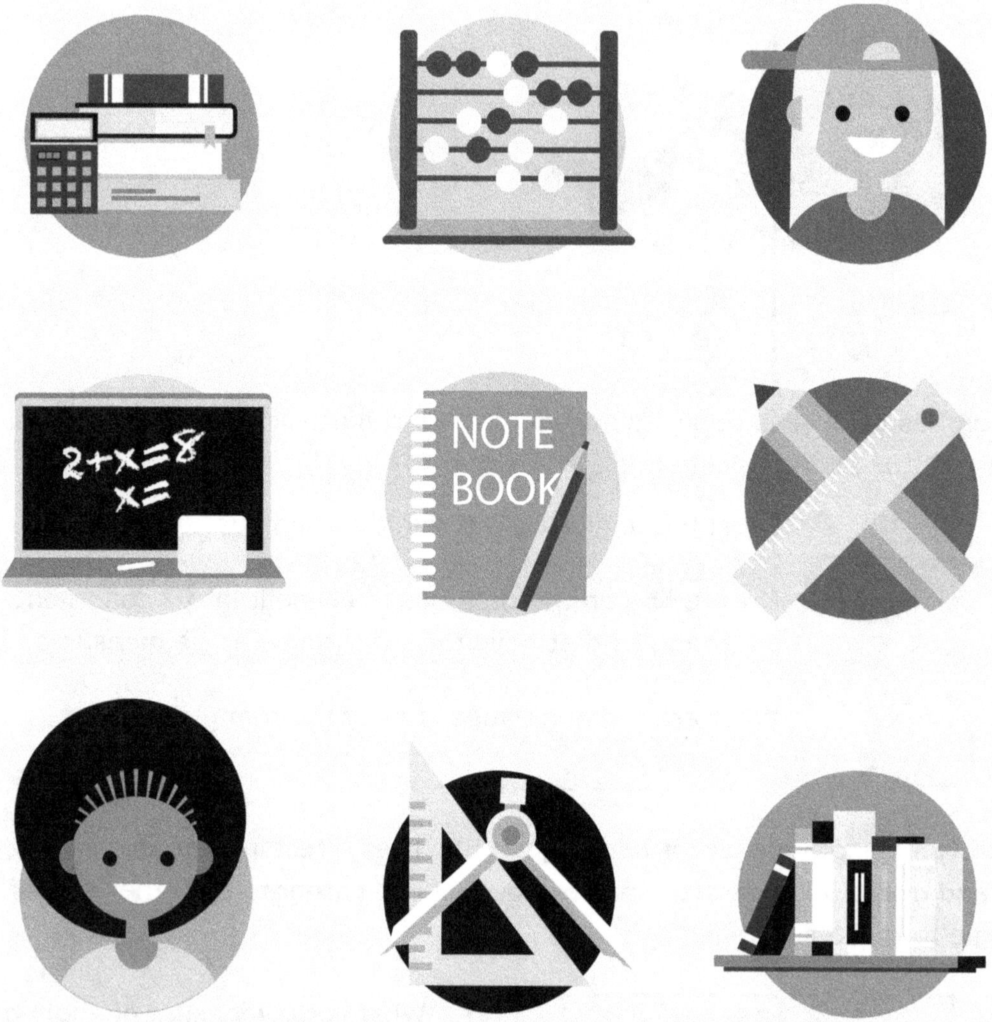

# DRAW AND IDENTIFY POINTS, LINES, RAYS, AND ANGLES

**G.A.1 Draw points, lines, line segments, rays, angles (right, acute, obtuse), and perpendicular and parallel lines. Identify these in two-dimensional figures.**

1. Which word describes the lines below?

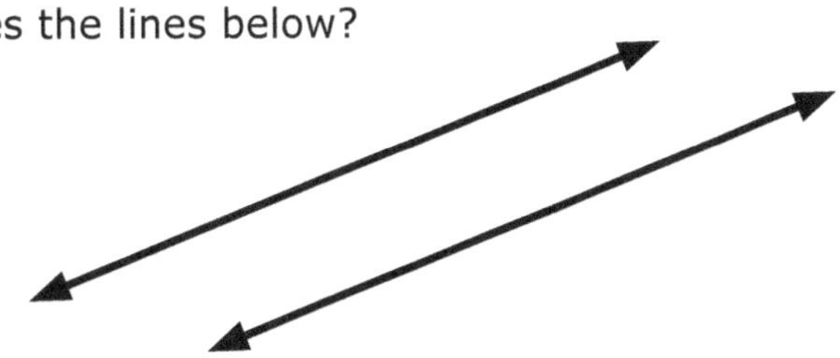

**A.** perpendicular
**B.** intersecting
**C.** parallel
**D.** line segment

2. Which word describes the lines below?

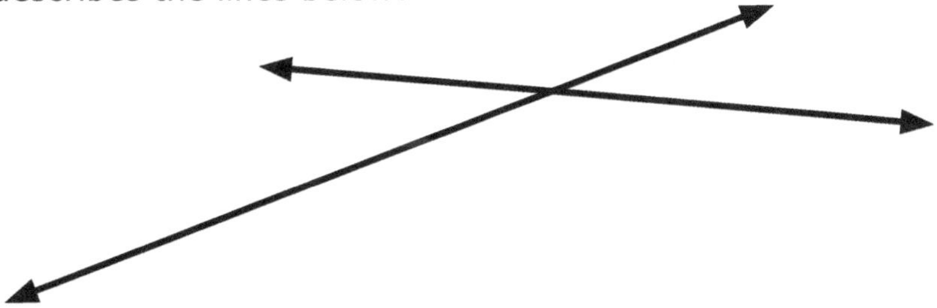

**A.** perpendicular
**B.** intersecting
**C.** parallel
**D.** line segment

3. Which phrase describes the shape below?

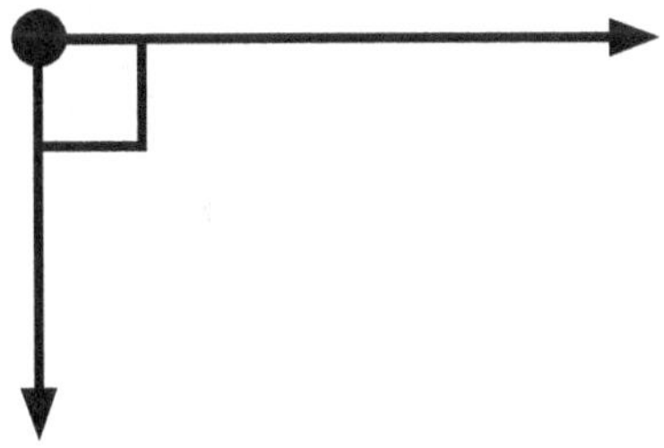

**A.** two rays forming a right angle
**B.** two line segments forming a right angle
**C.** two parallel lines forming an angle
**D.** two rays forming an obtuse angle

4. Identify the line formed by points A and B on the shape below.

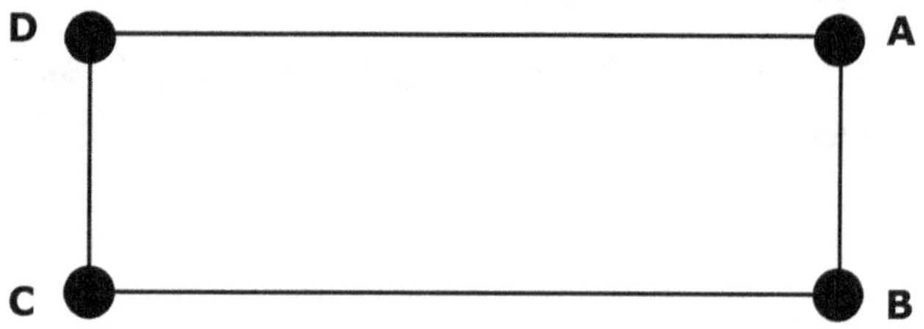


**A.** ray
**B.** angle
**C.** line
**D.** line segment

5. Which shape below has 2 obtuse angles?

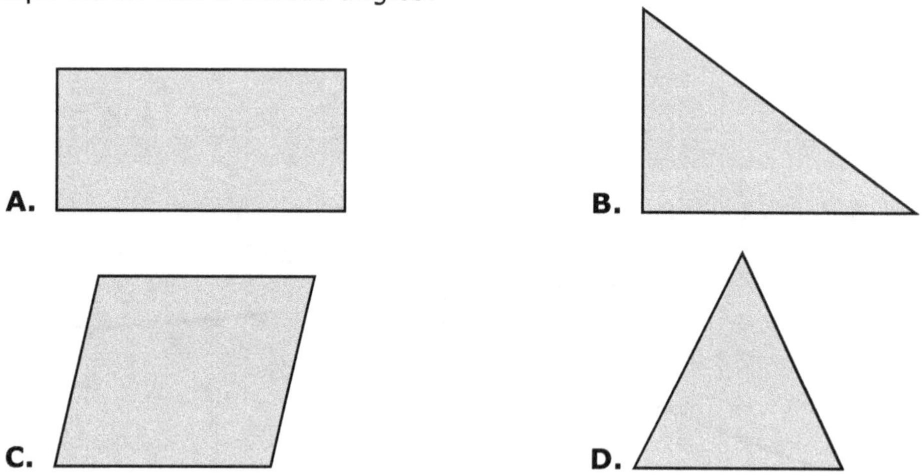


6. Identify a ray shown in this diagram.

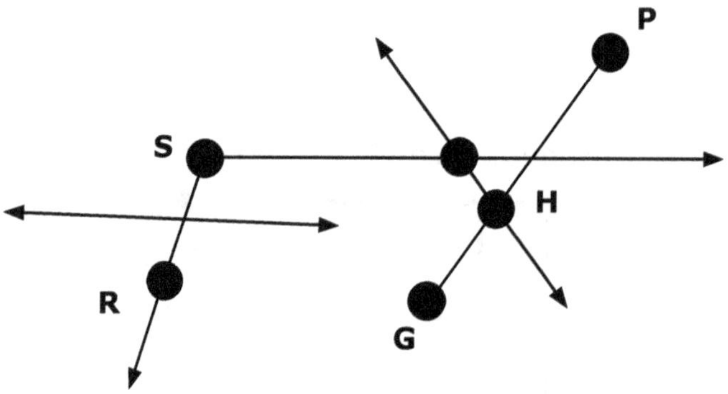


**A.** PH
**B.** SR
**C.** GH
**D.** PS

7. Which shape has 1 set of parallel sides and 2 acute angles?

**A.** 

**B.** 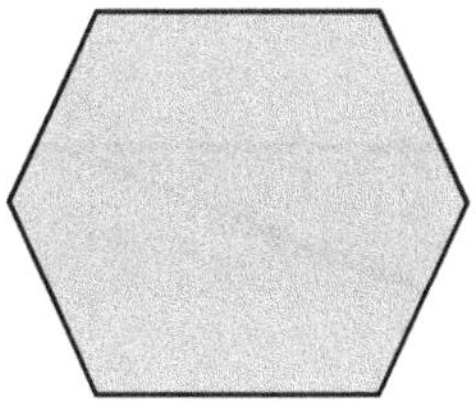

**C.** 

**D.** 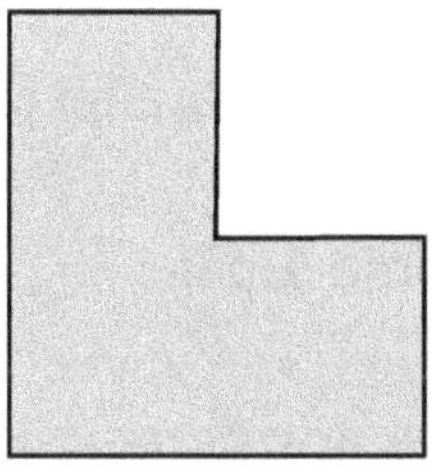

8. Which shape has 1 pair of perpendicular line segments and 2 acute angles?

**A.** 

**B.** 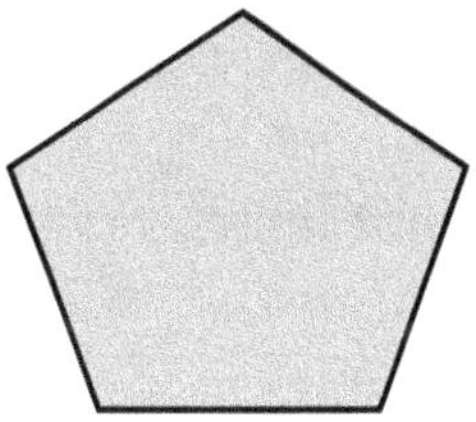

**C.** 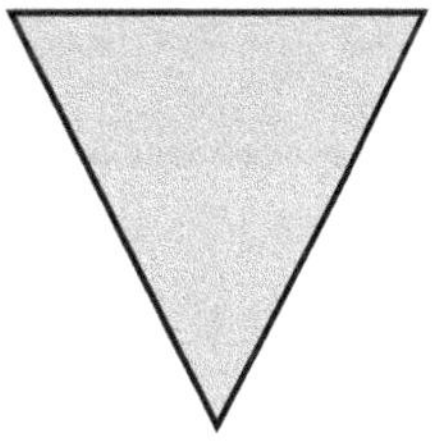

**D.** 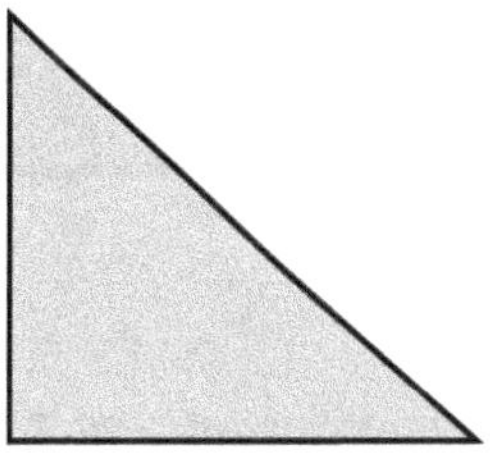

9. What is the measure of each angle in a triangle if the triangle has all sides the same length?
   - **A.** 45°
   - **B.** 90°
   - **C.** 60°
   - **D.** 50°

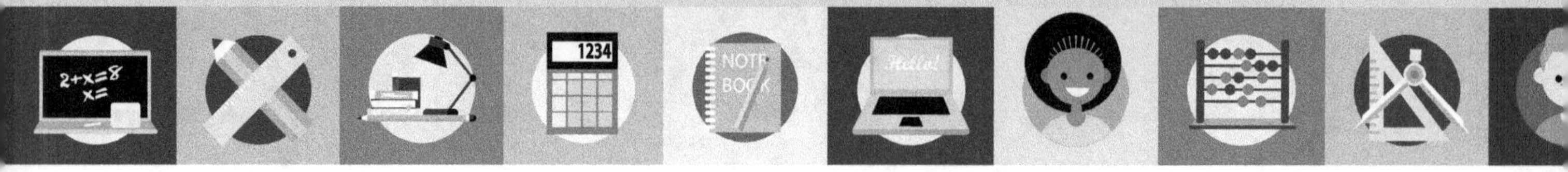


10. Use this figure to answer the questions below.

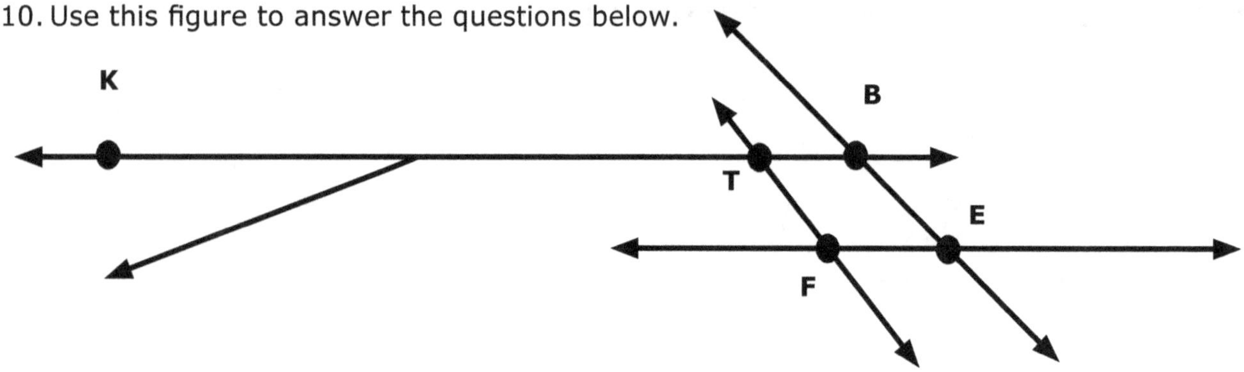


A. Are there any parallel lines? _______________

If so, name 1 pair: _______________ and _______________

B. Are there any perpendicular lines? _______________

If so, name 1 pair: _______________ and _______________

C. Is angle B acute, right or obtuse? _______________

11. Draw a line that intersects the line below but is not perpendicular to it.

A. What types of angles are formed where the line intersects?

B. Would the angles formed from the intersecting line be different if the line drawn was perpendicular to the current line? Why or why not?

12. Draw a quadrilateral with one acute angle, one obtuse angle, and two right angles.

What shape did you draw? ____________

# CLASSIFY TWO-DIMENSIONAL FIGURES

**G.A.2 Classify two-dimensional figures based on the presence or absence of parallel or perpendicular lines, or the presence or absence of angles of a specified size. Recognize right triangles as a category, and identify right triangles.**

1. Which statement describes a square?
   **A.** Opposite sides are not parallel
   **B.** Opposite sides are parallel and all 4 angles are right angles
   **C.** Opposite sides are parallel and only 2 angles are right angles
   **D.** Does not have any perpendicular lines

2. Triangle D has angles that are the same measure. What must be true about triangle D?
   **A.** It is a right triangle
   **B.** It is a scalene triangle
   **C.** It is an isosceles triangle
   **D.** It is an equilateral triangle

3. Which type of triangle has at least one obtuse angle?

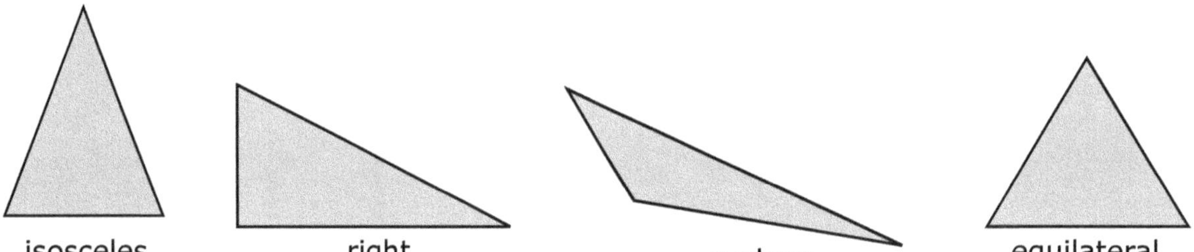

**A.** isosceles **B.** right **C.** scalene **D.** equilateral

4. Which polygon has all sides the same length, but does not have all angles the same measure?
   **A.** rhombus
   **B.** rectangle
   **C.** square
   **D.** triangle

5. Which quadrilateral only has 1 pair of parallel sides?
   **A.** parallelogram
   **B.** trapezoid
   **C.** rectangle
   **D.** rhombus

6. Which polygon has:

- **2 sets of parallel sides**
- **2 pairs of sides of equal lengths**
- **4 right angles**

  **A.** rhombus
  **B.** trapezoid
  **C.** rectangle
  **D.** parallelogram

7. Which polygon has:

- **1 right angle**
- **2 acute angles**
- **3 sides**

  **A.** equilateral triangle
  **B.** isosceles triangle
  **C.** rhombus
  **D.** right triangle

8. Which polygon could have only 1 pair of perpendicular sides?
  **A.** right triangle
  **B.** obtuse triangle
  **C.** rectangle
  **D.** square

9. Which statement below is true?
  **A.** A rhombus is a rectangle, but a rectangle is not a rhombus.
  **B.** A rhombus can be a square, but a square cannot be a rhombus.
  **C.** A rectangle is a parallelogram, and a parallelogram can be a rectangle.
  **D.** A trapezoid is not a quadrilateral.

10. Draw a polygon with:

- **2 obtuse angles**
- **2 acute angles**
- **2 pairs of parallel sides**

11. There are two groups of polygons below:

**Group 1**

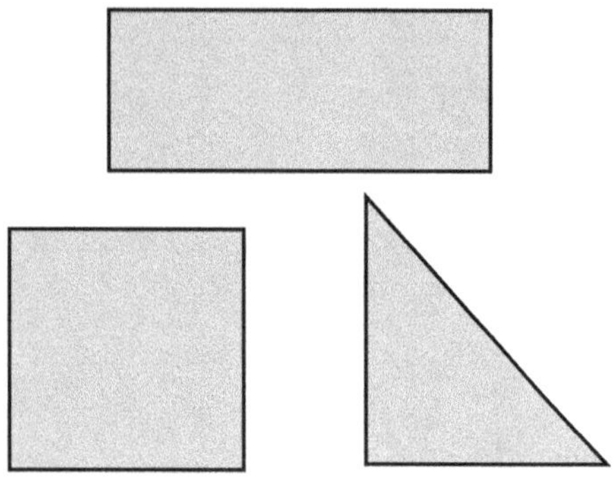

**Group 2**

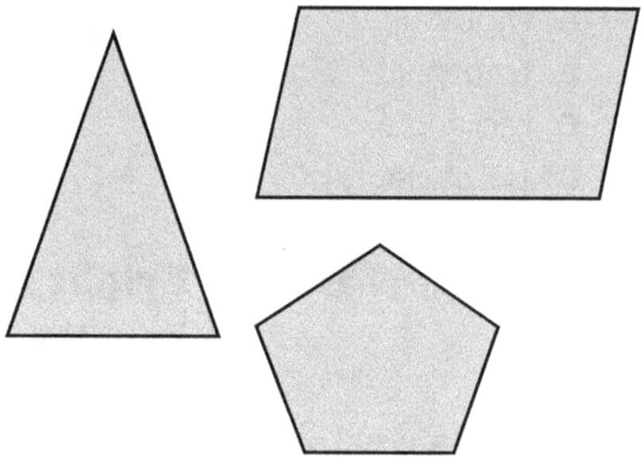

How are the groups sorted?

_______________________________________________

_______________________________________________

Add another polygon to each group with the same attributes.

12. Fill in the chart with the names of the polygons listed below. The shapes may fit into more than one category.

**right triangle** **square** **rectangle** **rhombus**

**parallelogram** **trapezoid**

| Polygons with at least one pair of parallel sides | Polygons with at least one pair of perpendicular sides | Polygons with at least one right angle |
|---|---|---|
| | | |
| | | |
| | | |
| | | |

# DRAW AND IDENTIFY LINES OF SYMMETRY

**G.A.3 Recognize a line of symmetry for a two-dimensional figure as a line across the figure such that the figure can be folded along the line into matching parts. Identify line-symmetric figures and draw lines of symmetry.**

1. Which shape below has a line of symmetry?

**A.** 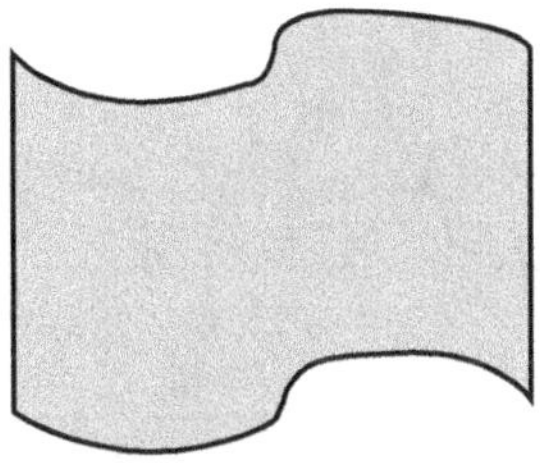

**B.** 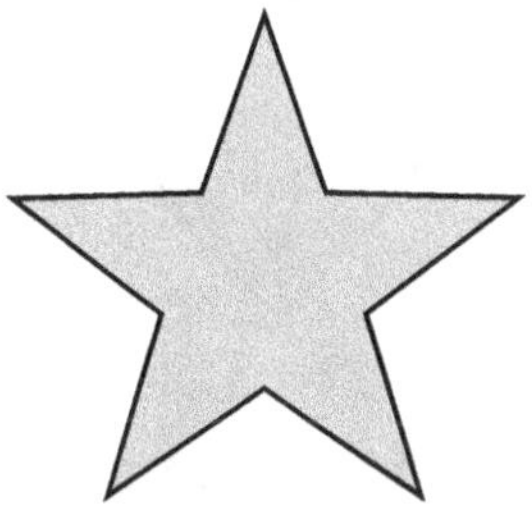

**C.** 

**D.** 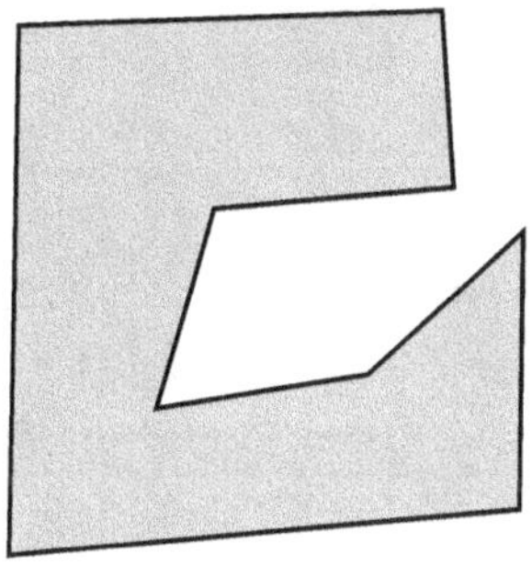

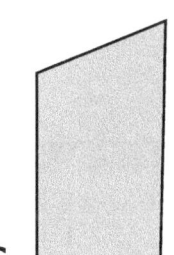

2. Which figure shows a line of symmetry?

**A.** 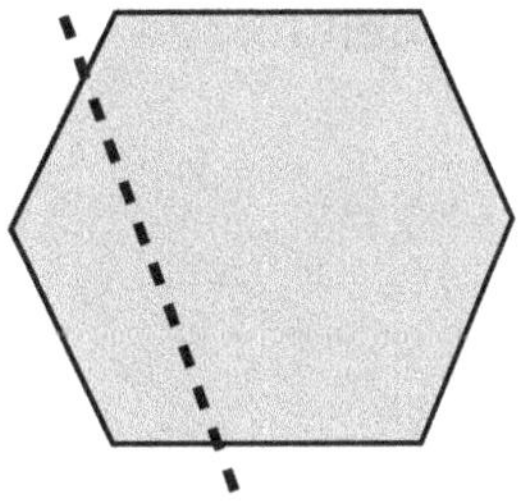

**B.** 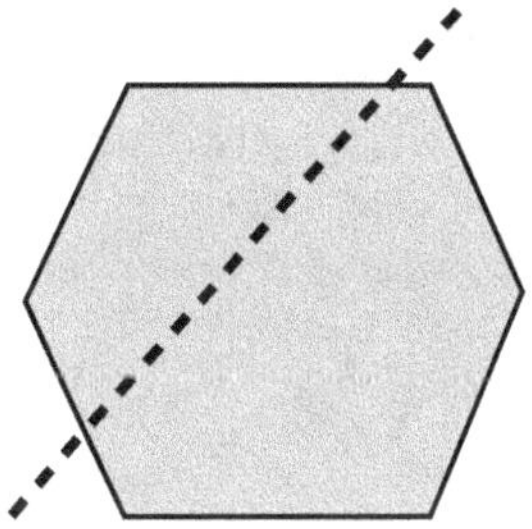

**C.** 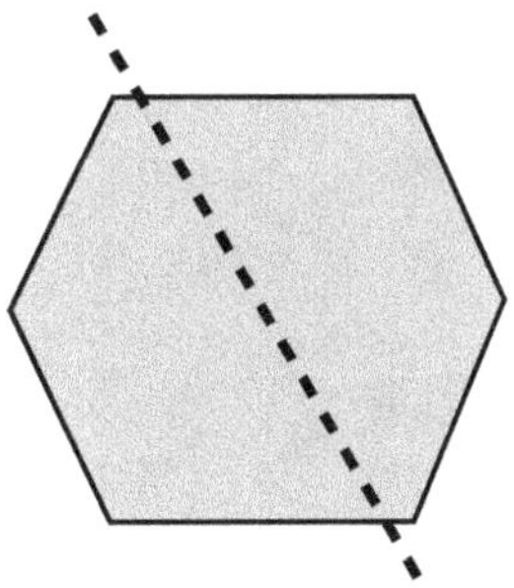

**D.** 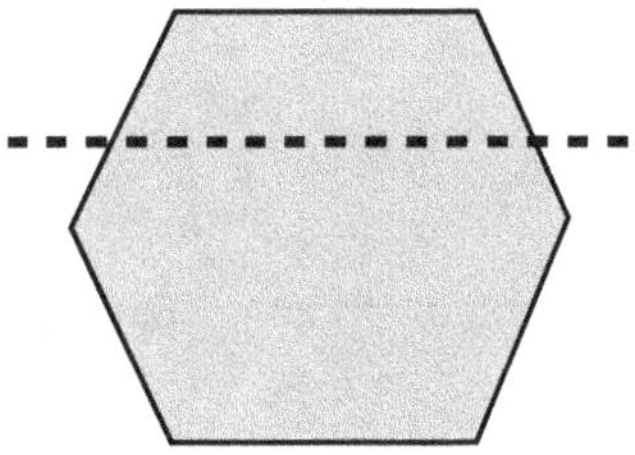

3. Which figure has more than 1 line of symmetry?

A. 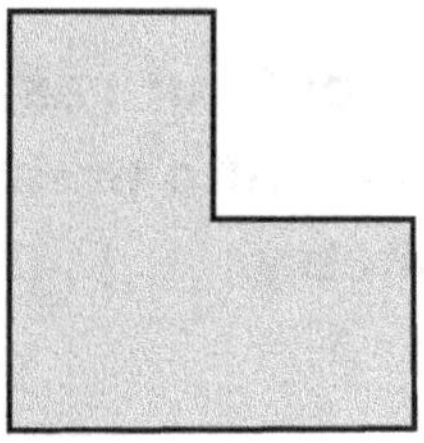

B. 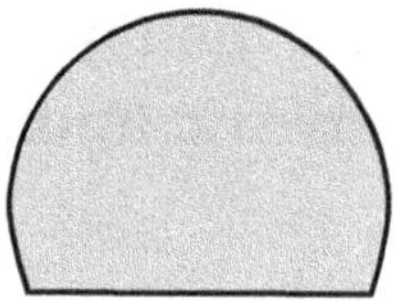

C. 

D. 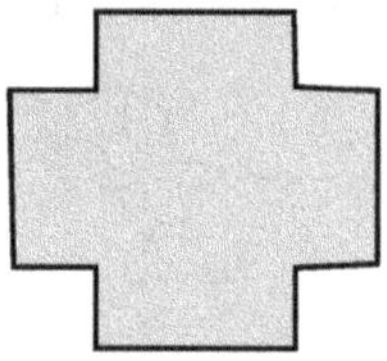

4. Which figure does not have a line of symmetry?

A. 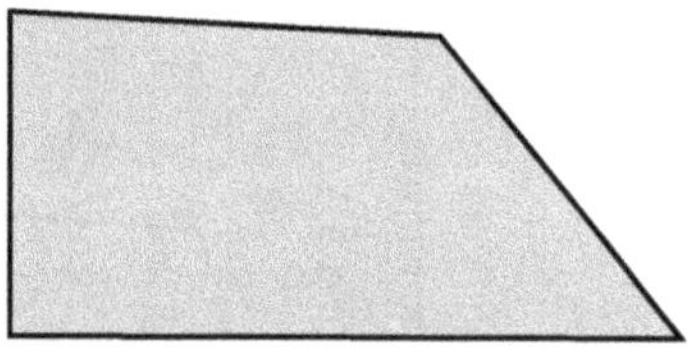

B. 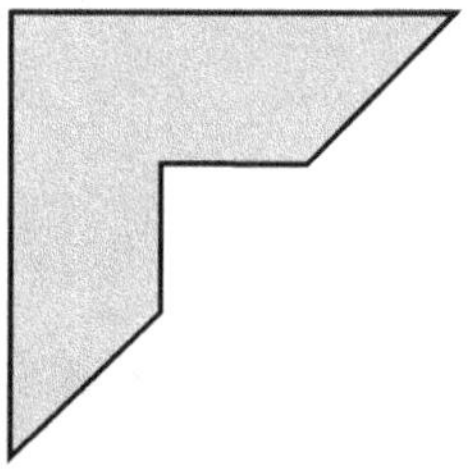

C. 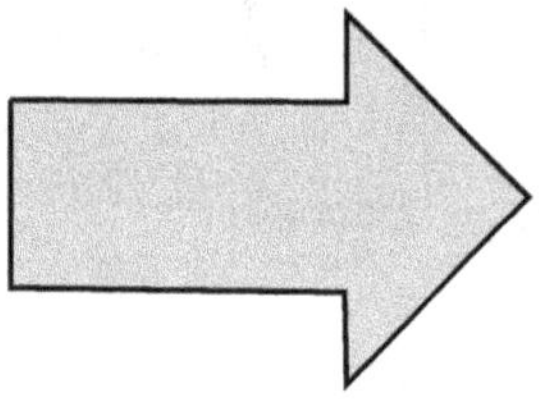

D. 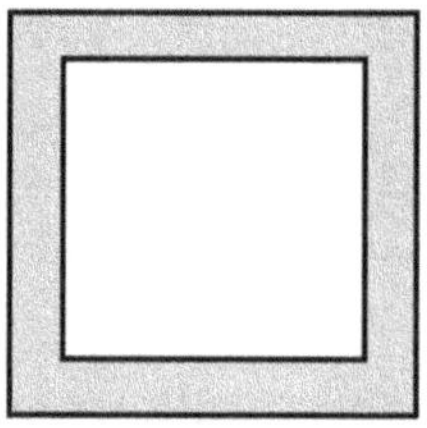

5. What would the other half of the figure below look like when folded over the line of symmetry, the dotted line?

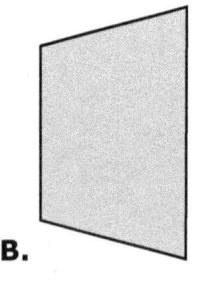

A. 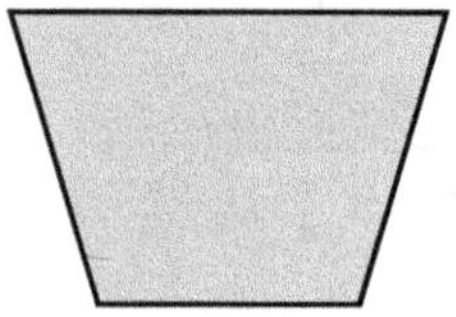

B. 

C. 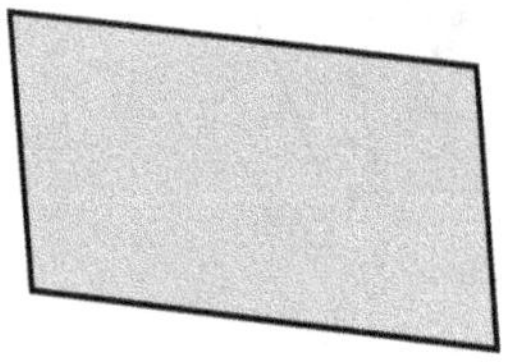

D. 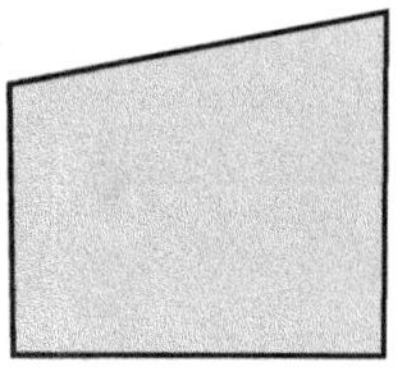

6. Which figure only has 1 line of symmetry?

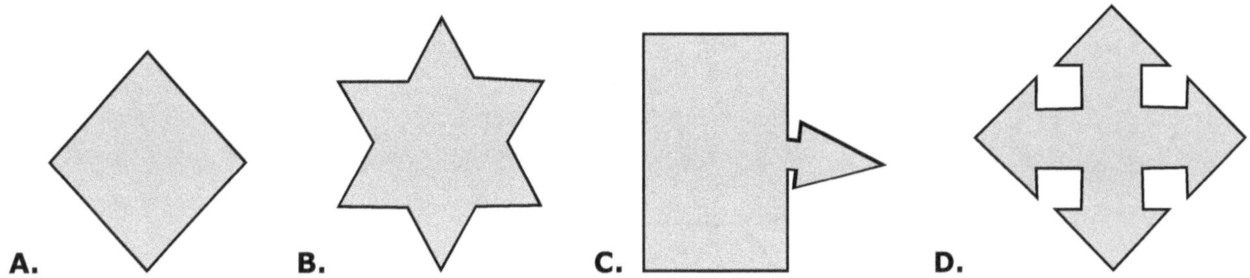


7. Which letter has more than 1 line of symmetry?

**A.** A **B.** M **C.** D **D.** X

8. What is the best way to describe the line of symmetry in the letter B?

B

**A.** horizontal
**B.** vertical
**C.** diagonal
**D.** none

9. How many lines of symmetry are in an equilateral hexagon?

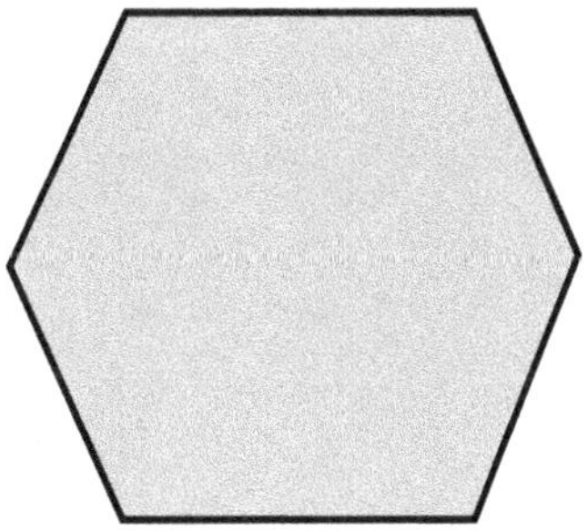

**A.** 4
**B.** 6
**C.** 2
**D.** 8

10. Draw the rest of this shape over the line of symmetry.

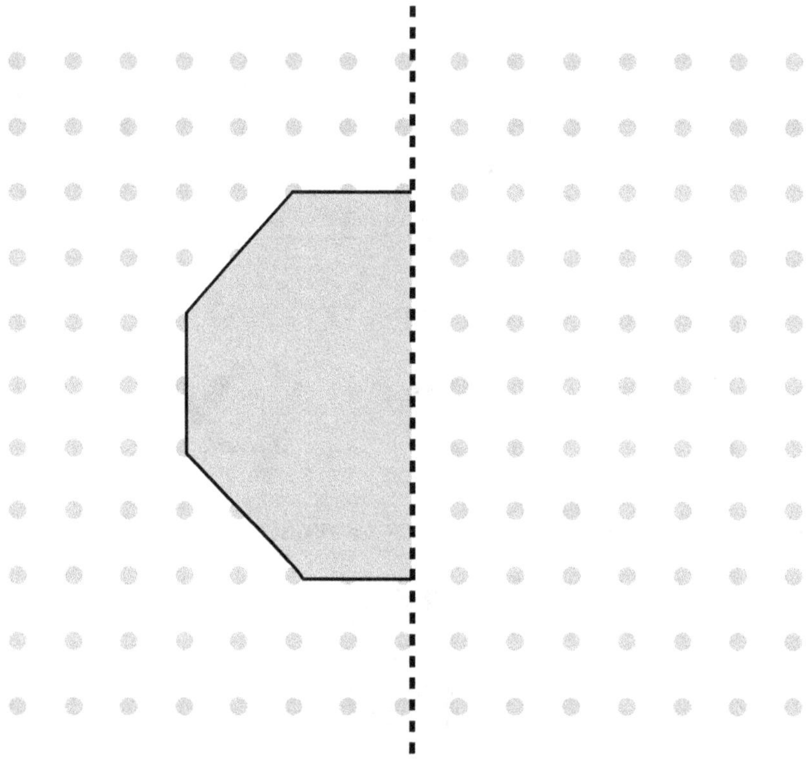

11. Use the dotted grid below to solve parts A and B.

A. Draw a shape with exactly 2 lines of symmetry.

B. Draw a shape with exactly 4 lines of symmetry.

12. Fill in the chart below to show the number of sides in each polygon and the number of lines of symmetry for each shape.

| Polygon | Equilateral triangle 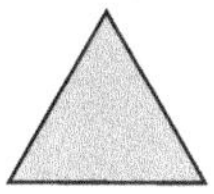 | Square  | Regular hexagon 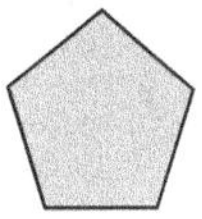 | Regular octagon 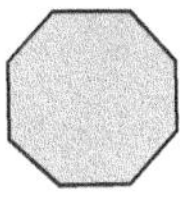 |
|---|---|---|---|---|
| Number of sides | | | | |
| Number of lines of symmetry | | | | |

A. What do you notice about the relationship between the number of sides in a regular polygon and number of lines of symmetry?

B. How many lines of symmetry does a circle have when the line passes through the center of the circle?

# ANSWER KEY

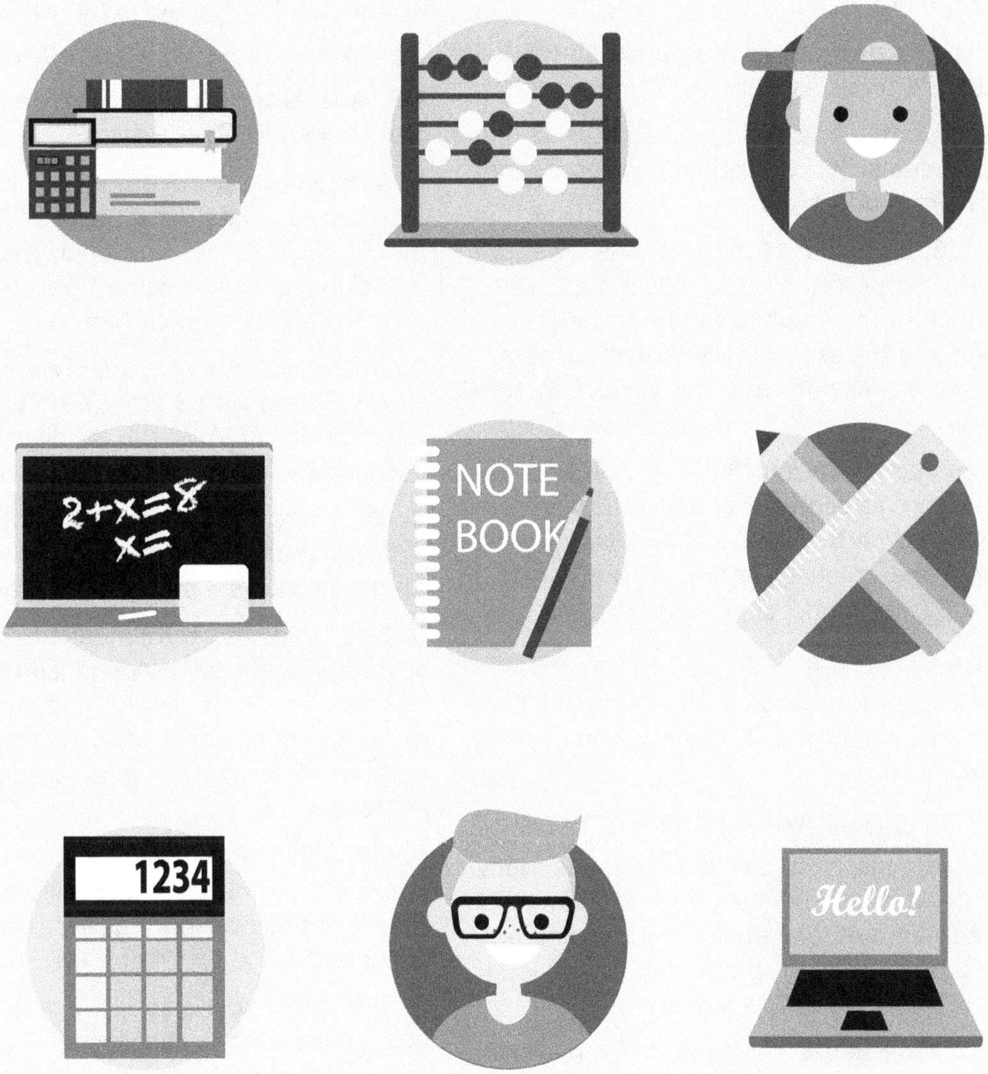

## OPERATIONS AND ALGEBRAIC THINKING

### OA.A.1 Understand Multiplication

**1. B.** The model in choice *B* shows 3 groups with 4 circles in each group. This can be counted as 4 + 4 + 4 which is 3x4=12. Using the phrase "3 times as many as 4" is the same as saying "3 times 4".

**2. C.** The phrase "5 times as many as 6" is the same as 5 x 6 so choice *C* is correct. Choices *B* and *D* do not have the correct products and choice *A* does not match the comparison phrase.

**3. A.** 24 = 6 x 4 is the same as saying 24 is 6 times as many as 4 or 6 times 4 is 24. Having the product at the beginning of the equation does not change the value of the numbers.

**4. D.** 15 is 5 times as many as 3 because 15 = 5 x 3 or 5 x 3 = 15. "5 times as many as 3" means 5 x 3.

**5. C.** "9 times as many as 4" is the same as saying 9 x 4 which equals 36. The other choices do not have the correct product.

**6. D.** 18 = 6 x 3 and 18 = 3 x 6 shows the Commutative Property of Multiplication, which means the factors in a multiplication equation can change order, and the product will remain the same. The other choices do not have the correct factors and products.

**7. A.** Twice as many means multiply by 2. If Paul has twice as many pens as pencils, that means he has more pens. To solve, multiply the number of pencils by 2 since Paul has twice the amount pencils. So the equation would be: 2 x 5 (the number of pencils)=10 pens

Distractors:

-Choice *C* is incorrect because it shows the addition equation and does not match the multiplication wording "twice as many"

- Choice *D* is incorrect because 2 x 5 does not equal 12

**8.** Part A: **B;** Sam picked twice (or 2 times) as many apples as Kate. Kate picked 6 apples and 2 times as many as Kate's amount of 6 apples is 12 apples. So Sam picked 2 times as many because Kate's amount of 6 apples x 2 = 12. Part B: **6 x 2 = 12**

Part C: **A.** Olive picked 2 apples and Robin picked 18 apples. 9 times as many as 2 = 18 which is the same as 9 x 2 =18 so Robin picked 9 times as many apples as Olive because Olive has 2 apples and we know 9 x 2 =18. Part D: **9 x 2 = 18.**

**9. 21 years old.** Joey is 3 times older than Jenna, who is 7 years old. That means Joey is 3 times as much as 7 which is the same as 3 x 7 so Joey is 21 years old.

**10.** Part A: **2 x 10 = 20** If we know the fish costs $2 and the bird costs $20, think: how are those numbers related? Is the cost of one animal a certain times as much as the cost of another animal? I know 2 x 10 = 20 so that means the cost of the bird ($20) is 10 times as much as the cost of the fish ($2) because

2 (the fish) x 10 = 20 (the bird).

Part B: **Yes, she is correct.** Sarah recognizes that 4 times as much as the $5 gerbil is the cost of the $20 bird because 4 x 5 = 20. Another way to think of this is 4 times as many as 5 = 4 x 5, which equals 20.

A bird ($20) is 4 times as much as $5 (the gerbil)

20 = 4 x 5, so Sarah is correct in her reasoning.

### OA.A.2 Use Multiplication & Division To Solve Word Problems

**1. A.** Each bag has 5 oranges in it and Simon needs 3 times as many. The phrase "3 times as many" means multiply by 3. Simon needs 3 bags so the model in choice A is correct because it shows 3 bags with 5 oranges in each bag.

Distractor: Choice C is incorrect because the model shows 5 bags with 3 oranges in each bag. Although the product (15) is the same, this is not correct because each bag has 5 apples, not 3.

**2. D.** There are 4 chairs set up and Tom needs 5 times that amount which means multiply by 5. Choice *D* shows 5 sets with 4 chairs in each set.

**3. B.** 3 times as many means multiply by 3. James scored 4 goals last season and 3 times as many this season so you would multiply 4 x 3 to compare the number of goals from this season (12) to the number of goals from last season (4). 4 goals last seasons x 3 = 12

**4. C.** In this problem, we are given the product or total amount of money in the comparison. Kelly has $24 which is 3 times as much as her sister. One way to think about this is 3 x ? = 24 or 24 is 3 times as many as?

So the bar model shows 3 boxes with an unknown amount in each box equaling 24. 24 is 3 times as much as 8 so we can use division to solve and think 24 ÷ 3 = 8 because we know 3 x 8 = 24

Distractor: Choice A is a distractor since there are 4 boxes shown in the model so you might think 4 x 6 = 24 or 24 ÷ 4 = 6. This is not correct because Kelly has 3 times as much money which means 3 x ? = 24, not 4 x ? = 24

**5. Chris: 10**

**John: 10, 10, 10, 10 = 40.**

**10 x 4 = 40 pages, so John read 40 pages.**

To fill in the chart, Chris read 10 pages so the box next to Chris is 10. Then there are 4 boxes next to John to represent 4 times as many. In those 4 boxes, write the number 10 to show 4 times as many as Chris, which is 10.

John read 4 times as many pages as Chris so 4 times as many means multiply Chris' amount (10) by 4. The equation is Chris' amount **10 x 4 times as many = 40**.

**6. B.** There are 5 times as many more students in the grade than in Charlie's class. This means multiply the number of students in Charlie's class 20 by 5 because the total amount of students in the grade is unknown. 20 x 5 = n, the number of students in 4th grade.

Distractor: Choice A is incorrect because 5 x n = 20 would represent a problem that has 20 total students in 4th grade since the equation shows 20 as the product.

**7. D.** Mrs. Smith travel 6 times as many hours as Mr. Jones because Mrs. Jones' travel time, 4 x 6 = 24, Mrs. Smith's travel time. In this problem we know the largest amount time traveled was 24 hours (the product) so we are missing one of the factors; think 4 times what equals 24?

**8. C.** In this problem, we have the product or total number of runs scored as 12 runs. The Blue Jays scored 6 times as many runs as the losing team, which we don't know so we can represent the unknown factor with a letter "r". 6 times as many as the losing team can be represented as 6 x r = 12 (the amount the Blu Jays scored) so 6 x 2 = 12, the losing team scored 2 runs.

**9.** Part A: **Brendan has 5 cards.** Part B: If Logan has 45 cards, which is 9 times as many as Brendan, we can represent Brendan's unknown number of cards as "c". 9 times as many as c as an equation is

9 x c = 45 because 9 times Brendan's amount of cards equals Logan's amount of 45. So Brendan has 5 cards, 9 x 5= 45.

**10. Lucy = 105**

**Samantha = 35**

**Kristen = 20.**

Start with what we know: we know Kristen played for 20 minutes. Samantha played for 15 more minutes, which means add 15 to Kristen's time to find Samantha's time on the playground. 15 + 20 = 35, so Samantha played for 35 minutes. Lucy played for 3 times as long as Samantha, which means multiply by 3 so Samantha's time 35 minutes times 3 = 105. Lucy played for 105 minutes.

**11. 1st and 3rd Choices.** This problem is asking you to compare the multiplicative relationship between 12 and 36. The question is asking: Mike biked how many more times father than Josh? Mike biked 36 miles which is 3 times farther than Josh because 12 (Josh's amount) x 3 = 36 (Mike's amount) OR 36 (Mike's amount) ÷ 3 = 12 (Josh's amount). Both a multiplication and division equation can be used to solve because we think about the multiplication and division relationship between the numbers: 12 x 3 = 36, 3 x 12 = 36, 36 ÷ 3 = 12 and 36 ÷ 12 = 3.

**12. 4 times as many students voted for Dragons than Tigers.** Think: 4 times which number of votes equals another number of votes in the chart. 4 times as many students voted for Dragons than Tigers. This is true because 4 times as many as the 12 Tiger votes equals 48, the Dragon votes. 12 x 4 = 48 or 48 ÷ 4 = 12.

## OA.A.3 Solve & Represent Multi-Step Word Problems with Equations

**1. Alyssa has $14 left; C.** First, to find out how much money Alyssa made babysitting, multiply 4 x 5 because she was paid $5 for every hour and worked 4 hours. Then, take the amount of money she made, $20, and subtract 6 because she spent $6. The parenthesis around 4 x 5 mean complete that operation first and then subtract 6.

**2. B.** If Steve worked 2 hours in the morning and 1 hour in the afternoon, first add to find the number of hours he worked each day. (2 +1) Then multiply by 5 (because he worked 3 hours each day) to find the total number of hours he worked last week.

**3. C.** Carol first needs to find the total price of the wood. If each piece costs $9 and she buys 3 pieces, multiply 3 x 9. Then subtract the cost of the wood from the amount paid, $40. So parentheses are needed around 3x9 since that is the first step. Then subtract 40 - 27 to find the change received.

**4. D.** First subtract the total numbers of pages and subtract the number of pages read (300-120) in parenthesis first. Then the remaining amount is divided by the 3 remaining days.

**5. A.** 2 times as much as the amount the plant grew in July means multiply 2 x 4 - the amount the plant grew in July (2 x 4 =8). Then add the amounts the plant grew together: 35 + 4 + 8 = 47 inches.

**6. D.** First, find the total number of chairs at the party (6 x 4). Then subtract the number of people going to the party to find the number of empty chairs. If Tommy and Kate are going with 19 other people then add 19 + 2 (Tommy and Kate) to find the number of people going to the party. Finally subtract the chairs and the number of people at the party to find the empty chairs (6 x 4) - (19 + 2) = 3

**7. A.** Jordan makes 6 large omelets with 3 eggs in each so multiply to find the number of eggs needed for the large omelets (3 x 6). Then Jordan makes 3 small omelets with 2 eggs in each so multiply to find the number of eggs needed for the small omelets (2 x 3). Add the products together to find the total number of eggs needed. (3 x 6) + (2x3) = 24 eggs.

**8.** Part A: **(28 + 31) ÷7 = 8 remainder 3 books so Mrs. Peterson needs 9 boxes to fit all the books.** First add 28 + 31 to find the total number of books Mrs. Peterson needs to pack. Then divide by 7 to find the number of boxes she needs because 7 books can fit into a box. 28 + 31 = 59, 59 ÷ 7 = 8 remainder 3. The remaining 3 books need to be placed in another box so Mrs. Peterson needs 9 boxes to fit all the books.

Part B: Estimate: I know the total number of books, 59, is not divisible by 7 so round 59 to a compatible number that is divisible by 7, which is 63. 63 ÷ 7 is 9 so I know my answer should be around 9.

**9. A.** 50 is the correct answer because if there were twice as many adult tickets than children's tickets sold, twice means multiply the number of children's tickets (25) by 2. 25 x 2 = 50 so there were 50 adult tickets sold. 25 x 6 equals the price of the 25 children's tickets and 50 x 9 equals the price of the adult tickets. Adding the price of the adult and children's tickets (25 x 6) + (50 x 9) = the total cost of the tickets sold on Friday.

**10. C.** First subtract 75-32 to find how much money Jessica still needs to earn. 75-32 = $43. If she earns $8 for each time she walks the dog, then divide 43÷8 to find how many times she needs to walk the dog to earn $3. Since this does not divide evenly, 43 ÷ 8= 5 remainder 3, she needs to walk the dog 6 times (6 x 8 = 48) in order to have enough money to buy the video game because $40 is not enough since she needs $43.

**11.** Part A: **False.** To find out how "2 more than 7 times the amount on Monday" is, multiply the amount of toys sold on Monday $4 x 7 = 28 + 2 (because 2 more means add 2) which equals 30. 30 is not the amount of toys sold on Friday so "False" is the correct answer here.

Part B: **True.** The toys sold on Wednesday and Thursday were 9 + 13 = 22. Twice as much as 22 is 2 x 22 = 44, which is the amount sold on Friday. So the correct answer here is "True".

**12. (15 x 5) + (43 x 11) + (19 x 8) = $700 on Friday.**

**Saturday: 4 x 700 = $2800 was made on Saturday's show.**

First find the amount of money made on the Friday night show. Multiply to find the amount of each ticket: child (15 x 5) + adult (43 x 11) + senior (19 x 8) which equals $700 when you add the products for Friday's show. Then multiply the amount of money from Friday night by 4 since the Saturday night show made 4 times as much. $700 x 4 = $2800 was made on Saturday night.

## OA.B.4 Understand and Use Factors and Multiples

**1. C.** The factors are the numbers that are multiplied to find the product. 1 x 8 = 8, and 2 x 4 = 8 so the factors of 8 are 1, 2, 4, 8

**2. B.** A multiple of a number is that number multiplied by an integer. So 7 x 2 = 14 so 14 is a multiple of 7. You can also skip count by 7s to get to 14, so 14 is a multiple of 7.

**3. A.** First list the factors of each number; 1 x6 and 2 x 3 = 6 so the factors of 6 are 1, 2, 3, 6

1 x 24, 2 x 12, 3 x 8, 4 x 6 all equal 24 so the factors of 24 are 1, 2, 3, 4, 6, 8, 12, 24

1 x 30, 2 x 15, 3 x 10, 5 x 6 all equal 30 so the factors of 30 are 1, 2, 3, 5, 6, 10, 15, 30

The factors 6, 24, and 30 have in common are 1, 2, 3, 6

**4. C.** 16 is a factor of 32 because 2 x 16 = 32

16 is a multiple of 4 because you can multiply 4 x 4 to equal 16 or skip count by 4s; 4, 8, 12, 16, 20 and you can see 16 is a multiple of 4

**5. D.** $12 is the cost of one ice cream cake because 12 is a factor of 96. 96 ÷ 12 = 8 so the ice cream shop could have sold 8 cakes for $12 each and made $96.

**6. C.** 17 is prime because it only has 1 factor pair; 17 x 1 = 17. A factor pair is the two factors that are multiplied to equal a product, such as 1 x 17 make one factor pair of 17.

**7. D.** Gavin could not have run 16 miles if he runs 6 miles everyday because 16 is not a multiple of 6. 6 x 2 = 12 and 6 x 3 =18 so there is no way Gavin could have run 16 miles if he runs 6 miles every day.

**8. C.** 27 ÷9 = 3 proves 27 is a composite number

because you can think of this division equation as multiplication: 9 x 3 = 27. This shows 27 has more than 27 and 1 as factors. The factors of 27 are 1, 3, 9, 27 so this means 27 is composite.

**9.** Part A: **12, 24, 36**

Part B: **The numbers I circled are *multiples* of 12.**

Lisa could have made 12 cupcakes, which would be one tray. She could have also made 24 cupcakes and baked 2 trays because 12 x 2 = 24. Or she could have made 36 cupcakes and baked 3 trays of cupcakes because 12 x 3 = 36.

12, 24, and 36 are multiples of 12 because 1 tray of 12 cupcakes makes 12 cupcakes. 2 trays of 12 cupcakes makes 24 cupcakes. 3 trays of 12 cupcakes makes 36 cupcakes. When you count by 12s, you are listing the multiples of 12.

**10.** Part A: **One way: 2 groups of 8 people on each team OR 8 groups with 2 people on each team.**

**Another way: 4 groups with 4 people on each team**

16 can be divided into 2 groups of 8 people because 2 x 8 = 16 OR 8 groups with 2 people in each group because 8 x 2 =16. OR

16 can be divided into 4 groups with 4 people in each group because 4 x 4 = 16.

Part B: **16 is composite because it has more than 1 factor pair.** 16 is composite because there are more than 2 factors fo 16. 1 x 16 = 16, 2 x 6 = 16, and 4 x 4 = 16 so the factors of 16 are 1, 2, 4, 8, 16.

**11. B.** A factor pair of 12 is 4 and 3 because 4 x 3 =12 and the number line shows 3 jumps of 4 which are factors of 12.

**12.**

| Hayden's Cookies | Rows | Columns |
|---|---|---|
| Option 1 | 6 | 6 |
| Option 2 | **2** | **18** |
| Option 3 | **3** | **12** |
| Option 4 | **4** | **9** |

**OR**

| Hayden's Cookies | Rows | Columns |
|---|---|---|
| Option 1 | 6 | 6 |
| Option 2 | **18** | **2** |
| Option 3 | **12** | **3** |
| Option 4 | **9** | **4** |

I know Hayden has 36 cookies to arrange on the tray because 6 rows of 6 cookies represents 6 x 6 = 36.

The other factors of 36 are 2 x 18 so Hayden can make 2 rows of 18 cookies in each row.

3 x 12 = 36 so Hayden can make 3 rows with 12 cookies in each row.

4 x 9 = 36 so Hayden can make 4 rows with 9 cookies in each row.

Or the rows and columns could be reversed but it would still represent the same factors of 36.

## OA.C.5 Generate & Identify Arithmetic & Shape Patterns

**1. C.** The pattern is decreasing by 9 because 95 - 86 = 9, 86 - 77 = 9 so 59 -9 = 50

**2. B.** Multiply the previous number by 2.

20 x 2 = 40

40 x 2 = 80

80 x 2 = 160

**3. D.** Add 3, then multiply by 2 is a 2-step rule.

5 + 3 = 8

8 x 2 = 16

16 + 3 = 19

So the pattern is 5, 8, 16, 19. 19 is the 4th number in this pattern.

**4. 1st and 4th Choices.** The numbers in the patters are multiple of 12 because 12 x 2 = 24, 12 x 3 =36, 12 x 4 = 48 and 12 x 5 = 60.

They are also multiples of 4 because 4 x 3 = 12, 4 x 6 = 24, 4 x 9 = 36, 4 x 12 = 48, and 4 x 15 = 60.

**5. B.** The number of vases x 8 = the number of flowers in each vase. 2 vases x 8 = 16 flowers, 5 vases x 8 = 40 flowers. The each vase holds 8 flowers.

**6. Set 4 should have 3 circles and Set 5 should have 1 circle.** The pattern is decreasing by 2. The first set has 9 circles, set 2 has 7 circles, set 3 has 5 circles so each set decreases by 2.

**7.** Part A: **16 is composite because it has more than 1 factor pair. 69, 78, 87, 96;** Part B: **16 is composite because it has more than 1 factor pair. The pattern is n+9 or add 9 to the previous number.**

The pattern is add 9 to each number so the next numbers in the sequence would be 69, 78, 87, and 96.

60 + 9 = 69

69 + 9 = 78

78 + 9 = 87

87 + 9 = 96

**8. B.** If Jackson doubled his score each time he played, add 100 + 100 = 200, the second score. 200 + 200 = 400, his 3rd score. 400 + 400 = 800, his 4th score.

**9. A.** 900 would be the 90th number in the pattern. The rule is adding 10 to every number in the sequence and to find a certain number in the sequence, multiply by 10.

1 x 10 =10

2 x 10 = 20

3 x 10= 30 and so on. To find the 90th number, multiply by 10: 90 x 10 = 900

**10. B.** The pattern in this sequence is add 6. You can continue adding 6 to each number until you reach 72 or you can think: 72 is a multiple of 6 because 6 x 12 = 72 so yes, 72 will be a number in this pattern.

**11. D.** There will be 7 rounds of games and then 2 teams remain for the final championship game. Start with 44 teams, subtract 6 after each set of games.

44, 38, 32, 26, 20, 14, 8 shows 7 rounds of games. 8 - 6 = 2, the last round.

**12.** Part A: **16 is composite because it has more than 1 factor pair. 13 x 12 = 156 students.** A. The pattern shows for every 1 adult, there are 12 students. To find the relationship between the numbers, look at how 4 and 48 are related: 4 x 12 = 48, 6 x 12 = 72, so for every 1 adult, there are 12 students on the field trip.

To find the number of students there would be with 13 adults, multiply by 12. 13 x 12 = 156.

Part B: **16 is composite because it has more than 1 factor pair. 180 ÷ 12 = 15 adults.** Use the pattern adults x 12 = students to help solve part B.

If there are 180 students, and we need to find the number of adults, insert the given numbers into the equation: adults x 12 = 180 students.

To find the number of adults, think what number times 12 equals 180. OR use the opposite (inverse) operation to solve: 180 ÷ 12 = 15, so there are 15 adults with 180 children.

## NUMBERS AND OPERATIONS IN BASE 10

### NBT.A.1 Understand Place Value

**1. C.** 4 in the thousands place is worth (has a value of) 4000 because 4 x 1000= 4000

**2. A.** 4 in the tens place has a value of 40. 10 times 4 in the tens place or 40 = 400 so the equation would be 10 x 40 = 400

**3. D.** 4 in the thousands place is equal to 4000.

4000 is 10 times the value of the 4 in the hundreds place because 4,000 is 10 x 400 or 10 x 400 is 4,000.

**4. B.** 15, 000 is 1,000 times greater than 15 because 15 x 1,000 = 15,000

**5. C.** The value of the 8 in 48,921 is 8,000 so ten times the 8000 would be 80,000. The answer that has an 8 in the ten thousands place is 86,502.

**6. A.** 450 x 1000 = 450,000. Another way to think about this is to think 10 x 10 x 10 is 1000 so move 3 place values to the left on the place value chart since each place value is ten times the previous place value.

**7. C.** 3,200,000 ÷ 32,000 = 100 because 32,000 x 100 = 3,200,000.

**8. 2400 and 14**

**14,922 and 87,341**

**40,135 and 9,477.** The 4 in 2400 is in the hundreds place and has a value of 400. 4 in 14 is in the ones place and has a value of 4. 400 is 100 x 4.

The 4 in 14,922 is in the thousands place and has a value of 4,000. The 4 in 87,341 is in the tens place and has a value of 40. 4,000 is 100 x 40.

The 4 in 40,135 is in the ten thousands place and has a value of 40,000. The 4 in 9,477 is in the hundreds place and has a value of 400. 40,000 is 100 x 400.

**9. B.** 320 groups of 100 equals 32,000 because 320 x 100 = 32,000.

100 is two groups of 10 or 10 x 10 so 320 x 1o moves into the 3 hundreds into the thousands place and 3,200 x 10 moves the 3 thousands into the ten thousands place.

**10. D.** 10,007 x 100 = 1,000,700

1 in millions place is 100 times 1 in the ten thousands place.

**11. 100 glue sticks.** 130,000 ÷ 1,300 = 100 or you can use multiplication to solve and think 1,300 x 100 = 130,000 so 100 glue sticks were in each box.

**12.**Part A: **50,000 ÷ 100 = 500**

Part B: **50,000 ÷ 1,000 = 50.**

50,000 bouncy balls divided into 100 bouncy balls per box equals 500 boxes.

50,000 bouncy balls divided into 1000 bouncy balls per box equals 500 boxes so the store should order 1,000 bouncy balls per box so they receive 50 boxes and not 500 boxes.

### NBT.A.2 Understand & Compare Multi-Digit Numbers

**1. C.** 10,043 in words is ten thousands, forty-three

**2. D.** Separate the number in separate place values: 358,201

The 3 is in the hundred thousands place so it's worth 300,000.

The 5 is in the ten-thousands place, so it's worth 50,000.

The 8 is in the thousands place, so it's worth 8,000.

The 2 is in the hundreds place so it's worth 200.

The 1 is in the ones place so it's worth 1.

**3. A.** Multiply each set of numbers in the parenthesis and add the products together.

2 x 10,000 = 20,000

3 x 1,000 = 3,000

9 x 100 = 900

4 x 10 = 40

20,000 + 3,000 + 900 +40 = 23,940

**4. C.** 14 thousands = 14 x 1000 = 14,000

5 thousands = 5 x 1000 = 5,000

8 tens = 8 x 10 = 80

6 ones = 6 x 1 = 6

14,000 + 5,000 + 80 +6 = 19,086

**5. B.** 487,912 is greater than 478,953 because the digit 8 in the ten thousands place in 487,912 has a value of 80,000, which is more than the digit 7 in the ten thousands place in 478,953. 80,000>70,000 so the 8 in the ten-thousands place proves 487,912 > 478,953

**6. D.** Seven tens is the same as 7 groups of 10 or 70. The digit in the tens place 789,498 is 9, so 7 tens (70) less than 90 or 9 tens is 2 tens (20) which is letter D. 789,428

9 - 7 =2

**7. B.** 400 tens is the same as 400 groups of 10 or 400 x 10 which equals 4000. So 4,000 can be renamed as 400 tens or 400 groups of 10.

**8. B.** 8 ten thousands = 8 x 10,000 = 80,000

and 97 tens = 97 x 10 = 970

80,000 +970 = 80,970

(800 x 1,000) + (70 x 100) + (2 x 1000) + (40 x 10) = 800,000 + 70,000 + 400 = 870,400

80 ten thousands = 80 x 10,000 = 800,000

70 hundreds = 70 x 100 = 7,000

20 tens= 20 x 10 = 200

9 ones =9

800,000 + 7,000 + 200 + 9 = 800,729

These numbers are less than B: 872,498

**9.** Part A: 40 hundreds is the same as 40 x 100 = 4,000

56 tens is the same as 56 x 10 = 560

3 ones= 3 so 4,000 + 560 + 3 = 4,563

Part B: **A.** 4,536 is less because 3 tens is less than 6 tens in 4,563

**10. C, D, E.** 7 thousands + 62 tens + 9 ones = 7,000 + (62 tens = 62 x 10 or 620) 620 + 9 = 7,629

(70 x 100) + (60 x 10) + (2 x 10) + (9 x 1) = 7000 + 600 + 20 + 9 = 7,629

76 hundreds = 76 x 100 = 7,600

2 tens = 2 x 10 = 20

9 ones = 9 x 1 = 9

7,600 + 20 + 9 = 7,629

**11.** Part A: How many hundreds are in 700,000? 7,000 hundreds because 7,000 x 100 = 700,000

Part B: How many thousands are in 700,000? 700 thousands because 700 x 1,000 = 700,000

Part C: How many tens are in 700,000? 70,000 tens because 70,000 x 10 = 700,000

**12.** Part A: 3 hundred thousands, 1 ten thousands, 7 thousands, 5 hundreds, 6 tens, 8 ones = 317,568

Part B: 3 hundred thousands = 300,000

1 ten thousand = 10,000

75 hundreds = 75 x 100= 7,500

6 tens = 60

8 ones = 8

300,000 + 10,000 + 7,500 + 60 + 8 = 317,568

Part C: 31 ten thousands= 31 x 10,000 = 310,000

75 hundreds = 75 x 100= 7,500

68 ones =68

310,000 + 7,500 + 60 = 317,568

## NBT.A.3 Round and Compare Multi-Digit Numbers

**1. B.** 875,235 rounded to the nearest ten thousand is 880,000 because the 75,235 falls between 70,000 and 80,000 and is closer to 80,000.

**2. C.** 78,432 rounded to the nearest hundreds is 78,400 because 432 falls between 400 and 500 and is closer to 400.

**3. D.** 843 rounds to 840. Since the question asks to round to the nearest tens' place, look at the number in the tens' place – 43. Think of the surrounding tens around 43. 43 is between 40 and 50 and is closer to 40 so 843 rounds to 840.

**4. A.** In 499,839 the red 9 is in the thousands' place. 9,800 is between 9,000 and 10,00 and it's closer to 10,000. Since 10,000 is the next place value after thousands, the digit in the ten thousands' place increases by 1 so the red 9 in the ten thousands' (499,839) will become a 10, which changed the 4 in the hundred thousands' place to 500,000. This rounding of 9 in the thousands and ten thousands raises each value by 1 which is 10 and moves to the next place value.

**5. B.** 983 rounds to 1000 because when rounding to the nearest hundreds, think 983 is between 900 and 1,000. Is it closer to 1,000 so it rounds up to 1,000.

**6. C.** 35,671 will round up to the next hundred. Look at the number in the hundreds' place 671 and think 671 is between 600 and 700. It is closer to 700 so 671 rounds up to 700.

**7. D.** 68,457 rounded to the thousands' place is 68,000 because the 8,457 is between 8,000 and 9,000 and is closer to 8,000 so 68,457 rounded to the nearest thousands' place is 68,000.

**8. B.** 1,357 does not round to 1300 when rounded to the hundreds' place. In 1,357, 357 is between 300 and 400 and is closer to 400 so 1,357 rounds to 1,400

**9. C.** 134,948 rounds to 130,000 when rounding to the ten thousands' place. In 134,948, the number in the ten thousands is 34,000. 34,000 is between 30,000 and 40,000 and it's closer to 30,000 so 134,948 rounds to 130,000

**10. 413,802 → 414,000**

**413,734 → 414,000**

**414,498 → 414,000**

**414,258 → 414,000**

413,802 when rounded to the thousands' place is 414,000 because 3,802 is between 3,000 and 4,000 and is closer to 4,000.

413,734 when rounded to the thousands' place is 414,000 because 3,734 is between 3,000 and 4,000 and is closer to 4,000.

414,498 when rounded to the thousands' place is 414,000 because 4,498 is between 4,000 and 5,000 and is closer to 4,000.

414,258 when rounded to the thousands' place is 414,000 because 4,258 is between 4,000 and 5,000 and is closer to 4,000.

**11. 4,320 → 4,315 and 4,324**

**17,660 → 17,655 and 17,664**

**812,710 → 812,705 and 812,714**

4,315 and 4,324 are the lowest and highest possible number that would round to 4,320 because 15, 16, 17, 18, 19, 20, 21, 22, 23, 24 all round to 20 with 15 and 24 being the lowest and highest possible number.

17,655 and 17,664 are the lowest and highest possible number that would round to 17,660 because 55, 56, 57, 58, 59, 60, 61, 62, 63, 64 all round to 60 with 65 and 64 being the lowest and highest possible number.

812,705 and 812,714 are the lowest and highest possible number that would round to 812,710 because 5, 6, 7, 8, 9, 10, 11, 12, 13, 14 all round to 10 with 5 and 14 being the lowest and highest possible number.

**12.** Part A: **Friday and Saturday:** Friday: $9,730 rounds to 10,000 because 9,730 is between 9,000 and 10,000 and is closer to 10,000 which is more than the actual sales.

Saturday: $10,569 rounds to $11,000 because 569 is between 0 and 1,000 when rounding to the thousands' place. 569 is closer to 1,000 so the rounded number $11,000, which is more than the actual sales.

Part B: **Thursday:** $10,048 rounded to the nearest thousand is $10,000 because 48 is between 0 and 1,000 and is closer to 10. The rounded number 10,000 is very close to the actual number 10,048.

Part C: **Saturday:** $10,569 rounds to $11,000 because 569 is between 0 and 1,000 when rounding to the thousands' place. 569 is closer to 1,000 so the rounded number is $11,000. 11,000-10,569 = 431 which is the largest difference between the rounded and actual number.

## NBT.B.4 Add & Subtract Multi-Digit Numbers

**1. A.** 9,237 + 5,871 = 15,108

9,000 + 5,000= 14,000

200 + 800 = 1,000

30 + 70 = 100

7+1 =8

14,000 + 1,000 + 100 + 8 = 15,18

**2. D.** 7,652 - 4,239 = 3,413

**3. C.** 45,873 + 139,592 = 185,465

**4. B.** $1299 less than the normal price means subtract $1299 from the original price.

$13500-$1299 = $12,201

**5. A.** To find the total number of people who visited the park over the weekend, add up all the visitors.

5,398 + 7,450 + 8,957 = 21,805 people

**6. C.** 1,463 + 537 = 2,000

**7. D.** 20 hundreds is the same as 20 groups of 100 or 20 x 100 = 2,000. 2,000 less means subtract. 5,975,321 - 2,000 = 5,973,321

**8. B.** To find the missing addend, subtract the total 28,754 and the known addend 5,763, 28,754 - 5,763 = 22,991

**9. A.** In order to find the missing part to this subtraction problem, start with the total 112,572 and subtract the known difference 39,678.

112,572 - 39,678 = 72,894

**10. C.** To find how much the rent increases each year, compare one year to the next by subtracting since you are looking for the difference between the cost of rent each year.

$20,720 -$19,350 = $1,370 OR

$22,090 - $20,720 = $1,370

**11. Kennedy's score: 1,839 Total score: 5,054** First find Kennedy' score by subtracting 3,215 - 1,376 because she scored less than Aiden. 3,215 - 1,376 = 1,839. Kennedy's score is 1,839. To find how many points they scored, add up both their scores, 1,839 + 3,215 = 5,054 points total.

**12.** Part A: **The movie theater made $7,237 more in the winter and fall than in the spring and summer.** First add the amount of money made in winter and fall: 24,671 + 22,319 = 46,990. Then add the amount of money made in spring and summer: 19,255 + 20,498 = 39,753. Finally, subtract winter and fall's amount 46,990 and summer and spring's amount 39,753 to find how much more money the theater made in the winter/fall. 46,990 - 39,753 = $7,237.

Part B:**The difference between the highest selling season, winter, and the lowest selling season, spring, is $5,416.** The highest selling season is winter $24,671 and the lowest season was spring $19,255. Subtract $24,671 - $19,255 = $5,416

## NBT.B.5 Multiply Multi-Digit Numbers & Represent Multiplication

**1. C.** 549 x 8 = 4,392

**2. A.** 2,974 x 5 = 14,870

**3. B.** If there are 24 students in the class and they each receive 15 stickers can be counted as 24 groups of 15 or 24 x 15 = 360 stickers. Mrs. Rogers needs to buy 360 stickers.

**4. D.** Break apart 45 into (40 + 5) Multiply each place value by 5: (40 x 5) and (5 x 5) Add the products together.

**5. B.** (9 x 7) must be completed first since it is in parenthesis. 9 x 7 = 63, the complete the equation by multiplying 63 x 10 = 630

**6.**

| | |
|---|---|
| **80 X 70** | **3 X 70** |
| **9 X 80** | **9 X 3** |

**5600 + 210 + 720 + 27 = 6,557.** Multiply each separate place value. Then add the products together.

83 = 80 + 3

79 = 70 + 9

Multiply each place value: (80 x 70) + (70 x 3) + (80 x 9) + (9 x 3) = 6,557

**7. A.** To find the relationship between the numbers: Number A x 100 = Number B

10,007 x 100 = 1,000,700

**8. C.** 37 x 52

(30 x 50) + **(30 x 7)** + (30 x 2) + ( 7 x 2)

30 x 7 is incorrect because in the number 37, you would not multiply itself: 30 x 7, it should be 50 x 7.

**9. B.** First, multiply to find how many pastries were sold on the first 3 days. 3 x 147 = 441, then add 441 and the number of pastries sold on the 4th day, 138. 441 + 138 = 579 pastries total over the 4 days.

**10. D.** Step 1: Find out how many cookies were ordered: 28 x 25 = 950 cookies .

Step 2: Each person eats one cookie and there are 935 people at the restaurant. Subtract to find the number of cookies left over: 950-935 = 15

**11. (2x3) x 64 = 384 square feet.** If the garden has 2 rows with 3 sections in each row, multiply to find the total number of sections: 2 x 3 = 6. If each section is 64 square feet, multiply the area of each section by the number of sections: 64 x 6 = 384 sq. feet total.

**12. 1,536 ounces total.** First find the number of gallons Jordan brings to the game. If Jordan brings 3 times as many gallons of water as Bennett (3 gallons), multiply 3 x 3 = 9. If one gallon contains 128 ounces, multiply the number of gallons by the number of ounces in each gallon.

Bennett: 3 gallons x 128 ounces = 384 ounces

Jordan: 9 gallons x 128 ounces = 1,152 ounces

To find the total number of ounces, add the 2 products: 1,152 + 384 = 1,536 ounces total

## NBT.B.6 Divide Multi-Digit Numbers & Represent Division

**1. B.** 966 ÷ 3 = 322

**2. C.** 7200 ÷ 9 = 800

9 x 8 = 72 so 9 x 800 = 7200

**3. A.** Mario's total amount of money made last week was 264. He earns $8 and we need to find the number of hours we worked. Since we have the total, 264 divide to find the number of hours he worked.

264 ÷ 8 = 33

33 x 8 = 264

**4. D.** To find the missing divisor, use the reverse operation to solve. 77 x _____ = 462?

77 x 6 = 462 so 462 ÷ 6 = 7

**5. A.** 7 x *n* = 196 So find the missing number *n*, use the inverse operation to solve.

196 ÷ 7 = 28 so 7 x 28 = 196

**6. 4 x 6 = 24**

**6 x 4 = 24**

**24 ÷ 6 = 4**

**24 ÷ 4 = 6**

The array shows 4 rows with 6 circles in each row.

So the fact family of 6, 4, and 24 shows this array.

4 x 6 = 24

6 x 4 = 24

24 ÷ 6 = 4

24 ÷ 4 = 6

**7. C.** 60 muffins divided into 8 bags 60 ÷ 8 = 7 remainder 4 because 8 x 7 = 56 and 60 -56 = 4

**8. B.** 23 ÷ 5 = 4, remainder 3

23 buttons divided into 5 groups equals 4 buttons in each group and 3 buttons remaining

**9. A.** Addison shaded a total of 148 squares with 4 rows on one side and a unknown number of columns (think array =rows x columns) so divide 148 ÷ 4 = 37 find the number of squares in each row. 4 x 37 = 148

**10. D.** Peyton spends $9 a day, so divide by 9 to find how many days it will take him to spend his money.

256 ÷ 9 = 28 with 4 remaining, so it will take Peyton 28 days to spend his money (28 x 9 = 252) and he will have $4 left over that he can't buy lunch with. 256-252 = 4

**11.** Part A: **350 ÷ 5 = 70**

Lola rounded 353 to 350 and divided by 5, 350 ÷ 5 = 70

Part B: **600÷ 3 = 200.** Lola rounded 614 to 600. 600 ÷ 3 = 200

**12.** Part A: **5785 ÷ 5 = 1,157 VIP adult tickets**

5 times fewer means divide by 5 so 5785 ÷ 5 = 1,157 VIP adult tickets.

Part B: **3624 ÷ 4 = 906 VIP children's tickets.** 4 times fewer means divide by 4 so 3624 ÷ 4 = 906 VIP children's tickets.

Part C: **5,785 + 1,157 = 6,942.**

**6,942 ÷ 2 = 3, 471 adults cheering for the home team.**

First find the total number of adult tickets sold (regular + VIP)

5,785 + 1,157 = 6,942 total adult tickets

Half of the adults were cheering for the home team and half means divide by 2 so 6,942 ÷ 2 = 3,471 adults cheering for the home team.

# NUMBERS AND OPERATIONS – FRACTIONS

## NF.A.1 Understand, Identify & Generate Equivalent Fractions

**1. B.** The shaded model shows $^1/_4$. $^2/_8$ is equivalent to $^1/_4$ because you can divide the numerator and denominator in $^2/_8$ by 2

2 ÷ 2 = 1

8÷ 2 = 4 so the resulting fraction is ¼

**2. D.** The shaded model represents $^3/_6$ . $^1/_2$ is equal to $^3/_6$ because you can divide the numerator and denominator by 3

3÷ 3 = 1

6 ÷3= 2

$^1/_2$ is the resulting equivalent fraction

**3. C.** The bar model shows the fraction $^2/_8$.

$^1/_4$ is equivalent to $^2/_8$ because

2÷ 2 = 1

8÷ 2 = 4 so the resulting fraction is $^1/_4$

**4. A.** The fraction shown on the number line is $^8/_{10}$

$^4/_5$ is equivalent to $^8/_{10}$ because you can divide the numerator and denominator by 2:

8÷2 = 4

10÷2 = 5

the resulting fraction is $^{4}/_{5}$

**5. C.** The fraction that represents the amount of striped stickers is $^{4}/_{12}$ because there are 4 out of 12 stickers shaded. The fraction equivalent to $^{4}/_{12}$ is $^{1}/_{3}$ because you can divide the number and denominator by 4:

$4 \div 4 = 1$

$12 \div 4 = 3$

so the resulting fraction is $^{1}/_{3}$

**6. D.** $^{2}/_{5}$ is equivalent to $^{6}/_{15}$ because you can multiply the numerator and denominator of $^{2}/_{5}$ by 3 and the resulting fraction will be $^{6}/_{15}$.

OR you can divide the numerator and denominator of $^{6}/_{15}$ by 3 and the resulting fraction will be $^{2}/_{5}$

$2 \times 3 = 6$

$5 \times 3 = 15$

so the resulting fraction is $^{6}/_{15}$

**7. B.** $^{1}/_{10}$ and $^{10}/_{100}$ are equivalent because you can multiply the numerator and denominator by 10 to get $^{10}/_{100}$

$1 \times 10 = 10$

$10 \times 10 = 100$

so the resulting fraction is $^{10}/_{100}$

**8. A.** $^{4}/_{32}$ can be simplified into $^{2}/_{16}$ or $^{1}/_{8}$ as equivalent fractions:

$4 \div 2 = 2$

$32 \div 2 = 16$ so the resulting equivalent fraction is $^{2}/_{16}$

OR

$4 \div 4 = 1$

$32 \div 4 = 8$ so the resulting equivalent fraction is $^{1}/_{8}$

**9. $^{2}/_{5}$ $^{8}/_{20}$ $^{12}/_{30}$.**

The fraction that is shaded on the model is $^{4}/_{10}$

$^{2}/_{5}$ is equivalent to $^{4}/_{10}$ because

$2 \times 2 = 4$

$5 \times 2 = 10$ so the resulting fraction is $^{4}/_{10}$

$^{8}/_{20}$ is equivalent to $^{4}/_{10}$ because

$4 \times 2 = 8$

$10 \times 2 = 20$ so the resulting fraction is $^{8}/_{20}$

$^{12}/_{30}$ is equivalent to $^{4}/_{10}$ because

$4 \times 3 = 12$

$10 \times 3 = 30$ so the resulting fraction is $^{12}/_{30}$

**10. B.** The fraction that represents the muffins in each group is 6/18 since there are 6 muffins out of 18 muffins in each group. 1/6 is equivalent to 3/18 because:

$1 \times 6 = 6$

$6 \times 3 = 18$, so the resulting fraction is $^{3}/_{18}$

**11. The number lines should be divided into equal pieces given the denominator, with an X at $^{1}/_{4}$, $^{2}/_{8}$, $^{3}/_{12}$** These fractions are equivalent because you can multiply the same number to the numerator and denominator of $^{1}/_{4}$ and the resulting fraction will be $^{2}/_{8}$ and $^{3}/_{12}$

$1 \times 2 = 2$

$4 \times 2 = 8$ so the resulting fraction is $^{2}/_{8}$

$1 \times 3 = 3$

$4 \times 2 = 12$ so the resulting fraction is $^{3}/_{12}$

**12. 1 white button.** 5 out of the 30 buttons are white so $^{5}/_{30}$ are white. If she adds 6 buttons with the same fractional amount being white, think:

$$\frac{5}{30} = \frac{\square}{6}$$

You can solve this problem using multiplication or division.

$6 \times 5 = 30$ so multiply the unknown numerator by 5 to equal 5, ___ $\times 5 = 5$

The unknown numerator is 1 so 1 out of the 6 buttons are white

Using division:

Divide the numerator and denominator of $^{5}/_{30}$ by 5:

$5 \div 5 = 1$

$30 \div 5 = 6$, which results in the fraction $^{1}/_{6}$

So 1 out of the 6 buttons are white.

## NF.A.2 Compare Fractions

**1. C.** $^{3}/_{12}$ is equivalent to $^{1}/_{4}$. Of $^{1}/_{4}$, $^{1}/_{2}$, $^{1}/_{6}$ and $^{3}/_{4}$, the smallest fraction is $^{1}/_{6}$. When comparing the fractions with a numerator of 1, the larger denominator indicates a smaller size fractional part.

**2. D.** $^{9}/_{10}$ is the largest fraction because it is the closest to one whole.

**3. B.** $^{2}/_{6} = {^{1}/_{3}}$

$^{1}/_{3}$ can be changed to an equivalent fraction with a denominator of 6:

$1 \times 2 = 2$

$3 \times 2 = 6$

$^{1}/_{3} = {^{2}/_{6}}$, and $^{2}/_{6} = {^{1}/_{3}}$

**4. A.** $^{3}/_{6}$ is larger than $^{1}/_{3}$.

Change $^{1}/_{3}$ to have a common denominator of 6:

$1 \times 2 = 2$

$3 \times 2 = 6$

So the new equivalent fraction to $^1/_3$ is $^2/_6$

$^3/_6 > {^2/_6}$

**5. D.** $^2/_8$ is larger than $^1/_5$

To compare, use a common denominator of 40:

$^2/_8 = {^{10}/_{40}}$

$2 \times 5 = 10$

$8 \times 5 = 40$

$^1/_5 = {^8/_{40}}$

$1 \times 8 = 8$

$5 \times 8 = 40$

so $^{10}/_{40}$ is larger than $^8/_{40}$

$^2/_8 > {^1/_5}$

**6. C.** $^1/_6$ is smaller than $^1/_2$.

To compare, use a common denominator of 6.

$^1/_2 = {^3/_6}$

$1 \times 3 = 3$

$2 \times 3 = 6$

so $^1/_6$ is smaller than $^3/_6$ (or $^1/_2$ ).

**7. B.** To compare $^8/_{10}$ and $^{75}/_{100}$, change $^8/_{10}$ to a denominator of 100 to compare.

$8 \times 10 = 80$

$10 \times 10 = 100$ so $^{80}/_{100}$ can be compared with $^{75}/_{100}$ since they have a common denominator.

**8. A.** Compare $^2/_6$ and $^3/_5$ by using a common denominator of 15.

$2 \times 5 = 10$

$3 \times 5 = 15$

so $^2/_3 = {^{10}/_{15}}$

$3 \times 3 = 9$

$5 \times 3 = 15$

so $^3/_5 = {^9/_{15}}$

$^{10}/_{15} > {^9/_{15}}$

**9. C.** To compare $^5/_6$, $^2/_4$ and $^9/_{12}$, use the common denominator of 12.

$5 \times 2 = 10$

$6 \times 2 = 12$

so $^5/_6 = {^{10}/_{12}}$

$2 \times 3 = 6$

$4 \times 3 = 12$

so $^2/_3 = {^6/_{12}}$

Colby read the least because he read $^6/_{12}$ which is less than $^{10}/_{12}$ and $^9/_{12}$

**10. $^4/_{20}$, $^1/_4$, $^{40}/_{100}$, $^3/_5$.** To compare, use the common denominator of 100.

$^3/_5 = {^{60}/_{100}}$

$3 \times 20 = 60$

$5 \times 20 = 100$

$^1/_4 = {^{25}/_{100}}$

$1 \times 25 = 25$

$4 \times 25 = 100$

$^4/_{20} = {^{20}/_{100}}$

$4 \times 5 = 20$

$20 \times 5 = 100$

Now you can compare $^{20}/_{100}$, $^{25}/_{100}$, $^{60}/_{100}$ and $^{40}/_{100}$

**11. No, Alexa did not practice long enough.**

**$^{16}/_{20} > {^{15}/_{20}}$ so she did not practice enough.**

Compare $^4/_5$ and $^3/_4$ by using a common denominator of 20.

$4/5 = 16/20$

$4 \times 4 = 16$

$5 \times 4 = 20$

$^3/_4 = {^{15}/_{20}}$

$3 \times 5 = 15$

$4 \times 5 = 20$

Alexa was supposed to practice for $^4/_5$ of an hour (or $^{16}/_{20}$) and she practices ¾ of an hour (or $^{15}/_{20}$)

$^{16}/_{20} > {^{15}/_{20}}$ so she did not practice enough.

**12. Sean spent more money.**

**$^9/_{18} > {^4/_{12}}$ OR**

**$^1/_2 > {^1/_3}$**

Raquel spent 4 out of 12 dollars, $^4/_{12}$ of her money. Sean spent 9 out of 18 dollars, $^9/_{18}$ of his money. To compare the fractions, reduce $^9/_{18}$ to $^1/_2$:

$9 \div 9 = 1$

$18 \div 9 = 2$

$^4/_{12}$ can be reduced to $^1/_3$

$4 \div 4 = 1$

$12 \div 4 = 3$

Compare $^1/_2$ and $^1/_3$: $^1/_2$ is larger than $^1/_3$ so Sean spent more money.

## NF.B.3, NF.B.3.A, NF.B.3.B, NF.B.3.C, NF.B.3.D. Understand & Use Fractions: Decompose Fractions, Add and Subtract Fractions, Add & Subtract Mixed Numbers, Solve Word Problems With Fractions

**1. B.** The first fraction models shows 2 out of 6 or $^2/_6$ shaded and the second model shows 3 out of 6 or $^3/_6$ shaded.

**2. C.** $^3/_8 + ^4/_8 = 7/8$

When adding fractions, add the numerators.

**3. D.** $^8/_{10} - ^5/_{10} = ^3/_{10}$ When subtracting fractions, subtract the numerators.

**4. A.** The grid has 10 equal parts and 3 parts are shaded so the fraction representing the shaded amount is $^3/_{10}$ . $^3/_{10}$ can be expressed as $^1/_{10} + ^1/_{10} + ^1/_{10}$

**5. B.** Add the numerators: 4 + 2 = 6 so the sum = $^6/_5$ , which is larger than 1 whole $^5/_5$

**6. C.** To find the remaining pizza, subtract the pizza Dane ate from the whole pizza amount $^7/_7$

$^7/_7 - ^4/_7 = ^3/_7$

**7. D.** $3\ ^3/_4 + 2\ ^2/_4$

add the whole numbers 3 + 2= 5

$^3/_4 + ^2/_4 = ^5/_4$

$^5/_4 = ^4/_4 + ^1/_4$ and $^4/_4$ is the same as 1 whole so add the 1 whole to the whole numbers. 5 + 1 = 6 and add the remaining $^1/_4$: 6 ¼

**8. B.** $4\ ^2/_6 + 2\ ^4/_6 = 7$

add the whole numbers 4 +2 = 6

$^2/_6 + ^4/_6 = ^6/_6$ , $^6/_6$ is the same as 1 whole. 6 + 1 = 7

**9. A.** 13 miles total minus the miles ran 8 ¼ = the remaining miles.

13 - 8 ¼ = x

Rename 13 as 12 and $^4/_4$ in order to subtract.

$12\ ^4/_4$ - 8 ¼ = 4 ¾

Subtract the whole numbers 12-8 = 4

Subtract the fractions $^4/_4 - ^1/_4 = ^3/_4$

**10.** Part A: **$3 - 1\ ^1/_3 = 1\ ^2/_3$ cups**

To find how many more cups of flour was used than sugar, subtract $3 - 1\ ^1/_3$

Rename 3 as $2\ ^3/_3$, then subtract:

2 - 1 = 1

$^3/_3 - ^1/_3 = ^2/_3$ which is $1\ ^2/_3$ more cups of flour

Part B: **$3 + 1\ ^1/_3 + 1\ ^2/_3 = 6$ cups.**

To find the total, add $3 + 1\ ^1/_3 + 1\ ^2/_3$

Add the whole numbers: 3 + 1 + 1 = 5

Add the fractions: $^2/_3 + ^2/_3 = ^3/_3$ or 1 whole

Add 1 + 5 = 6 cups

**11. $^1/_6$ of the apple pie is left over.** To find the fraction of the pie that is left over, first add up the pieces that were eaten:

$^1/_6 + ^1/_6 + ^1/_2$

Change $^1/_2$ to $^3/_6$ to add:

$^1/_6 + ^1/_6 + ^3/_6 = ^5/_6$

Subtract 1 (the whole apple pie) – $^5/_6 = ^1/_6$ of the apple pie is left over.

**12.** Part A: **2 ½ + $1\ ^3/_8 + 2\ ^3/_4 = 6\ ^5/_8$ eaten.**

To find the total amount that was eaten, add 2 ½ + $1\ ^3/_8$ + 2 ¾ by using the common denominator of 8.

2 ½ = $2\ ^3/_8$

2 ¾ = $2\ ^6/_8$ by

3 x 2 = 6

4 x 2 = 8

$2\ ^4/_8 + 2\ ^6/_8 + 1\ ^3/_8 = 6\ ^5/_8$

Add the whole numbers

2 + 2 + 1 = 5

Add the fractions: $^4/_8 + ^6/_8 + ^3/_8 = 1\ ^3/_8 = 1\ ^5/_8$

$5 + 1\ ^5/_8 = 6\ ^5/_8$

Part B: **1 and $^3/_8$ of the cakes were left over.** If there were 3 chocolate cakes and 2 ½ was eaten, subtract 3 – 2 ½ to find the remaining amount: ½ chocolate cake.

If there were 2 vanilla cakes and $1\ ^3/_8$ was eaten, subtract 2 – $1\ ^3/_8$ to find the remaining amount $^5/_8$ of vanilla cake.

If there were 3 ice cream cakes and 2 ¾ were eaten, subtract 3 - 2 ¾ to find ¼ of the ice cream cake remaining.

Then add the remaining pieces of cake ½ + $^5/_8$ + ¼

Use the common denominator of 8

½ = $^4/_8$ and ¼ = $^2/_8$

Then add:

$^4/_8 + ^2/_8 + ^5/_8 = ^{11}/_8 = 1\ ^3/_8$ of the cakes were left over.

## NF.B.4, NF.B.4.A, NF.B.4.B, NF.B.4.C Multiply Fractions: Multiply Fractions by Whole Numbers, Solve Word Problems By Multiplying Fractions

**1. C.** There are 3 cakes. Each cake has icing on 2 out of the 4 pieces or $^2/_4$ of it.

Multiply 3 x $^2/_4$ because there are 3 cakes with $^2/_4$ icing.

**2. B.** Two models are shown in choice B. Each model has 1 part of out 3 parts shaded; $^1/_3$

So the model shows 2 groups of $^1/_3$ or 2 x $^1/_3$

**3. D.** Another way to express 3 x $^2/_3$ is to use repeated addition to show multiplication.

3 groups of $^2/_3$ is the same as adding $^2/_3$ 3 times:

$^2/_3 + ^2/_3 + ^2/_3$

**4. A.** 3 x $^2/_3$ = $^6/_3$

Count how many thirds are shaded. 6 pieces out of the third-sized pieces are shaded. 6 thirds are shaded = $^6/_3$

OR Use repeated addition to solve by adding $^2/_3 + ^2/_3 + ^2/_3 = ^6/_3$

**5. B.** The model shows 4 squares with $^1/_4$ of each square shaded. 4 groups of ¼ is the same as 4 x $^1/_4$ = $^4/_4$ or 1 whole

**6. C.** 5 x $^2/_5$ is the same as thinking 5 groups of $^2/_5$ or:

$^2/_5 + ^2/_5 + ^2/_5 + ^2/_5 + ^2/_5 = ^{10}/_5$

In 5 x $^2/_5$ multiply the whole number $^5/_1$ x $^2/_5$

5 x 2 =10

1 x 5 = 5 so the product is $^{10}/_5$

**7. D.** 6 x ½ = $^6/_2$ or as a whole number 3.

6 groups of ½ = ½ + ½ + ½ + ½ + ½ + ½ = $^6/_2$

$^6/_2$ can be changed into a whole number by thinking 6 half-sized pieces is the same as having 3 wholes because 6 ÷ 2 = 3 or:

½ + ½ = 1

½ + ½ = 1

½ + ½ = 1

1 + 1 + 1 = 3

**8.** Part A: **The first model should have $^2/_6$ shaded. The product should have 1 whole rectangle shaded and $^2/_6$ in the next rectangle shaded** because 4 x $^2/_6$ = $^8/_6$

Part B: **$^8/_6$**

4 x $^2/_6$ = $^8/_6$ or:

$^2/_6 + ^2/_6 + ^2/_6 + ^2/_6 = ^8/_6$

Part C: **1 and $^2/_6$**

As a mixed number, think: $^8/_6 = ^6/_6 + ^2/_6$

$^6/_6$ = 1 so the mixed number is 1 $^2/_6$

**9. A.** 5 smoothies with $^1/_3$ cup of milk means add $^1/_3$ 5 times, which equals 5 and a $^1/_3$

5 $^1/_3$ = $^5/_3$

$^5/_3 = ^3/_3 + ^2/_3$

so $^5/_3$ = 1 $^2/_3$

**10. ¾ x ____= 6**

To find the number of plants Mia can fit in her garden, think: (3 x n) ÷ 4 = 6

3 x 8 = 24 ÷ 4 = 6 so Mia can fit **8 plants.**

**11. C.** He will need an even number of tiles.

1 ½ + 1 ½ + 1 ½ = 4 ½

Because ½ + ½ = 1 whole, Josh will always need 2 halves to equal a whole number.

If Josh uses 4 tiles, he will have a length that is a whole number: 1 ½ + 1 ½ + 1 ½ + 1 ½ = 6

**12. Carly ran the farthest** because ¾ x 5 = $^{15}/_4$

$^{15}/_4$ = 3 ¾ miles

**Lucy ran the least** because $^2/_6$ x 8 = $^{16}/_6$

$^{16}/_6$ = 2 $^4/_6$ which can be reduced to 2 and $^2/_3$ miles.

## NF.C.5 Understand & Use Equivalent Fractions Involving Denominators of 10 to 100

**1. B.** The model shows 3 out of 10 columns shaded or $^3/_{10}$

**2. C.** The model shows 30 out of 100 cubes shaded or $^{30}/_{100}$

**3. A.** $^{30}/_{100}$ is the same as $^3/_{10}$

3 x 10 = 30

10 x 10 = 100

so $^3/_{10}$ times $^{10}/_{10}$ = $^{30}/_{100}$

**4. D.** $^{40}/_{100}$ is the same as $^4/_{10}$

4 x 10 = 40

10 x 10 = 100, $^{40}/_{100}$

So, $^4/_{10}$ times $^{10}/_{10}$ = $^{40}/_{100}$

**5. A.** $^{80}/_{100}$ can be simplified to a denominator of 10.

80 ÷ 10 = 8

100 ÷10 = 10

So the reduced fraction is $^{80}/_{10}$ ,

$^{80}/_{10} = ^{80}/_{100}$

**6. B.** $^{7}/_{10} + ^{20}/_{100} = ^{90}/_{100}$

$^{7}/_{10} = ^{70}/_{100}$

7 x 10 = 70

10 x 10 = 100

$^{70}/_{100} + ^{20}/_{100} = ^{90}/_{100}$

**7. C.** $^{3}/_{10} + ^{5}/_{100} = ^{35}/_{100}$

$^{3}/_{10} = ^{30}/_{100}$

3 x 10 = 30

10 x 10 = 100

$^{30}/_{100} + ^{5}/_{100} = ^{35}/_{100}$

**8. D.** $^{3}/_{10} + ^{55}/_{100} = ^{85}/_{100}$

$^{3}/_{10} = ^{30}/_{100}$

3 x 10 = 30

10 x 10 = 100

$^{30}/_{100} + ^{55}/_{100} = ^{85}/_{100}$

**9. A.** $^{6}/_{10} = ^{60}/_{100}$

6 x 10 = 60

10 x 10 = 100

$^{60}/_{100} + ^{25}/_{100} = ^{85}/_{100}$

**10.** Part A: **Model should have 40 out of 100 shaded and 33 out of 100 shaded, so 73 cubes out of 100 cubes shaded.**

$^{4}/_{10} = ^{40}/_{100}$ so 40 cubes should be shaded since there are 100 cubes in the model. $^{33}/_{100}$ means shade 33 out of 100 cubes. So 73 cubes should be shaded.

Part B: **$^{73}/_{100}$**

$^{4}/_{10} = ^{40}/_{100}$

4 x 10 = 40

10 x 10 = 100

$^{40}/_{100} + ^{33}/_{100} = ^{73}/_{100}$

Part C: **$^{27}/_{100}$**

To find the remaining number of cards subtract the whole $^{100}/_{100} - ^{73}/_{100} = ^{27}/_{100}$

**11.** Part A: $^{3}/_{10} + ^{4}/_{100} = ^{34}/_{100}$

Lisa added the numerators without creating a common denominator. $^{3}/_{10} = ^{30}/_{100}$

In order to create the correct equation, she needs to find a common denominator.

3 x 10 = 30

10 x 10 = 100

Now she can add $^{30}/_{100} + ^{4}/_{100}$ because they have a common denominator = $^{34}/_{100}$

Part B: Equation: $^{30}/_{100} + ^{4}/_{100} = ^{34}/_{100}$

**12. She has $22 left.** Add the cost of the items to find how much money she spent. $^{58}/_{100} + ^{2}/_{10} = ^{78}/_{100}$

$^{2}/_{10} = ^{20}/_{100}$

2 x 10 = 20

10 x 10 = 100

Subtract to find the amount of money remaining:

$^{100}/_{100} - ^{78}/_{100} = ^{22}/_{100}$

So she has $22 out of $100 remaining.

## 4 NF.C.6 Convert Fractions to Decimals

**1. B.** $^{4}/_{10}$ is the same as 0.4 – with the digit 4 being in the tenths place.

**2. C.** 37 out of 100 cubes are shaded. As a decimal this is written as 0.37. There are 3 tenths shaded and 7 hundredths shaded in the model.

**3. A.** 1 whole square is shaded. 34 out of 100 squares are shaded in the next model. As a decimal, the whole 1 is in the ones place 1.0 and 34 hundredths is 0.34 – 3 tenths are shaded and 4 hundredths are shaded. The decimal 1.34 is the same as 1 $^{34}/_{100}$

**4. C.** The model shows 62 squares shaded out of 100 squares. As a decimal, this is 0.62 hundreds or 62 hundredths.

**5. D.** 2 ones is shown as 2.0

$^{6}/_{100}$ or 6 out of 100 is 0.06 as a decimal – the 6 is in the hundredths place.

**6. B.** $^{8}/_{10}$ (or 8 out of 10) is the same as 0.80 because the 8 in the decimal is in the tenths place. The zero place holder in the hundredths place does not change the value of the decimal.

**7. A.** 0.2 or 2 tenths can be written as 2 out of 10 $^{2}/_{10}$ or 20 out of 100 $^{20}/_{100}$

$^{20}/_{100} = ^{2}/_{10}$ because

2 x 10 = 20

10 x 10= 100 so either fraction represents 0.2

$^{20}/_{100} = 0.20$

**8. C.** Point A is located at 0.7. The number line is divided into 10 equal parts. Point A is on the 7th dash mark out of 10 dash marks so $^{7}/_{10}$ = 0.7.

**9. D.** Point B is located at 0.6. The number line is divided into 5 equal parts. Each part or dash mark represents $^{2}/_{10}$. Skip count by 2's 5 times, 2, 4, 6, 8, 10 and you reach the end of the number line $^{10}/_{10}$ or 1.

Point B is at $^{6}/_{10}$ or 0.6.

**10. Fractions equivalent to 0.5:**

$^{1}/_{2}$

$^{6}/_{12}$

$^{2}/_{4}$

$^{5}/_{10}$

$^{50}/_{100}$

All of these fractions represent one half or 5 tenths. One half is the same as 5 tenths because 5 is half of 10, $^{5}/_{10} = ^{1}/_{2}$

**11. $^{2}/_{5} = ^{4}/_{10}$ = 0.4**

**2 $^{1}/_{2}$ = 2 and $^{5}/_{10}$ = 2.5**

**$^{3}/_{4} = ^{75}/_{100}$ = 0.75**

**$^{12}/_{20} = ^{60}/_{100}$ = 0.60**

2/5 = 4/10

2 x 2 = 4

5 x 2 = 10

$^{4}/_{10}$ = 0.4

2 $^{1}/_{2}$ = 2 $^{5}/_{10}$

$^{1}/_{2} = ^{5}/_{10}$

1 x 5 = 5

2 x 5 = 10

2 $^{5}/_{10}$ = 2.5

$^{3}/_{4} = ^{75}/_{100}$

3 x 25 = 75

4 x 25 = 100

$^{75}/_{100}$ = 0.75

$^{12}/_{20} = ^{60}/_{100}$

12 x 5 = 60

20 x 5 = 100

$^{60}/_{100}$ = 0.60

**12. 16.47 meters**

**16 $^{47}/_{100}$ meters**

(10 x 1)= 10

( 6 x 1) = 6

( 4 x $^{1}/_{10}$) = 0.4

( 7 x $^{1}/_{100}$) = 0.07

10 + 6 + 0.4 + 0.07 = 16.47 meters

OR 16 $^{47}/_{100}$ meters

## NF.C.7 Compare Decimals

**1. B.** 0.62 is less than 0.65 because 2 hundredths is less than 5 hundredths.

**2. D.** 0.51 is less than 0.52 because 1 hundredth is less than 2 hundredths.

**3. C.** The decimal represented in the model is 1.34.

Choice C- 1.38 is greater than 1.34 because 8 hundredths is greater than 4 hundredths.

**4. A.** 0.8 is greater than 0.76 because 8 tenths is larger than 7 tenths.

**5. B.** 0.6 > 0.59 because 6 tenths is greater than 5 tenths.

**6. D.** 0.70 < 0.89 because $^{70}/_{100}$ is less than $^{89}/_{100}$ or 8 tenths is more than 7 tenths.

**7. C.** 0.7 = 0.70 because 7 tenths is equal to 7 tenths.

**8. A.** 0.28 is greater than 0.03 because 2 tenths is greater than 0 tenths. 0.28 is less than 0.3 because 2 tenths is less than 3 tenths.

**9. B.** 0.08, 0.84, 0.9

8 hundredths is the smallest decimal, 0.84 is smaller than 0.9 because 8 tenths is less than 9 tenths.

0.9 is the largest because 9 tenths is larger than 8 tenths (0.8) and 0 tenths (0.08).

**10.** Part A: **Decimals should be at the proper spot on the number line. 0.04, 0.16, 0.22, 0.31**

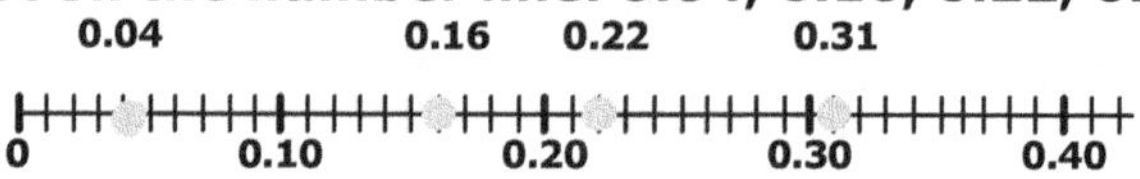


Part B: **0.04, 0.16, 0.22, 0.31 are ordered from least to greatest.**

**11.**

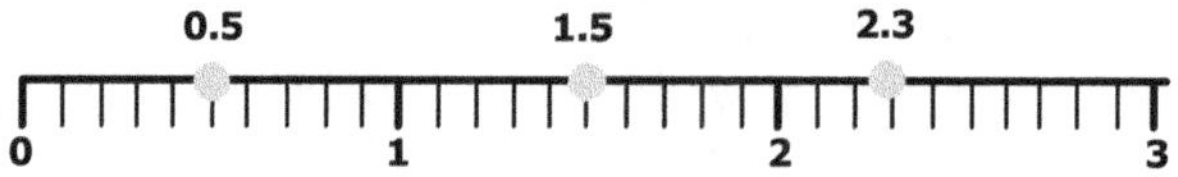


Part A: **possible answers: 0.6, 0.7, 0.8, 0.9, 1.0, 1.1, 1.2, 1.3, 1.4**

The decimals are in between 0.5 and 1.5: 0.6, 0.7, 0.8, 0.9, 1.0, 1.1, 1.2, 1.3, 1.4

Also any of those decimals with a number in the hundredths would be possible: 0.75, 1.24, etc.

Part B: **possible answers: 2.4, 2.5, 2.6, 2.7 and so on.** Any decimal greater than 2.3 is possible for part B.

**12. 10.07 > 10.4 is incorrect because 0.07 hundredths is less than 0.4 tenths.**

**If you compare the tenths places, 0.0 tenths is less than 0.4 tenths.**

**The correct comparison is 10.07 < 10.4**

## MEASUREMENT AND DATA

### MD.A.1 Compare, Contrast & Record Units of Measurement

**1. A.** In the Metric System of linear measurement, kilometers are the largest unit.

**2. C.** In the US Customary system of linear measurement, inches are the smallest unit.

**3. B.** 6 inches is a reasonable estimate for the hot dog. The other options would not be reasonable given the object - a hot dog.

**4. D.** 2 tons is 4,000 pounds because 1 ton is 2,000 pounds. 4,000 pounds (or 2 tons) is a reasonable estimate for the weight of a car.

**5. B.** 4 pints are equal to half a gallon or 2 quarts. There are 8 pints in 1 gallon so there are 4 pints in a half-gallon.

**6. A.** 5 kilometers = 5,000 meters.

1 kilometer = 1,000 meters so to find the number of meters in 5 kilometers, multiply 5 x 1,000 = 5,000

**7. C.** 480 minutes are equal to 8 hours.

1 hour = 60 minutes so to find the number of minutes in 8 hours, multiply 8 x 60 = 480 minutes.

**8. D.** 1 liter = 1,000 milliliters so Caylee drank 1,000 milliliters of soda.

**9. B.** 120 feet = 40 yards.

If 3 feet equal 1 yard, to find the number of yards in 120 feet, divide by 3:

120 ÷ 3 = 40 yards.

**10. 800 milliliters of soda each day.** 4 liters equals 4,000 milliliters because if 1 liter = 1,000 milliliters, then multiply 4 liters x 1000 to find the total number of milliliters in 4 liters = 4,000

4,000 milliliters split between 5 days means divide

4000 ÷ 5 = 800 milliliters each day.

**11.** Part A: **1 yard = 3 feet = 36 inches.**

**2 yards = 6 feet = 72 inches.**

**3 yards = 9 feet = 108 inches.**

**4 yards = 12 feet = 144 inches.**

If 1 yard = 3 feet, multiply the number of yards times 3 to find the number of feet in each yard: 2 yards x 3 feet in each yard = 6 feet in 2 yards, and so on.

To find the number of inches in 3 feet, multiply the number of feet by the number of inches in each foot: 3 feet x 12 inches in each foot = 36 inches in 3 feet; 6 feet x 12 inches =72 inches in 2 yards, and so on.

Part B: **1 foot is 12 times as long as 1 inch.**

**1 yard is 3 times as long as 1 foot.**

**1 yard is 36 times as long as 1 inch.**

**12. See explanation.** 5 foot sandwich is 60 inches long because 1 foot = 12 inches so multiply 5 feet x 12 inches to find the length of the 5 foot sub = 60 inches.

60 inches can be divided in to 10 pieces, each piece is 6 inches.

60 inches can be divided into 5 pieces, each piece is 12 inches.

60 inches can be divided into 12 pieces, each piece is 5 inches.

60 inches can be divided into 20 pieces, each piece is 3 inches.

60 inches can be divided into 15 pieces, each piece is 4 inches.

### MD.A.2 Solve Word Problems Using Measurements

**1. B.** There are 16 ounces in a pound. The Chihuahua gained 2 points so add 9 + 2 = 11 pounds. To find the weight in ounces, multiply 11 x 16 = 176 ounces.

**2. C.** Carlos is 5 feet tall. To convert 5 feet to inches, think there are 12 inches in 1 foot. 5 feet x 12 inches in each foot = 60 inches in 5 feet.

Carlos is 60 inches tall, which is 5 inches taller than the required 55 inches. 60 - 55 = 5 inches.

**3. A.** 1 centimeter is equal to 10 millimeters so multiply 6 cm x 10 millimeters in each centimeter = 60 millimeters in 6 cm.

6 centimeters is equal to 60 millimeters.

**4. D.** 6 liters = 6,000 milliliters.

1 liter = 1,000 milliliters so multiply 6 x 1000 to find the number of milliliters in 6 liters.

To find the amount of lemonade she used to fill up the pitchers, multiply 550 x 8 since she filled 8 pitchers. 550 x 5 = 4,400

To find the amount of lemonade remaining, subtract the amount of lemonade 6,000 minus the lemonade she used in pitchers 4,400.

6,000 – 4,400 = 1,600

**5. B.** First, convert 5 kilograms to grams. If there are 1,000 grams in one kilogram, multiply 5 x 1000 = 5,000 grams.

If each of the 10 bags weighs the same amount, divide 5,000 grams ÷ 10 = 500 grams, so each bag weighs 500 grams.

**6. C.** Add the total hours Jordan drove, 5 + 2 = 7 hours.

Then, multiply the number of miles traveled each hour by the number of hours.

60 x 7 = 420 miles

**7. A.** If the apples cost $2.60 per pound and Maggie buys 2.5 pounds, multiply to find the cost of the apples.

2.60 x 2.5 = $6.50

Subtract to find the amount of change she received:

$10.00 - $6.50 = $3.50

**8. D.** First, convert the gallons and quarts to pints since she is using pint-sized glasses.

1 gallon = 8 pints.

1 quart = 2 pints.

½ gallon soda is equal to 4 pints because 8 pints in 1 gallon divided by 2 (half a gallon) = 4 pints.

1 gallon of lemonade = 8 pints.

3 quarts of orange juice equals 6 pints because 3 quarts times 2 pints in each quart = 6 pints.

Add all the amounts in pints: 8 + 4 + 6 = 18 pints.

**9. C.** First, convert 3.5 tons to pounds. 1 ton = 2,000 pounds so multiply 2,000 x 3.5 = 7,000 pounds. 7,000 pounds + 1,500 pounds = 8,500 pounds for the lights and stage props.

Subtract 10,000 – 8,500 to find the remaining weight that is allowed on the stage = 1,500 pounds.

**10.** Part A: **60 ounces of cheese** Part B: **5 bags of cheese**

He needs 5 pounds of cheese. Convert 5 pounds into ounces. 1 pound = 16 ounces so multiply 5 pounds by 16 ounces to find the total number of ounces in 5 pounds. 5 x 16 = 80. David needs 80 ounces but has a 20 ounce bag, so subtract to find out how many more ounces of cheese he needs 80 -20 = 60. He needs 60 more ounces of cheese.

The bags of shredded cheese only come in 12-ounce bags so divide to find the number of bags David needs.

60 ÷ 12 = 5. He needs 5 bags.

**11. 1 hour 15 minutes.** First, add all the time Levi spent running errands. 35 + 25 + 1 hour + 45 minutes.

1 ¾ hour = 105 minutes.

¾ of 60 minutes = 45 minutes.

25 + 35 + 60 + 45 = 165 minutes.

Subtract the time Levi has 4 hours, from the time he spent, 165 minutes.

4 hours = 240 minutes because there are 60 minutes in 1 hour, multiply 4 x 60 = 240.

240 – 165 = 75 minutes.

75 minutes is 1 hour 15 minutes.

75 – 60 (1 hour) = 15 minutes.

**12.** Part A: **The train comes at:**

**5:30**

**6:15**

**7:00**

**7:45**

**8:30**

**9:15**

In order to find what times the train will come, count 45 minutes on the number line. Between each hour there are 4 sections so 60 ÷ 4 = 15, so each increment or section on the timeline is 15 minutes. Start at 5:30 and count 45 minutes to 6:15 and so on to find the times.

Part B: **Jane will wait 15 minutes.**

Jane will wait 15 minutes because she arrives at 7:30 and the next train is at 7:45, 45 – 30 = 15 minutes.

Part C: **Kip will wait 30 minutes.**

Kip will wait 30 minutes because he arrives at 8:45 and the next train is at 9:15. The amount of time between 8:45 and 9:15 is 30 minutes.

## 4 MD.A.3 Find Area and Perimeter; Solve Problems Involving Area and Perimeter

**1. C.** To find the area of a rectangle, multiply length x width. 12 x 7 = 84 square inches.

**2. D.** To find the perimeter, add all the sides.

15 + 9 + 15 +9

**3. B.** To find the area of a rectangle, multiply length x width. If we know the length is 12 x w = 48, then

12 x 4 = 48 so the width is 4 feet.

**4. A.** To find the perimeter, add all the sides or add the length and width, then double it (or multiply by 2) since there are 2 lengths and 2 widths to the rectangle.

**5. C.** 14 x 9 = 126 so the length and width of the garden is 14 yards by 9 yards.

**6. D.** The perimeter is 62 meters and the length is 16 meters. Set up an equation with the lengths:

16 + 16 + w + w = 62

32 + w + w = 62 to find the remaining widths, subtract

62 – 32 = 30; 30 divided by the 2 widths is 15 so the width is 15 meters

**7. B.** Larry's rectangle has a perimeter of 42 inches: 2 x (8 + 13) = 42

A rectangle that is 9 inches by 12 inches has a perimeter of 42 inches: 2 x (12 +9) = 42

**8. A.** Find the area of each rectangle and add them together: 18 x 9 = 162, 10 x 15 = 150. 150 + 162 = 312 sq. cm

**9. C.** First, find the unknown width. If the perimeter is 64 and the length is 14, set up an equation.

14 + 14 + w + w = 64

28 + w + w = 64

64 – 28 = 36. To find the remaining widths, divide by 2, 36 ÷ 2 = 18.

If the length is 14 and the width is 18, multiply to find the area: 252 sq. yards.

**10. 20 x 28 = 560**

**10 x 56 = 560**

**14 x 40 = 560**

**70 x 8 = 560**

Divide to find the missing factor:

560 ÷ 20 = 28

560 ÷10 = 56

560 ÷ 14 = 40

560 ÷ 70= 8

**11. Option 1: 10 inches by 2 inches**

**Option 2: 8 inches by 4 inches**

**Option 3: 7 inches by 5 inches**

**Option 4: 9 inches by 3 inches**

**Option 5: 11 inches by 1 inch**

**Largest area: 7 inches by 5 inches, 7 x 5 = 35 sq. inches.**

To find each of the possible dimensions with a perimeter of 24, start with 11 inches and complete the steps of adding 11 + 11 = 22, subtract 24 - 22 = 2, 2 divided between the remaining 2 sides is 1, 2 ÷ 2 =1, so one option is 11 by 1 inch. Then, do the same exercise with '10' instead of '11', and so on until you find all perimiter options for a rectangle.

The largest possible area is 7 by 5 because 7 x 5 = 35.

**12. Side P: 5 ft**

**Side J: 20 ft**

To find the side P, look at the opposite side, which is 10 feet so the side with the missing measurement side P will have to add up to 10. If one part of that side is 5, the missing side P will have to be 5 because 5 + 5 =10.

To find the bottom missing side J, look at the opposite side of the figure. The top part is 12 ft. and the other horizontal top part is 8ft, so 12 + 8 = 20 ft. for Side J.

Part B: **60 feet**

To find the perimeter, add up all the sides:

10 + 20 + 5 + 8 + 5 + 12 = 60 feet.

Part C:**160 sq. feet**

To find the area, split the large figure into 2 smaller rectangles. The rectangle on the left is 10 x 12 = 120 and the rectangle on the right side is 8 x 5 = 40.

Add the areas: 120 + 40 = 160 sq. feet.

## MD.B.4 Display and Interpret Data in Line Plots and Solve Problems Using Line Plots

**1. C.** Each X represents the vote of each child in the class. Add up all the Xs, and there are 15 votes so there are 15 children in the class.

**2. A.** 5 students have 2 pets and 1 student has 4 pets. Subtract to find the difference 5-1 = 4. Therefore, 4 more students have 2 pets than 4 pets.

**3. B.** The highest number of students have 2 pets. 5 students have 2 pets.

**4. A.** 2 feet of snow was not recorded since there is no data/markings above 2ft.

**5. C.** 1 ¼ ft. of snow was recorded 4 times because there are 4 Xs above 1 ¼, showing it was recorded 4 times.

**6. D.** Count up all the Xs in the line plot since each X represents a recording of the snowfall. There are 17 Xs listed here so the snowfall was recorded 17 times.

**7. Make the line plot:**

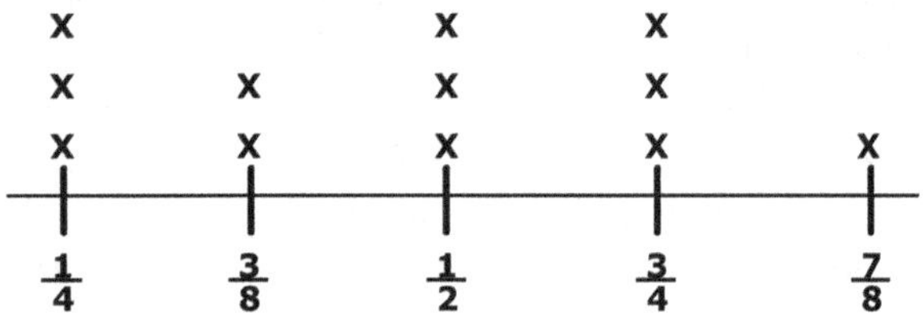


**8. D.** Count all the fractions that are ½ or more. There are 7 fractions or 7 students that ran ½ mile or more.

**9. C.** The longest distance run is $^{7}/_{8}$ and the shortest distance run is ¼ mile. To find the distance, subtract 7/8 – ¼ using a common denominator of 8. Change ¼ to a denominator of eighths:

1 x 2 = 2

4 x 2 = 8, so ¼ = $^{2}/_{8}$

$^{7}/_{8}$ - $^{2}/_{8}$ = $^{5}/_{8}$

**10. B.** Only one student ran $^{7}/_{8}$ mile in gym class so the least common distance is $^{7}/_{8}$

**11. Make the line plot:**

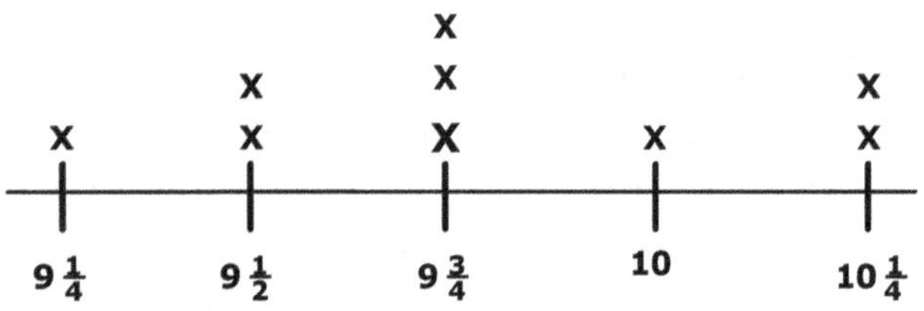


**12. No, he is incorrect.** Add up all the ages listed in the chart to find the combined age of 9 kids. First add the whole numbers (9 x 6) + (10 x 30) = 84. Then add the fractions:

¼ + ¾ + ¼ + ¾ + ¼ + ¾ = 3

½ + ½ = 1

84 + 3 + 1 = 88, the combined age of the 9 kids is 88 years old.

## MD.C.5, MD.C.5.A, MD.C.5.B. Recognize Angles & Understand Angles Measurement

**1. B.** The angle is larger than 90 degrees so it is obtuse.

**2. D.** The angle is less than 90 degrees so it is acute.

**3. A.** The angle is a square angle, 90 degrees which is a right angle.

**4. C.** The angle measures 50 degrees. One ray is at zero degrees and the other ray is on 50 degrees. The angle is an acute angle so the measurement is 50, not 130.

**5. B.** The angle measures 110 degrees. One ray is at zero degrees and the other ray is on 110 degrees. The angle is an obtuse angle so the measurement is 110, not 70.

**6. A.** The angle shown in choice A is acute or less than 90 degrees.

**7. D.** The measure of a circle all the way around is 360 degrees.

**8. C.** 77 one-degree angles is the same as 77 degrees.

**9. B.** ¼ of 360 degrees is 90 degrees. ¼ is a quarter turn. Divide 360 into 4 equal parts to represent each quarter or ¼. So each quarter turn on the circle would be 90 degrees.

**10.** Part A: **3 one-third size turns equal a full turn on the circle.**

Part B: **Each 1/3 size angle is 120°.** A. The circle is divided into thirds so it would take 3 one-third sized turns to make one full turn on the circle.

$^{1}/_{3}$ of 360 = 120 because 360 ÷3 = 120 so each of the $^{1}/_{3}$ sized angles on the circle measures 120°.

**11.** Part A: **For the circle divided into fifths, each angle is 72° For the circle divided into sixths, each angle is 60°.**

The measure of a circle in degrees is 360° and the circle is divided into 5 equal pieces, divide: 360÷ 5 = 72 so each fifth-size angle on the circle is 72°.

The measure of a circle in degrees is 360° and the circle is divided into5 6 equal pieces, divide: 360÷ 6 = 60 so each sixth-size angle on the circle is 60°.

Part B: **Yes, he is correct. 1/5 > 1/6 so 72°> 60°.**

1/5 of the circle is larger than 1/6 of the circle. 72° > 60° so he is correct.

**12. 90° = 4 turns**

**30° = 12 turns**

**40° = 9 turns**

**60° = 6 turns**

A full turn on a circle is 360°. It would take 4 90° turns

to make a full circle or 360° because 90 x 4 = 360.

It would take 12 30° turns to make a full circle or 360° because 30 x 12 = 360.

It would take 9 40° turns to make a full circle or 360° because 40 x 9 = 360.

It would take 6 60° turns to make a full circle or 360° because 60 x 6 = 360.

## MD.C.6 Measure and Sketch Angles

**1. A.** The angle measures 60 degrees when using a protractor.

**2. B.** The angle measures 45 degrees when using a protractor.

**3. D.** The angle measures 150 degrees when using a protractor.

**4. C.** The angle is a 90 degree angle or a square angle. The square marking in the center of the angle shows it is a right angle.

**5. A.** A straight angle measures 180°.

**6. C.** The protractor in choice C is used correctly. Both rays have an endpoint at the center vertex on the protractor. One ray starts at 0 and the other ray measures the angle.

**7. D.** The vertex is where 2 rays meet to form an angle. The vertex on the angle shown in number 7 is located at point D.

**8. A.** Point A is located at 80 degrees on the protractor so a ray can be drawn from the vertex to point A to create an 80 degree angle.

**9. B.** The points on the protractor in Choice B show 140-degree angle. One point is at zero, another point is at the vertex and the final point is at 140 degrees. Connect the dots to draw 140-degree angle.

**10. The triangle should have a 90°, 30° and 60°angle.** Check the angle measures of the triangle.

Add the angles: 30 + 90 + 60 = 180°

**11. Check the angles using a protractor.**

**12. Check the angles using a protractor.**

**The sum of the interior angles of a trapezoid equals 360 degrees.** Check the angles using a protractor.

## MD.C.7 Measure and Sketch Angles

**1. B.** x = 28° The angle shown is a 90 degree angle. One part is 62. We know 62 + x = 90. To the find the other angle, subtract 90 - 62 = 28, so the missing angle x is 28 degrees.

**2. A.** A straight angle is 180 degrees. One part is 135 degrees. 135 + x = 180, to find the missing part subtract 180-135 = 45 degrees.

**3. D.** A full circle measures 360 degrees so add both angles shown to equal 360. 230 + x = 360, subtract to find the unknown angle: 360 - 230 = 130. Angle x is 130 degrees.

**4. B.** The measure of a complete circle is 360. A 48-degree angle in the circle would be 48 out of 360 degrees of the circle.

**5. C.** A straight angle equals 180 degrees so we know that 40 + 40 + x = 180

Solve the problem by adding 40 +40 = 80

80 + x = 180, subtract to find x. 180 - 80 = 100, so the unknown angle is 100°.

**6. A.** The 3 interior angles of a triangle equal 180°. 40 + 90 + x =180. Add 40 + 90 = 130, the subtract to find the missing angle: 180-130 = 50, so the unknown angle is 50°.

**7. C.** A circle measures 360° so the 6 angles must add up to 360°. Each angle is the same size so divide 360 ÷ 6 = 60, each angle is 60°.

**8. D.** The total amount the door should open is 110°. The door is currently at 75°. In order to find the remaining amount the door needs to open, subtract 110 - 75 = 35. The door needs to open 35° more to open fully.

**9. B.** First find the amount of degrees Jeremy already turned his pencil: add 156 + 44 = 200. The total number of degrees in a circle is 360, subtract to find the remaining amount Jeremy needs to turn: 360 - 200 = 160.

**10. 60°.** If the larges swing was 100° and Kayla went 40° forward, subtract to find the amount the swing has to move to get to the original position. 100 - 40 = 60.

**11.**

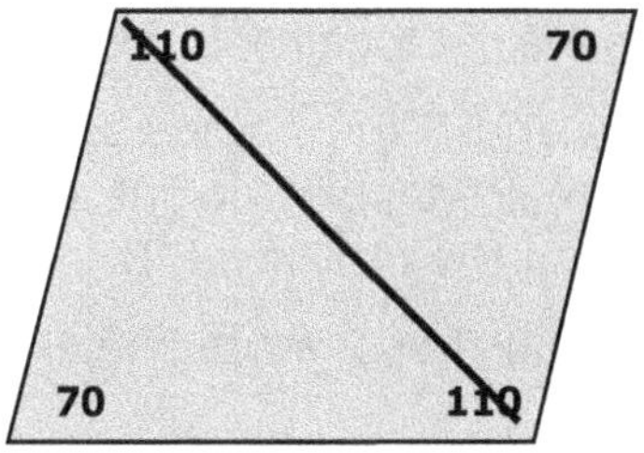


**Angles of the triangle: 70+ 55 + 55 = 180**

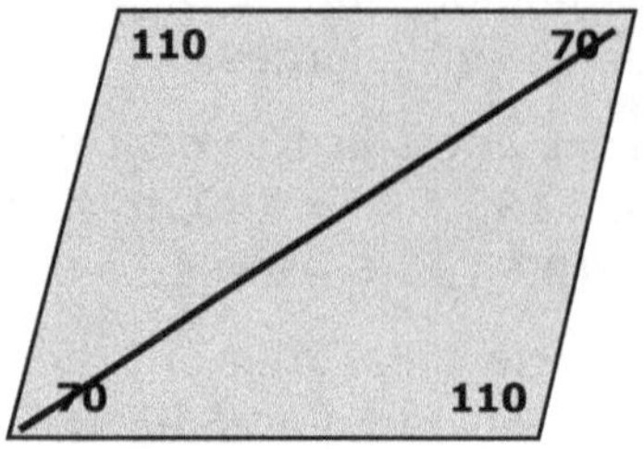


**Angles of the triangle: 110 + 35 + 35 = 180**

To find the angle measurement of the triangle, divide the 70 or 110 by 2 to find the measure of the angle depending on how the diagonal line was drawn.

110÷ 2 = 55

70 ÷ 2= 35

Then add the angle measures to find the sum of the interior angles of the triangle:

Angles of the triangle: 70+ 55 + 55 = 180

or Angles of the triangle: 110 + 35 + 35 = 180

**12.** Part A: **Angle B: 45°.** Angle B is on a straight line, which is 180°. One side of the angle is 135. Think 135 + b = 180, so subtract to find angle B: 180 – 135 = 45

Part B: **Angle Z: 45°.** Angle Z is part of a right angle. The shape is a rectangle so we know each angle in a rectangle is 90°. The line is directly in the middle of the right angle so 90 ÷ 2 = 45, angle Z is 45°.

## GEOMETRY

### G.A.1 Draw and Identify Points, Lines, Rays, and Angles

**1. C.** The lines are parallel – they are always the same distance apart and they never cross or touch.

**2. B.** The lines are intersecting because they cross at one point but the point at which they cross is not a 90° angle so they are not perpendicular.

**3. A.** Two rays form a right angle. Each line is a ray, starts at an endpoint and continues in one direct. In this picture, 2 rays are put together to form a right angle.

**4. D.** Points A and B form a line segment because the line has a start point at one end, A, and an ending point and the other end, B.

**5. C.** The rhombus has 2 acute angles and 2 obtuse angles.

**6. B.** SR forms a ray. S is the endpoint and the line continues in one direction past point R.

**7. A.** The trapezoid only has 1 set of parallel sides (top and bottom) and 2 angles are obtuse and 2 angles are acute. The other shapes shown here do not fit both requirements.

**8. D.** This right triangle has one set of perpendicular line segments that form the 90° angle in the left corner. The other 2 angles are acute.

**9. C.** The interior angles of a triangle equal 180°. If all sides are the same in the triangle, the triangle is equilateral and all the angles will be the same measure. Divide 180 into 3 equal parts for the 3 equal angles in the triangle. 180 ÷ 3 = 60, so each angle is 60°.

**10.** Part A: **Yes. KB and FE are parallel .** Lines KB and FE are the same distance apart and will never intersect.

Part B: **No perpendicular lines.** There are no 90 degree angles formed from perpendicular lines

Part C: **Angle B is obtuse.**

Angle B is obtuse because it is greater than 90.

**11.** Part A: **Answers may vary.**

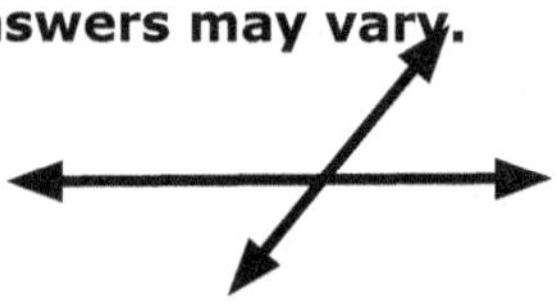

**There are 2 acute angles and 2 obtuse angles where the lines intersect.**

The angles formed from intersecting lines are 2 acute and 2 obtuse angles. Use a protractor to prove 2 angles are less than 90 and 2 angles are greater than 90.

Part B: **If the intersecting lines were perpendicular, the angles formed would be 90° angles.**

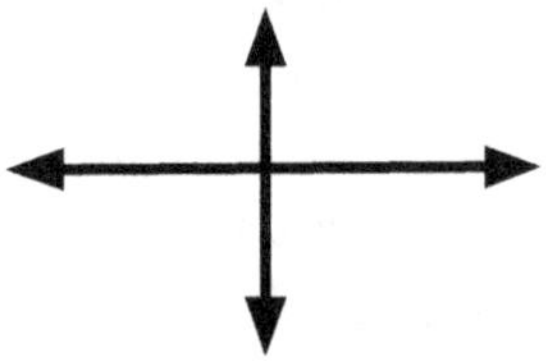

The definition of perpendicular lines is 2 lines forming a 90° angle so if the lines were perpendicular, as shown in the example, the angles would be 90° or right angles.

**12. Trapezoid.**

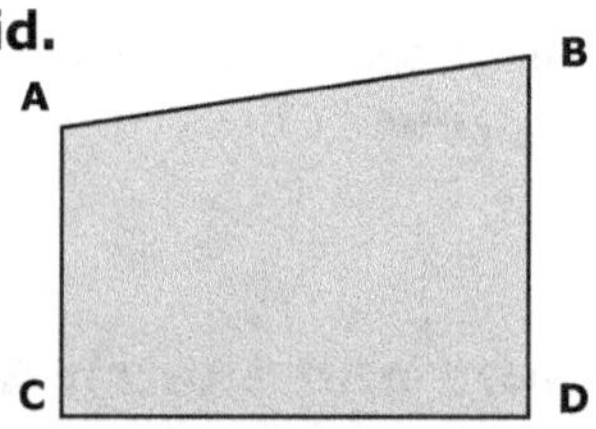


Angle C and D are right angles, angle A is obtuse and angle B is acute.

## G.A.2 Classify Two-Dimensional Figures

**1. B.** A square has 2 pairs or parallel sides (opposite sides) and all 4 angles are 90°.

**2. D.** All angles are the same in a triangle if all sides are the same length so the triangle is equilateral with all angles equaling 60°.

**3. C.** The scalene triangle has different measures for each angle and one is obtuse in the scalene triangle shown.

**4. A.**

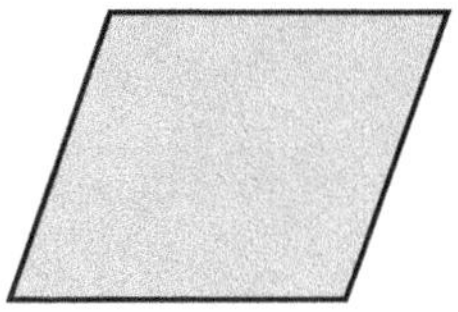

A rhombus has all sides the same length but not all angles are always equal. If the rhombus does have all the same angles, then it would be a square.

**5. B.** A trapezoid only has 1 pair of parallel sides. See the picture below: the top and bottom are parallel but the left and right side are not.

6**. C.** A rectangle has 4 right angles, 2 sets or parallel sides and opposite sides are equal in length. See the picture below:

**7. D.** A right triangle has one 90° angle the other 2 angles must be acute because the interior angles of a triangle add up to 180°. 180− 90 = 90 left to split between the remaining 2 angles and each would be less than 90°.

**8. A.** A right triangle has one right angle. The other 2 angles must be acute (see #7 explanation) so the right triangle only has 1 pair of perpendicular sides.

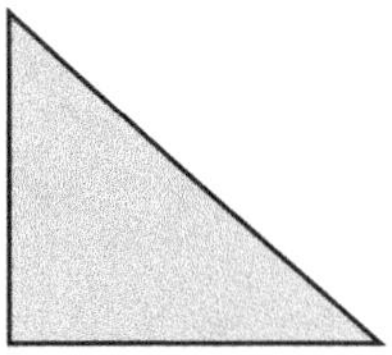

**9. C.** A rectangle always has 2 pairs of parallel sides, so it is a parallelogram, and a parallelogram can be a rectangle if it has 4 right angles.

**10. The shape could be a parallelogram**

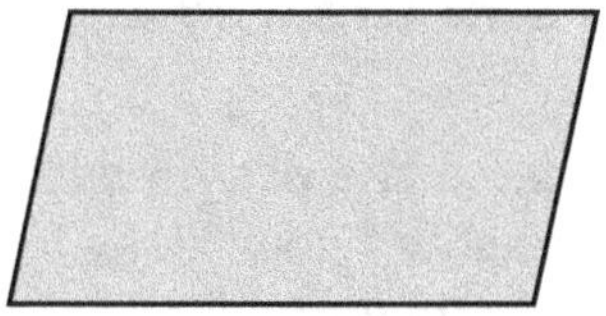

**The shape could be a rhombus**

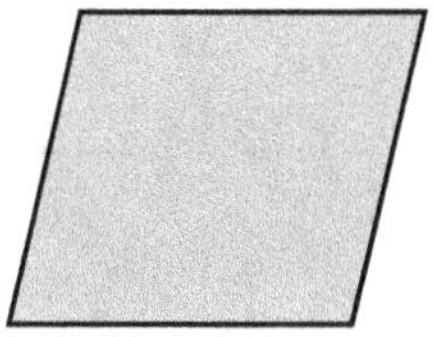

Both a parallelogram and a rhombus have 2 acute angles and 2 obtuse angels. They also have 2 pairs of parallel sides: top and bottom are parallel and left and right side are parallel.

**11. Group 1: Shapes with at least 1 right angle**

**Group 2: Shapes with no right angles.**

**Added shapes will vary.**

Group 1 shape: could be any other shape with a right angle

Group 2 shape: could be any other shape that does not have any right angles.

**12. Shapes with at least one pair of parallel sides:**

**square**
**rectangle**
**rhombus**
**parallelogram**
**trapezoid**

**Shapes with at least one pair of perpendicular sides:**

**square**
**rectangle**
**right triangle**

**Shapes with at least one right angle:**
**square**
**rectangle**
**right triangle**

A trapezoid can have a pair of perpendicular sides and at least one right angle, but does not need to.

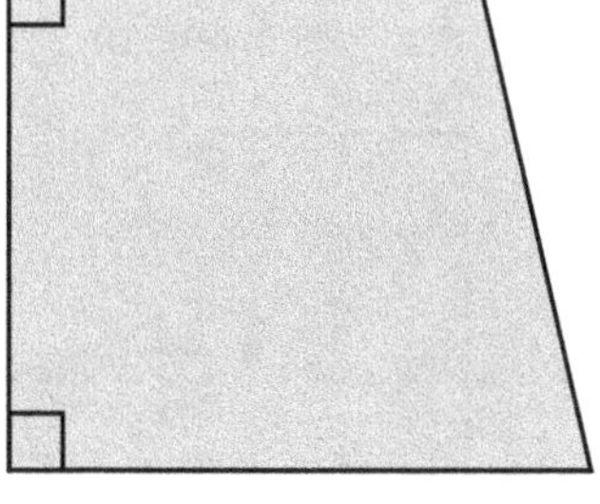

## G.A.3 Draw and Identify Lines of Symmetry

**1. B.** The star has a line of symmetry right through the middle of the star's point. The images on either side of the line are congruent:

**2. C.** The line of symmetry divides the hexagon into two congruent figures that match up perfectly when folded over the dotted line.

**3. D.** This shape has multiple lines of symmetry. The shape can be folded over the dotted line and the image on either side of the line would be congruent.

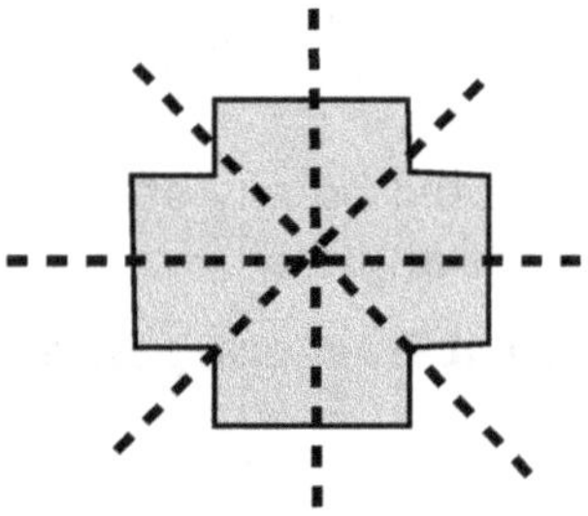

**4. A.** The shape in choice A does not have any lines of symmetry. It cannot be folded and form 2 congruent shapes.

**5. B.** The trapezoid folded over the line of symmetry would be the exact same shape and size of the trapezoid, just reflected over the line.

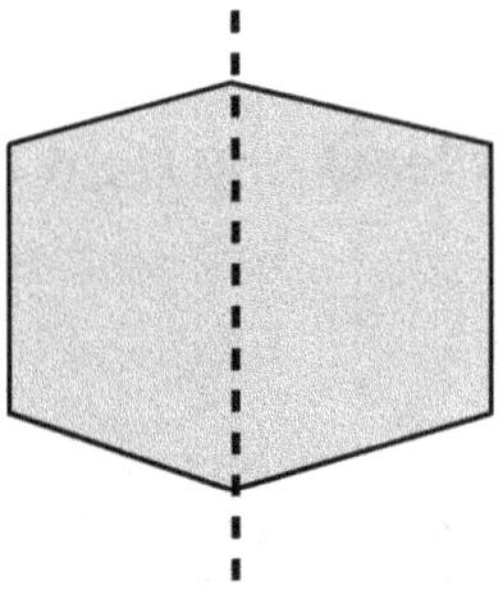

**6. C.** This shape only has 1 line of symmetry.

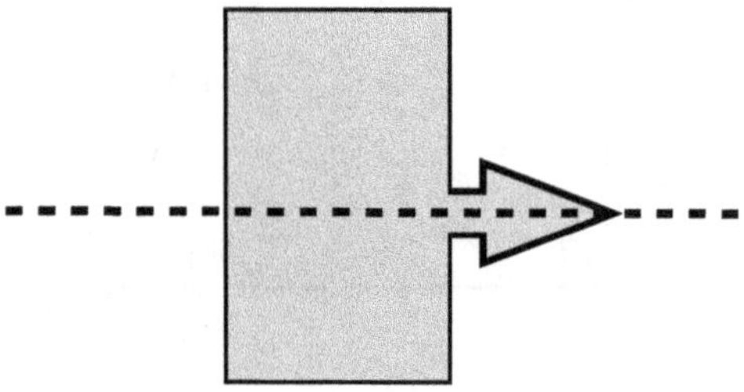

**7. D.** The letter X has a vertical and horizontal line of symmetry.

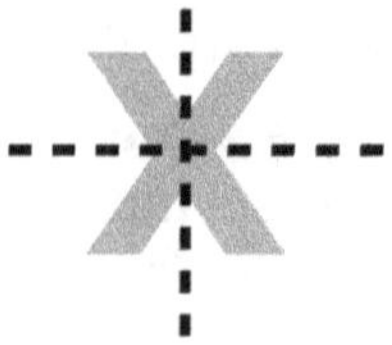


It also has diagonal lines of symmetry.

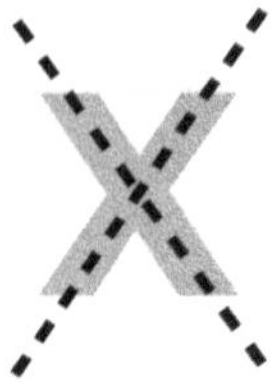


**8. A.** The letter B has a horizontal line of symmetry.

**9. B.** An equilateral hexagon has 6 lines of symmetry.

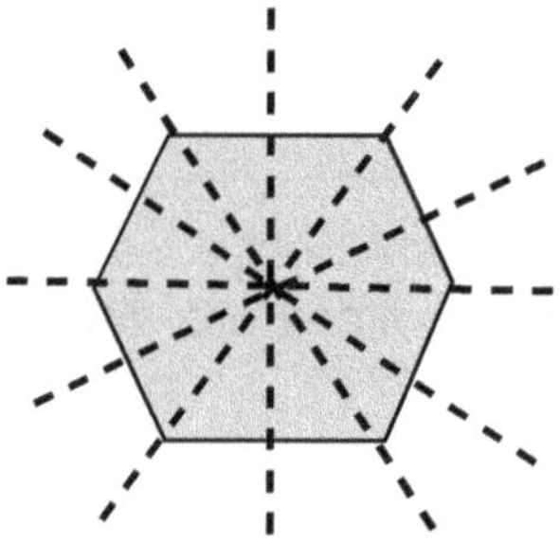

The six sides have the same length so the shape can be folded over 6 lines of symmetry.

**10.** Draw a symmetrical shape by counting the dots on the grid to make the exact same shape.

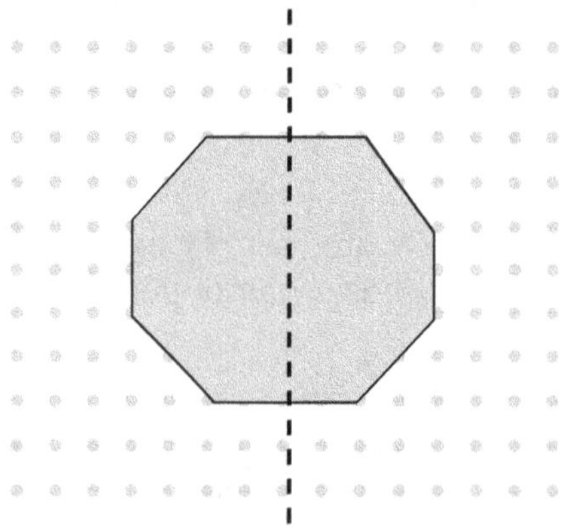

**11.** Part A: **2 lines of symmetry:**

**Answers will vary but some options are letters, polygon-like rectangles, or other shapes with2 lines of symmetry.** There are many shapes with 2 lines of symmetry.

Part B: **4 lines of symmetry: square rhombus and other shapes with sides of the same length like this one:**

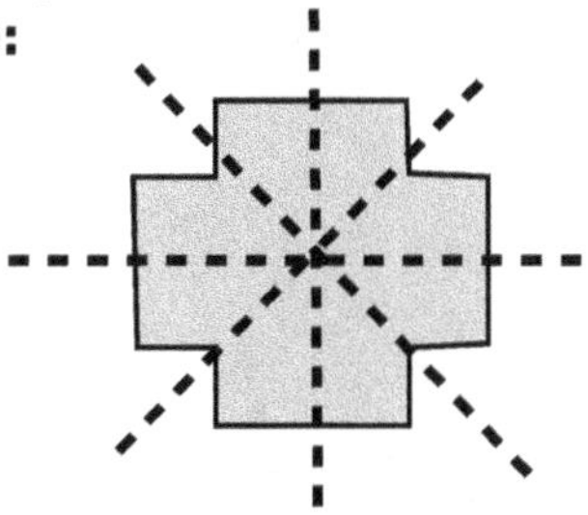

A shape with 4 lines of symmetry will have 2 sides of equal length like a square and a rhombus.

**12.**

Equilateral triangle:

Sides: **3** Lines of Symmetry: **3**

Square:

Sides: **4** Lines of Symmetry: **4**

Regular hexagon:

Sides: **6** Lines of Symmetry: **6**

Regular octagon:

Sides: **8** Lines of Symmetry: **8**

Part A: **A shape will have the same number of sides as number of lines of symmetry if the shape is a regular polygon or has all sides the same length.**

Part B: **A circle has an infinite number of lines of symmetry because a circle has the same radius from the center point of the circle to any point of edge of the circle, so there are an infinite number of lines that can be drawn through the center point of the circle.**

# PRACTICE TEST

# Mathematics
# Practice Test One
# Unit 1

1. What fraction is shaded below?

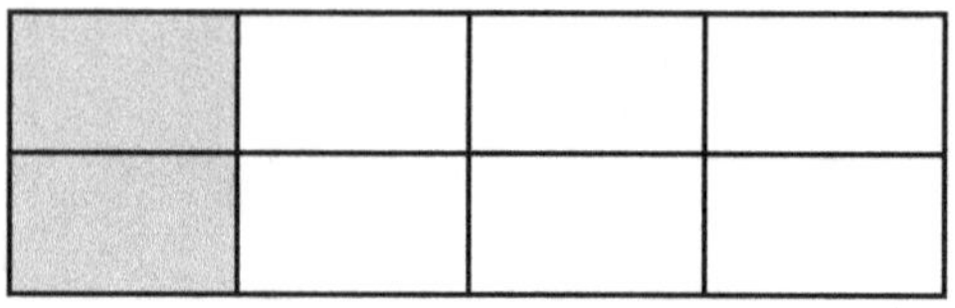

   Ⓐ $^{2}/_{2}$
   Ⓑ $^{1}/_{8}$
   Ⓒ $^{2}/_{6}$
   Ⓓ $^{1}/_{4}$

2. A pumpkin cost $0.60 per pound. Krista bought an 8-pound pumpkin. She paid with a $10 bill. How much change did she get back?
   Ⓐ $4.80
   Ⓑ $5.20
   Ⓒ $480
   Ⓓ $80

3. Sugar Bakery sold $75 worth of cupcakes on Saturday. Each cupcake costs the same amount. What could be the total cost of each cupcake? Choose **ALL** answers that apply.
   ☐ $2.00
   ☐ $5.00
   ☐ $3.00
   ☐ $4.00
   ☐ $15.00

4. Fill in the correct symbol, <, >, =, to make each number sentence correct.

   $^{3}/_{12}$ ☐ $^{1}/_{3}$ $^{50}/_{100}$ ☐ $^{1}/_{2}$ $^{7}/_{8}$ ☐ $^{3}/_{10}$

5. Which of the following comparisons is true?
   Ⓐ 10 thousands + 4 hundreds + 3 ones = 10, 403
   Ⓑ 10,900 = 10 ten thousands + 10 thousands, + 9 hundreds
   Ⓒ 1 thousand + 10 hundreds + 10 tens = 11,010
   Ⓓ 12 thousands + 12 hundreds + 12 ones = 121,212

6. The area of the school playground is 132 square yards.

**Part A**

The playground has a width of 11 square yards. What is the length of the playground?

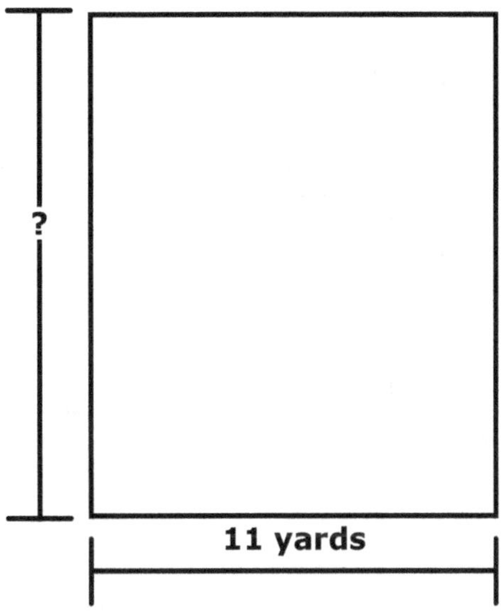


Answer: ______________________________ yards

**Part B**

What is the perimeter of the school playground?

Answer: ______________________________ yards

7. Which addition expression can be used to find the total amount of shaded portions of the fraction models below?

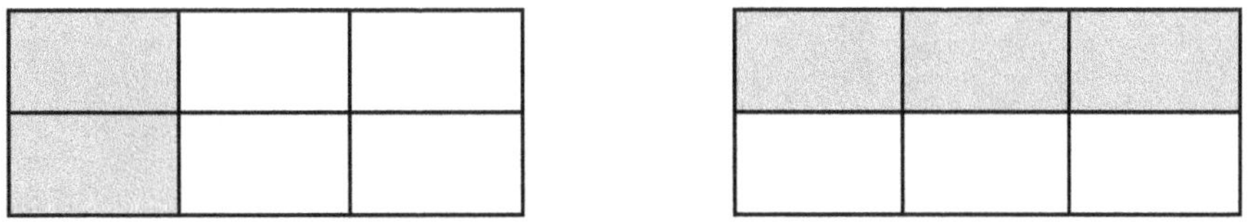

Ⓐ $1 + 3$
Ⓑ $\frac{6}{1} + \frac{3}{3}$
Ⓒ $\frac{6}{6} + \frac{6}{6}$
Ⓓ $\frac{2}{6} + \frac{3}{6}$

8. Is 11 a prime number of a composite number and why?
   Ⓐ Prime number, because it has 0 factor pairs.
   Ⓑ Composite number, because it has 1 factor pair.
   Ⓒ Prime number, because it has 1 factor pair.
   Ⓓ Composite number, because it has 0 factor pairs.

9. Complete the area model to find the product of 85 x 63.

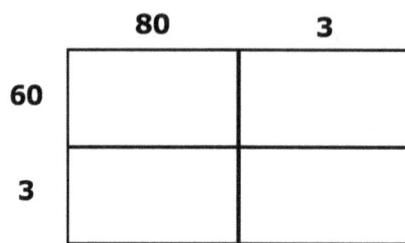

**Part A**

| | **80** | **3** |
|---|---|---|
| **60** | | |
| **3** | | |

**Part B**

Fill in the equation: ________ + ________ + ________ +________ = ________

10. Use the information provided to answer Part A and Part B for question 10. Two figures are shown. In Figure 1, the measure of angle *MPG* is 100°.

**Figure 1**

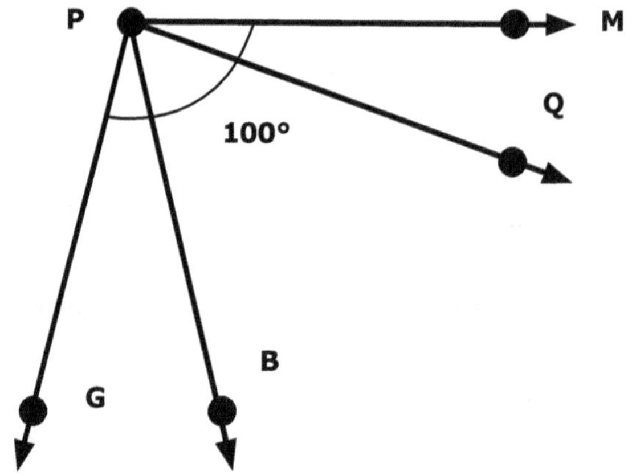


The measures of angle MPQ, angle QPB, and angle BPG are shown in Figure 2. The measure of angle MPG is still 100°.

**Figure 2**

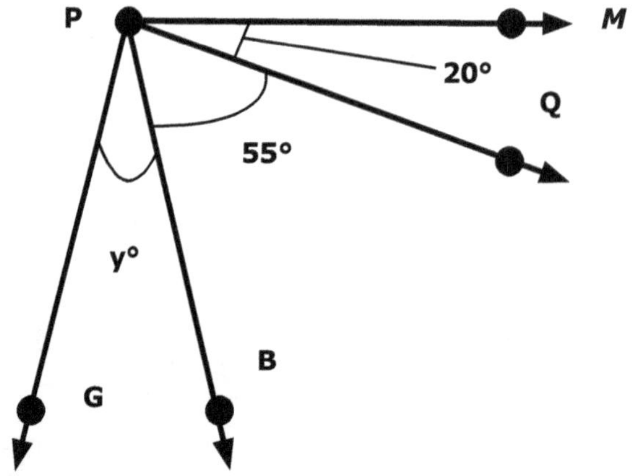


**Part A**

What equation can be used to find the value of y?

Ⓐ y + 55 + 20 = 100

Ⓑ y x 55 x 20 = 100

Ⓒ y - 55 - 20 = 100

Ⓓ y + 55 - 20 = 100

**Part B**

What is the value of y?

Answer: ______________________________

# Unit 2

11. Mrs. Mendez has a box of 72 crackers. She eats 5 crackers. Then she gives 3 crackers to each of her 21 students. Write an equation with an unknown variable that could be used to find out how many crackers Mrs. Mendez has left.

Equation: ______________________________________________

Show your work and solve the problem.

Answer: ______________________________ crackers.

12. Which statement below is NOT true?
   - Ⓐ All angles of an equilateral triangle have the same measure.
   - Ⓑ All three sides or angles of an isosceles triangle are equal.
   - Ⓒ A right triangle has one angle that measures 90°.
   - Ⓓ A scalene triangle does not have any sides that are the same length.

13. Find the pattern. Complete the table below.

| Input | Output |
|---|---|
| 1,000 | 250 |
| 800 | 200 |
| 400 | |
| | 50 |
| 80 | |

14. Write the fractions in order on the number line below.

$^{2}/_{16}$ $^{1}/_{4}$ $^{5}/_{16}$ $^{3}/_{8}$ $^{3}/_{4}$

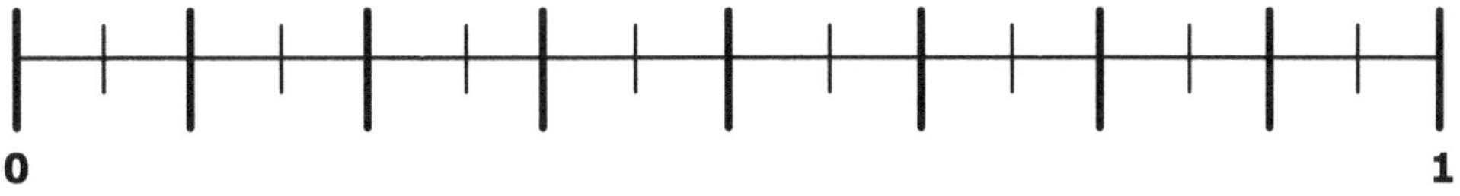

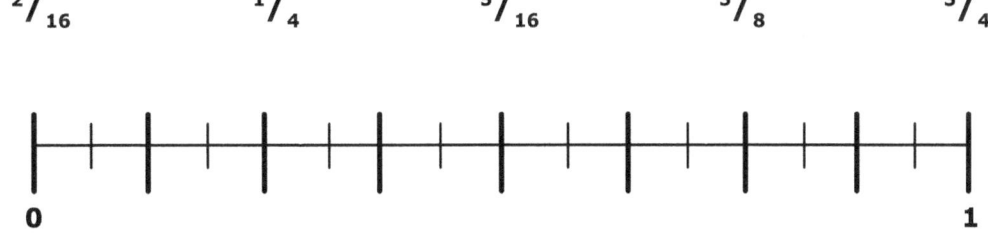

15. Each bottle of water contains 500 mL of water. If you drink 2 bottles every day, how many liters of water will you drink in 7 days?

Answer: ______________________________ liters

16. Jacob used an inch ruler to measure the length of 10 different pencils in the classroom. He measured each length to the nearest quarter inch. The table below shows the length of each pencil.

| Pencil # | Length |
|---|---|
| 1 | 7 in. |
| 2 | $7\,^{1}/_{4}$ in. |
| 3 | $6\,^{1}/_{2}$ in. |
| 4 | 5 in. |
| 5 | 7 in. |
| 6 | 7 in. |
| 7 | $5\,^{1}/_{2}$ in. |
| 8 | $6\,^{1}/_{2}$ in. |
| 9 | $4\,^{3}/_{4}$ in. |
| 10 | $6\,^{3}/_{4}$ in. |

Complete the table below to show how many pencils measure each length.

| Length of Pencil in Inches | Number of Pencils |
|---|---|
| $4\,^{3}/_{4}$ in. | |
| 5 in. | |
| $5\,^{1}/_{2}$ in. | |
| $6\,^{1}/_{2}$ in. | |
| $6\,^{3}/_{4}$ in. | |
| 7 in. | |
| $7\,^{1}/_{4}$ in. | |

Use the data in the table above to make a line plot. Make an X to show the length of each pencil.

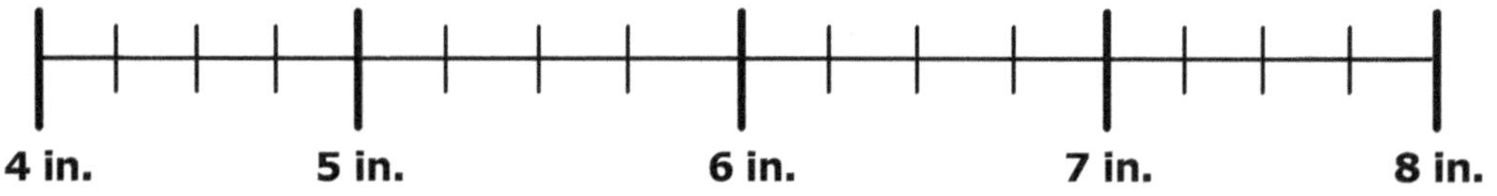


17. What number is 45,090 greater than 35,296?

Answer: ______________________________

18. Jackson ate $^{3}/_{12}$ of a whole pizza. What fraction of the pizza is left?

Ⓐ 9
Ⓑ $^{12}/_{9}$
Ⓒ $^{1}/_{4}$
Ⓓ $^{3}/_{4}$

19. Find the product of $5 \times {}^{2}/_{6}$ .

Ⓐ $5\ {}^{2}/_{6}$
Ⓑ $1\ {}^{2}/_{3}$
Ⓒ $5\ {}^{2}/_{3}$
Ⓓ $1\ {}^{2}/_{6}$

20. Which expression can be used to find the product of 5 x 17?

Ⓐ 5 x (10 x 7)
Ⓑ (5 x 10) x 7
Ⓒ (5 x 10) + (5 x 7)
Ⓓ 50 + 70

# Unit 3

21. Jane baked 3 dozen cookies. Fill in the chart below to show 5 possible ways Jane could arrange her cookies on the baking sheet.

| Number of Rows | Number of Columns |
|---|---|
| | |
| | |
| | |
| | |
| | |

22. Use the figure below to answer the questions in Part A, Part B, and Part C.

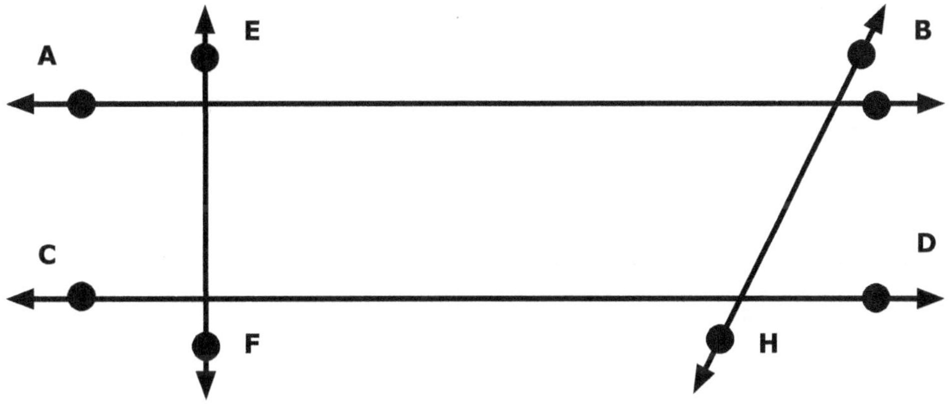


**Part A**

Line ____________________ is perpendicular to line ____________________.

**Part B**

Line ____________________ is parallel to line ____________________.

**Part C**

Line ____________________ intersects line ____________________.

23. What fraction of the model is shaded? Write the fraction.

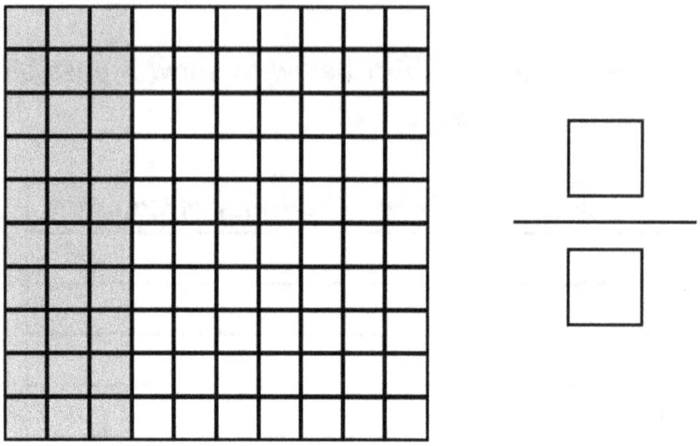

24. A t-shirt costs $9. A sweatshirt costs 4 times as much.

**Part A**

Which equation can be used to figure out the total cost, c, of 2 sweatshirts?

Ⓐ 9 + 4 + 2 = c
Ⓑ 9 x 4 = c
Ⓒ 2 x (9 x 4) = c
Ⓓ 9 − 4 − 2 = c

**Part B**

What is the total cost, c, of 2 sweatshirts?

______________________________

25. What unknown number makes this equation true?

$$486 \div \square = 54$$

Answer: ______________________________

26. Michael created the table below to show the relationship among inches, feet, and yards.

| # of Inches | # of Feet | # of Yards |
|---|---|---|
| 36 | 3 | 1 |
| 72 | 6 | 2 |
| 73 | 7 | 3 |
| 74 | 8 | 4 |

Did Michael complete the table correctly? Explain your answer below.

27. Charlotte used the following fraction bars to help her compare fractions.

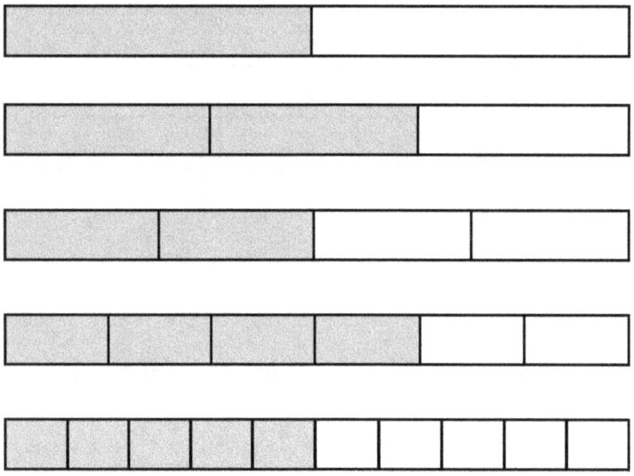

Based on the fraction bars above, which of the following statements are true? Choose **ALL** answers that apply.

- ☐ $\frac{1}{2} = \frac{4}{6}$
- ☐ $\frac{5}{10} > \frac{2}{3}$
- ☐ $\frac{2}{4} < \frac{4}{6}$
- ☐ $\frac{4}{6} = \frac{2}{3}$
- ☐ $\frac{1}{2} = \frac{5}{10}$

28. Valentina is adding $2\frac{4}{6} + 7\frac{1}{6}$. She uses these steps to find the sum.

**Step 1: 2 + 7 = 9**
**Step 2: 4/6 + 1/6 = 5/12**
**Step 3: 9 + 5/12 = 9 5/12**

Valentina made a mistake. Which mistake did she make?

Ⓐ In Step 2, Valentina added the denominators instead of keeping the denominators the same.

Ⓑ In Step 1, Valentina added the whole numbers instead of multiplying them.

Ⓒ In Step 2, Valentina added the numerators together, but she should have multiplied them.

Ⓓ Valentina is missing Step 4. She needs to simply the fraction.

29. Match each number in standard form to the correct number in expanded form.

| | |
|---|---|
| **120,500** | **100,000 + 2,000 + 50** |
| **12,500** | **100,000 + 200 + 50** |
| **102,050** | **10,000 + 5,000 + 200 + 20 + 5** |
| **100,250** | **10,000 + 5,000 + 200** |
| **15,225** | **100,000 + 20,000 + 500** |
| **15,200** | **10,000 + 2,000 + 500** |

30. Use the diagram to solve the problem.

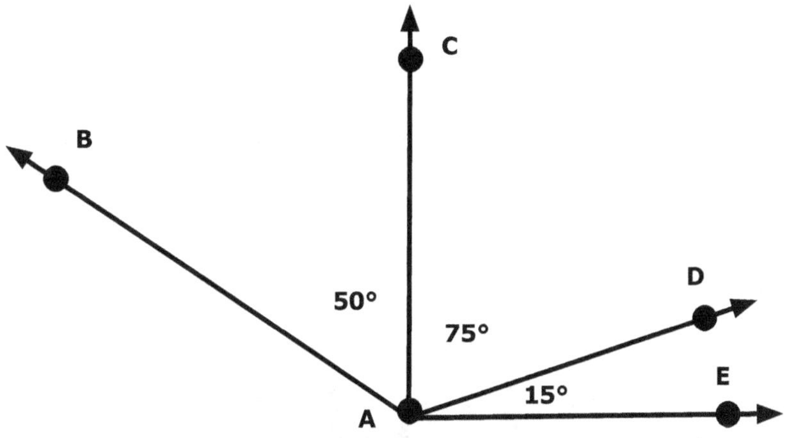


What is the measure of ∠ BAE?

_______________°

# Unit 4

31. The perimeter of the library measures 210 yards. The length of the library is 55 yards. What could the area of the library possibly be?

Ⓐ 3,600 square yards
Ⓑ 840 square yards
Ⓒ 52.5 square yards
Ⓓ 2,750 square yards

32. Label the number line below. Then complete the number line to represent the following equation:

$$^{1}/_{6} + ^{3}/_{6} = ^{4}/_{6}$$

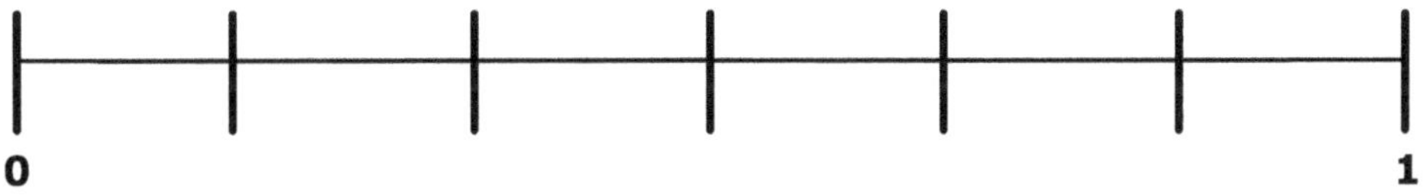


33. Fill in the correct symbol, <, >, =, to make each sentence true.

**right angle** ☐ **90°**  **straight line segment** ☐ **90°**  **circle** ☐ **90°**

34. Name the figure that has only one pair of parallel sides and exactly two right angles.

☐ rhombus
☐ right trapezoid
☐ regular pentagon
☐ regular hexagon

35. Write $^{60}/_{100}$ as an equivalent fraction with a denominator of 10.

$$\frac{\square}{\square}$$

36. Mrs. Calvin needs to make yellow paint. She mixes 4/10 liter of red paint with 50/100 liter of green paint. How many liters of yellow paint will she make?

$$\frac{\square}{\square}$$ **liter**

37. Washington Elementary School had a food drive to collect food for local food shelters. The school collected 1,649 items. The items will be divided equally among 2 shelters.

**Part A:** How many items will each shelter receive? Show your work below.

Answer: ______________________________ items

**Part B:** Will any items be left over? If so, how many? Show your work below.

Answer: ______________________________

38. Lila states that the following numbers are multiples of 12:

**12, 24, 36, 48, 60, 77, 84, 96**

Do you agree with Lila? Why or why not? Explain your reasoning.

_______________________________________________

_______________________________________________

_______________________________________________

_______________________________________________

_______________________________________________

_______________________________________________

_______________________________________________

39. Use the numbers to complete each number sentence. Each number can only be used once. Only 4 numbers will be used.

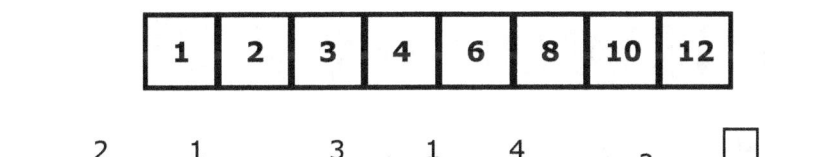

| | | | | | | | |
|---|---|---|---|---|---|---|---|
| **1** | **2** | **3** | **4** | **6** | **8** | **10** | **12** |

$1 > \frac{2}{\square} > \frac{1}{4}$  $\frac{3}{\square} < \frac{1}{2} < \frac{4}{4}$  $\frac{2}{6} = \frac{\square}{3} = \frac{4}{\square}$

40. Scott can run a mile in 7 minutes and 30 seconds. In how many seconds can he run a mile?

Answer: ______________________________ seconds

# Mathematics Practice Test One Answer Key & Explanations

## Mathematics Practice Test One

## Answer Explanations

1. **D.** The model shows the fraction $^2/_8$.

¼ is equivalent to $^2/_8$ because:

2÷ 2 = 1

8÷ 2 = 4 so the resulting fraction is ¼.

**Difficulty Level: Easy**
**Standard: 4.NF.A.1**

2. **B.** Before you can determine how much change Krista received, you must first find out how much money she spent. If she bought an 8-pound pumpkin and each pound costs 60 cents, you need to multiply: 8 x .60 = $4.80.

Next , you need to subtract $4.80 from $10.00 because Krista paid with a $10 bill.

$10.00 - $4.80 = $5.20

**Difficulty Level: Medium**
**Standard: 4.MD.A.2, 4.OA.A.3**

3. **2nd, 3rd, and 5th Choices.** Students should choose the 2nd, 3rd, and 5th answer choices. $5.00, $3.00, and $15.00 could be the cost of each cupcake because they are all factors of $75.00.

75 ÷ 5 = 15

75 ÷ 3 = 25

75 ÷ 15 = 5

**Difficulty Level: Medium**
**Standard: 4.OA.A.3, 4.NBT.B.6**

4. **<, =, >.** $^3/_{12} < {}^1/_3$ because if you were to reduce $^3/_{12}$ into simplest form, it would be $^1/_4$ and $^1/_4 < {}^1/_3$.

$^{50}/_{100} = {}^1/_2$ because if you were to reduce $^{50}/_{100}$ into simplest form, it would be $^1/_2$ .

$^7/_8 > {}^3/_{10}$ . You know that $^7/_8$ is greater than one-half, because one-half is $^4/_8$. You know that $^3/_{10}$ is less than one-half, because one-half is $^5/_{10}$. Therefore, $^7/_8 > {}^3/_{10}$ .

**Difficulty Level: Medium**
**Standard: 4.NF.A.2**

5. **A.** The statement: 10 thousands + 4 hundreds + 3 ones = 10, 403 is true.

The statement: 10,900 = 10 ten thousands + 10 thousands, + 9 hundreds is false. 10 ten thousands + 10 thousands + 9 hundreds = 110, 900

The statement: 1 thousand + 10 hundreds + 10 tens = 11,010 is false. 1 thousand + 10 hundreds + 10 tens = 2,100

The statement: 12 thousands + 12 hundreds + 12 ones = 121,212 is false. 12 thousands + 12 hundreds + 12 ones = 13,212

**Difficulty Level: Medium**
**Standard: 4.NBT.A.1, 4.NBT.A.2**

6. **12 yards; 46 yards.** Part A: If the area of the rectangle is 132 square yards and the width is 11 yards, you need to divide the width and the area to find the length: 132 ÷ 11 = 12 yards.

Part B: To find the perimeter of the shape, you need to add all four side lengths together: 11 + 12 + 11 + 12 = 46 yards

**Difficulty Level: Medium**
**Standard: 4.MD.A.3**

7. **D.** Both fraction models represent 6 equal parts in the whole. Therefore, you simply need to add the shaded portions, or the numerators, to determine the total amount of the shaded portions: $^2/_6 + {}^3/_6$

**Difficulty Level: Easy**
**Standard: 4.NF.B.3.a**

8. **C.** 11 is a prime number because it has 1 factor pair. A factor pair is the two factors that are multiplied to equal a product, such as 1 x 11 make one factor pair of 11.

**Difficulty Level: Easy**
**Standard: 4.OA.B.4**

9. **See detailed explanation; 1,035.** Part A: Student completed area models should look like the model below:

| X | 80 | 5 |
|---|---|---|
| 60 | 480 | 300 |
| 3 | 240 | 15 |

Part B: The addition equation that matches the area model above and can be used to find the product of 85 x 63 is: 480 + 300 + 240 + 15 = 1,035

**Difficulty Level: Medium**
**Standard: 4.NBT.B.5**

10. **A; 25°.** Part A: We know that the values of all 3 angles together is a total of 100°. We also know that <MPQ has a value of 20° and <QPB has a value of 55°. Therefore, the equation that shows the value the third angle, or *y* is: *y* + 20 + 55 = 100.

Part B: *y* = 25° because

25 + 20 + 55 = 100

**Difficulty Level: Medium**
**Standard: 4.OA.A.3, 4.MD.C.7**

11. **72 – [(21 x 3) + 5] = *c*; 4 crackers.** First you need to multiply 21 x 3 to determine how many crackers Mrs. Mendez will distribute to her students altogether. This should be done first because it is

written in parenthesis, according to the order of operations, multiplication needs to be completed first. 21 x 3 = 63. Next, you add 5 to 63 because Mrs. Mendez ate 5 crackers herself. 63 + 5 = 68. Last, you subtract the number of crackers eaten from the total number of crackers: 72 - 68 = 4 crackers left.

The equation: **72 – [(21 x 3) + 5] =c** can be used to solve this problem. The unknown variable, *c*, represents the number of crackers left.

**Difficulty Level: Hard**
**Standard: 4.OA.A.2, 4.OA.A.3, 4.NBT.B.5**

12. **B.** The statement 'All three sides or angles of an isosceles triangle are equal' is not true. An isosceles triangle has two sides that are of equal length. A scalene triangle doesn't have any equal side lengths or angles.

**Difficulty Level: Medium**
**Standard: 4.G.A.2**

13. **Correctly filled in table.** The rule of the table is to divide the Input number by 5. Student tables should be filled in as below:

| Input | Output |
|---|---|
| 1,000 | 250 |
| 800 | 200 |
| 400 | **100** |
| **200** | 50 |
| 80 | **20** |

**Difficulty Level: Medium**
**Standard: 4.OA.C.5, 4.NBT.B.6**

14. **Correctly labeled number line.** The number line begins at 0 and ends at 1 and is divided into 16 equal parts.

The fraction $^2/_{16}$ should be labeled on the 2nd tick mark.

The fraction $^1/_4$ is equivalent to $^4/_{16}$ and should be labeled on the 4th tick mark.

The fraction $^5/_{16}$ should be labeled on the 5th tick mark.

The fraction $^3/_8$ is equivalent to $^6/_{16}$ and should be labeled on the 6th tick mark.

The fraction $^3/_4$ is equivalent to $^{12}/_{16}$ and should be labeled on the 12th tick mark.

**Difficulty Level: Medium**
**Standard: 4.NF.A.1, 4.NF.A.2**

15. **7 Liters.** 1,000 mL = 1 L

If you drink two 500 mL bottles of water, you drink 1 L of water a day. To determine how many liters of water you drink in 7 days, you multiply 1 L x 7 days = 7 Liters

**Difficulty Level: 4.NBT.B.5, 4.MD.A.2, 4.OA.A.3**
**Standard: Medium**

16. **See detailed explanation.** Students should have the data table completed accordingly:

| Length of Pencil in Inches | Number of Pencils |
|---|---|
| 4 $^3/_4$ in. | 1 |
| 5 in. | 1 |
| 5 $^1/_2$ in. | 1 |
| 6 $^1/_2$ in. | 2 |
| 6 $^3/_4$ in. | 1 |
| 7 in. | 3 |
| 7 $^1/_4$ in. | 1 |

Students should complete the line plot according to the data table above. There should be one X above the 4 $^3/_4$ , 5, 5 $^1/_2$ , 6 $^3/_4$ , and 7 $^1/_4$ in. tick marks. There should be 2 X's above the 6 $^1/_2$ in. tick mark and 3 X's above the 7 in. tick mark.

**Difficulty Level: 4.MD.B.4**
**Standard: Medium**

17. **80,386.** To determine what number is 45,090 greater than 35,296 you need to add: 45,090 + 35,296 = 80,386.

**Difficulty Level: Medium**
**Standard: 4.NBT.B.4**

18. **D.** The clue word *left* indicates that you need to subtract. If Jackson ate $^3/_{12}$ of a pizza, that means the whole pizza was a fraction of $^{12}/_{12}$ .

$^{12}/_{12}$ - $^3/_{12}$ = $^9/_{12}$ .

Students then need to recognize that $^9/_{12}$ is equivalent to $^3/_4$ because 9 ÷ 3 = 3 and 12 ÷ 3 = 4.

**Difficulty Level: Medium**
**Standard: 4.NF.A.1, 4.NF.B.3.a**

19. **B.** 5 x $^2/_6$ = $^2/_6$ + $^2/_6$ + $^2/_6$ + $^2/_6$ + $^2/_6$ = $^{10}/_6$ .

$^{10}/_6$ is the solution as an improper fraction. To find the mixed number:

$^2/_6$ + $^2/_6$ + $^2/_6$ = 1 whole and $^2/_6$ + $^2/_6$ = $^4/_6$ , and $^4/_6$ can be reduced to $^2/_3$ . Therefore, 5 x $^2/_6$ = 1 $^2/_3$.

**Difficulty Level: Hard**
**Standard: 4.NF.A.1, 4.NF.B.3.a, 4.NF.B.4.c**

20. **C.** This question measures a student's ability to apply their understanding of the distributive property. 5 x 17 can be solved by decomposing the 17 into 10 + 7 and distributing the 5 to each number: (5 x 10) + (5 x 7) = 50 + 35 = 85

**Difficulty Level: Medium**

**Standard: 4.NBT.2.5**

21. **Correctly filled in table.** The table below shows all possible solutions. Students can have any 5 of the solutions below.

| Number of Rows | Number of Columns |
|---|---|
| 1 | 36 |
| 2 | 18 |
| 3 | 12 |
| 4 | 9 |
| 6 | 6 |
| 36 | 1 |
| 18 | 2 |
| 12 | 3 |
| 9 | 4 |

**Difficulty Level: Medium**
**Standard: 4.OA.A.3, 4.OA.B.4**

22. **See detailed explanation.** Part A: When 2 lines are perpendicular, they meet to create a right angle. In the figure line AB is perpendicular to line EF and line CD is perpendicular to line EF. Either answer choice is acceptable.

Part B: When 2 lines are parallel, they are 2 lines that are the same distance apart and will never touch. In this figure, line AB is parallel to line CD. This is the only acceptable answer choice.

Part C: When 2 lines intersect, they are 2 lines that share exactly one point. In this figure, line GH intersects line AB; line GH intersects line CF, line EF intersects line AB, and line EF intersects line CD. Any of these answer choices is acceptable.

**Difficulty Level: Medium**
**Standard: 4.G.1.1**

23. $^{30}/_{100}$, $^{3}/_{10}$ The figure has 100 equal parts. 30 parts are shaded, representing the fraction $^{30}/_{100}$. The fraction in simplest form is: $^{3}/_{10}$.

**Difficulty Level: Easy**
**Standard: 4.NF.A.1, 4.NF.C.5**

24. **C; $72.** Since 1 t-shirt costs $9 and a sweatshirt costs 4 times that amount, 1 sweatshirt = 9 x 4 = $36. The equation that can be used to find the total cost of 2 sweatshirts is:

2 x (9 x 4) = $72.

Students might mistakenly select letter *B*, which only finds the total cost of 1 sweatshirt.

**Difficulty Level: Medium**

**Standard: 4.OA.1.1, 4.OA.1.2, 4.OA.1.3**

25. **9.** Students can solve this problem using long division or the reverse equation. If students solve the problem using long division, their work may resemble the example below:

```
       9
 54 ⟌486
  -  486
       0
```

If students solve the problem using the reverse equation, their work may resemble the example below:

54 x N = 486
N = 9

**Difficulty Level: Hard**
**Standard: 4.NBT.B.6**

26. **No, appropriate explanation.** In this table, only the first 2 rows are filled in correctly. After that, Michael only counted by ones, rather than multiplying by the appropriate unit of measurement. An appropriate student explanation may state: No, Michael is not correct. I know this because there is 3 feet in 1 yard and there is 36 inches in 1 yard/3 feet. This means that every yard you add, you need to multiply the number of feet and the number of inches by that number of yards. For example, to find out how many feet in 4 yards, you need to multiply 4 x 3 = 12 feet. To find out how many inches in 4 yards, you need to multiply 4 x 36 = 144.

**Difficulty Level: Medium**
**Standard: 4.NBT.B.5, 4.MD.A.1**

27. **3rd, 4th, and 5th Choices.** Students should select the 3rd, 4th and 5th answer choices.

$^{2}/_{4} < ^{4}/_{6}$ because $^{2}/_{4}$ covers less space on the fraction bars than $^{4}/_{6}$.

$^{4}/_{6} = ^{2}/_{3}$ because they cover the same amount of space on the fraction bars.

$^{1}/_{2} = ^{5}/_{10}$ because they cover the same amount of space on the fraction bars.

**Difficulty Level: Medium**
**Standard: 4.NF.A.1, 4.NF.A.2**

28. **A.** The mistake in Valentina's work occurs in Step 2. In Step 2, she adds: $^{4}/_{6} + ^{1}/_{6} = ^{5}/_{12}$. However, when you are adding fractions, you are not supposed to add the numerators and the denominators. You are only supposed to add the numerators. The number sentence should say:

$^{4}/_{6} + ^{1}/_{6} = ^{5}/_{6}$

**Difficulty Level: Medium**

**Standard: 4.NF.2.3.a, 4.NF.2.3.c**

29. **See detailed explanation.** 120,500 should be matched to: 100,000 + 20,000 + 500

12,500 should be matched to: 10,000 + 2,000 + 500

102,050 should be matched to: 100,000 + 2,000 + 50

100,250 should be matched to: should be matched to 100,000 + 200 + 50

15,225 should be matched to: 10,000 + 5,000 + 200 + 20 + 5

15,200 should be matched to: 10,000 + 5,000 + 200

**Difficulty Level: Easy**
**Standard: 4.NBT.A.2**

30. **140°.** In order to determine the measure of ∠BAE, you need to add the given angle measures altogether:

∠BAC measures: 50°

∠CAD measures: 75°

∠DAE measures: 15°

50 + 75 + 15 = 140°

**Difficulty Level: Medium**
**Standard: 4.NBT.B.4, 4.MD.C.7**

31. **D.** In order to determine what the area of the library could be, students first need to determine what the width of the library is. You already know that the perimeter is 210 yards and the length is 55 yards. Since the library has 4 sides, you can add the length together to determine the part of the perimeter you already know:

55 + 55 = 110. If you subtract 210-110, you know that the width measurements have a *total* of 100 yards. You can divide 100 into 2 to determine the length of each side. 100 ÷ 2 = 50. Therefore, the width of the library is 50 yards and the length of the library is 55 yards. To find the area, you multiply: 50 x 55 = 2,750 square yards.

**Difficulty Level: Hard**
**Standard: 4.OA.A.3, 4.NBT.B.4., 4.NBT.B.5, 4.NBT.B.6, 4.MD.A.3**

32. **Correctly completed number line.** The number line begins at 0, ends at 1, and is divided into 6 equal parts. Students should label the first tick mark as $^{1}/_{6}$, the second tick mark as $^{2}/_{6}$, and so on, until $^{6}/_{6}$ or 1.

To demonstrate $^{1}/_{6} + ^{3}/_{6} = ^{4}/_{6}$

Students should show 1 jump from 0 to $^{1}/_{6}$. Then students should show 1 jump that is $^{3}/_{6}$ long, crossing 3 tick marks and stopping on $^{4}/_{6}$.

**Difficulty Level: Medium**
**Standard: 4.NF.2.3.a**

33. **=, >, >** A right angle is equal to 90° because they have the same measurement.

A straight line segment is greater than 90° because a straight line segment measures 180°.

A circle is greater than 90° because it measures 360°.

**Difficulty Level: Easy**
**Standard: 4.MD.C.7**

34. **B.** A right trapezoid has 2 right angles and 1 pair of parallel sides.

**Difficulty Level: Hard**
**Standard: 4.G.A.2**

35. **$^{6}/_{10}$.** $^{60}/_{100}$ = $^{6}/_{10}$ You need to divide the numerator, 60, and the denominator, 100, by 10 to determine the equivalent fraction.

60 ÷ 10 = 6

100 ÷ 10 = 10

**Difficulty Level: Medium**
**Standard: 4.NBT.B.6, 4.NF.C.5**

36. **$^{9}/_{10}$.** Before you can add the fractions $^{4}/_{10}$ and $^{50}/_{100}$ you need the fractions to have the same denominator. If you divide the numerator and denominator of $^{50}/_{100}$ by 10, you will get the fraction $^{5}/_{10}$. Then you can add: $^{4}/_{10} + ^{5}/_{10} = ^{9}/_{10}$

**Difficulty Level: Medium**
**Standard: 4.NBT.B.6, 4.NF.B.3.a, 4.NF.C.5**

37.Part A: **824 items;** Part B**: 1 leftover.** The key words *divided equally* indicate that you need to divide in to determine how many items each food shelter will receive.

1,649 ÷ 2 = N

If students solve the problem using long division, their work may resemble the example below:

```
   824  R 1
2 1,649
 - 16
    04
   - 4
     09
   -  8
      1
```

**Difficulty Level: Medium**
**Standard: 4.OA.A.3, 4.NBT.B.6**

38. **No, appropriate explanation.** Lila is incorrect because 77 is not a multiple of 12.

An appropriate student explanation may state: No, I do not agree with Lila. Lila is incorrect because 77 is not a multiple of 12. If 12 x 5 = 60, then 12 x 6 must be 72 because 60 + 12 = 72. The next multiple would be 84 because 12 x 8 = 84.

**Difficulty Level: Medium**
**Standard: 4.OA.B.4**

---

39. **See detailed explanation.**

$$1 > \frac{2}{\square} > \frac{1}{4}$$

Possible denominators for this question are: 3, 4, 5, 6

$$\frac{3}{\square} < \frac{1}{2} < \frac{4}{4}$$

Possible denominators for this question are: 7, 8, 10

$$\frac{2}{6} = \frac{\square}{3} = \frac{4}{\square}$$

Possible numerator for this question is: 1

Possible denominator for this question is: 12

**Difficulty Level: Hard**
**Standard: 4.NF.A.1, 4.NF.A.2**

---

40. **450 seconds.** To determine how many seconds it takes Scott to run one mile, you need to multiply the number of minutes it takes him to run a mile by 60.

(1 minute = 60 seconds)

It takes Scott 7 minutes and 30 seconds to run 1 mile: 7 x 60 = 420. You need to add 420 + 30 because Scott runs 1 mile in 7 minutes and 30 seconds.

420 + 30 = 450 seconds

**Difficulty Level: Medium**
**Standard: 4.OA.A.3, 4.NBT.B.4, 4.MD.A.1**

# BONUS

## FULL-LENGTH PRACTICE TEST

**GO TO THE FOLLOWING URL ADDRESS**

**TO ACCESS YOUR BONUS PRACTICE TEST.**

**https://originstutoring.lpages.co/parcc-math-grade-4/**

**Thank you for selecting this book.**

**We would be thrilled if you left us a review on the website where you bought this book!**

www.ingramcontent.com/pod-product-compliance
Lightning Source LLC
Chambersburg PA
CBHW081349080526
44588CB00016B/2426
*9781948255363*